W9-CAM-295

More praise for THE SHELTER OF EACH OTHER

"This new book is an expansion of [*Reviving*] *Ophelia* but offers more ideas for change. . . . Pipher's message about families is a combination of nostalgia and call to action."

—*The Washington Post Book World*

"Mary Pipher is that rarity in these days of culture wars: She can talk about values without self-righteousness. She reclaims some common sense in the dialogue about family."

—*The Seattle Times*

"Using her analytical and story-telling skills, Pipher lays out the cultural, technological and economic forces that are tearing families apart and creating a crisis of meaning and values in the society as a whole. . . . *The Shelter of Each Other* generates a feeling of warmth and a sense of possibility that families need not be doomed. What families need today, [Pipher] says, is hope—and her book succeeds in showing how to build it."

—*Milwaukee Journal Sentinel*

"Lively [and] straightforward . . . *The Shelter of Each Other* offers hope for the American family in a time that challenges its viability."—*Kirkus Reviews*

The Shelter
of Each Other

THE
SHELTER OF
EACH OTHER

Rebuilding Our Families

MARY PIPHER, Ph.D.

BALLANTINE BOOKS · NEW YORK

Copyright © 1996 by Mary Pipher, Ph.D.

All rights reserved under International and Pan-American Copyright Conventions. Published in
the United States by Ballantine Books, a division of Random House, Inc., New York, and
distributed in Canada by Random House of Canada Limited, Toronto.

Excerpt from "What a Friend We Have in Jesus," © 1855 by Fleming H. Revell Company.

http://www.randomhouse.com

Library of Congress Catalog Card Number: 96-97140

ISBN: 0-345-40603-6

This edition published by arrangement with G. P. Putnam's Sons.

Cover design by Barbara Leff
Cover photo © Tom Campbell/FPG International

Manufactured in the United States of America

First Ballantine Books Edition: April 1997

10 9 8 7 6 5 4

"It is in the shelter of each other that the people live."

IRISH PROVERB

To Bernard and Phyllis Pipher,
who have taught me about building strong families.
They have given me their loyalty and steadfastness.
Their love has held my life in place.

Acknowledgments

I want to thank my aunt Margaret Nemoede, whose book *And the Winds Blow Free* provided information about my grandparents. I thank all my clients and friends who told me their stories. I am grateful to Andrea Simon, Sherri Hanigan, Beatty Brasch, Laura Freeman, Rose Dame, Natalie Porter, Gertrude Fisher and Jan Stenberg for their conversations about the book. I thank my photographer friend Randy Barger and my two writers' groups—Prairie Trout and the Nebraska Wesleyan Writers' Group. I thank my readers—Jan Zegers, Herb Howe, Marge Saiser, Pam Barger, Sue Howe, Ellen Debas, Mary Kenning, Dave Iaquinta, Frank McPherson, Francis Baty and Paul Gruchow. Also, I appreciate the support of Joelle Delbourgo, Rachel Tarlow, Lisa Cahn, Cathy Fox, Kate Murphy, Judy Burns Miller, Susan Petersen and my beloved Jane Isay. Thanks to my agent, Susan Lee Cohen. Thank you to my three families, the Brays, Pages and Piphers, and to Sara, Zeke and Jim.

Contents

═══════

PART III
SOLUTIONS: WHAT WILL
SURVIVE OF US IS LOVE

The Shelter
of Each Other

INTRODUCTION

When my son was ten and my daughter four, we camped at Blue Stem Lake. In the afternoon Zeke landed a twelve-inch bass and Sara rescued a frog. While my husband played his guitar under a cottonwood, I lay reading on the shore. For dinner we ate hamburgers and beans. In the dark, we roasted marshmallows around a fire. We listened to cicadas and the motor of a small boat. A moon the shape and color of a pumpkin rose over the lake. Sara snuggled into her father and said a line so beautiful that I can quote it fifteen years later: "I'm melting into richness."

Zeke told us about a boy in his karate class who supposedly saved his mother from a mugger. He told us that he fell asleep nights hoping a robber would break in. He said, "Nothing would make me happier than saving our family from bad guys."

As I watched the stars come out and the moon climb into the sky, I thought about four million years of families. Lucky families have always had days like this—days outdoors fishing and swimming, feeling wind and sun, and later, eating together by a fire. A coyote wailed in the distance. We speculated how far away it was. I talked about the baby coyotes I had for pets when I was young. Jim played guitar and Zeke stirred the fire. I wanted to stop time and keep us this way forever. I felt the ghosts of a million mothers, each of whom must have had this same thought.

———

Magical moments are embedded in ordinary life. The joys and sorrows of family are as mixed together as salt and pepper can be mixed, and as inseparable. Those same children who delighted me around the camp-fire drove me wild a few years later when they were teens. Even today they can irritate me and vice versa on a regular basis. I have memories of sad and crazy times in both my family of origin and my current family. As a child I was upset by family problems, and as an adult I have lost a great deal of sleep worrying about my children. But I prefer to recall the happy memories.

I remember the day my husband invented car dancing. We were driving through snow to Minneapolis. The children were tired of car games and each other. Jim put on a Van Morrison tape and announced a car dancing competition. As Van sang, "The caravan is painted red and white, everyone is staying overnight," Jim twisted and swayed as much as he could while driving a van. Soon the kids were dancing in their seat belts, raising their hands high, oohing with the chorus. We moaned our way across the Middle Raccoon River in Iowa as the sun went down. Then it was dark and we were in Minnesota. We had all won the dance contest.

When I was five, my cousin Steve taught me to fish near his Ozark home. He baited my hook and took off the bluegills and perch that I pulled in one after another. I remember Sunday dinners at my grand-parents' home in eastern Colorado. Twenty people gathered around a table heaped with chicken, roast beef, homemade biscuits and water-melon pickles. My grandfather said grace, my grandmother poured tea into tall, sweaty glasses. I remember my mother in the 1950s, driving to see patients along county roads and telling stories of her childhood. And I can see Aunt Betty crawling through the Idaho woods for huckleber-ries to make pies. I see my aunt Margaret at sunset reciting poetry about the "wine dark sea" and the ocean that is "always changing and always the same."

At a family reunion, I looked at pictures of my father and his mother, both of whom died long ago. My father's eyes reminded me of my son's; my daughter's body was that of my grandmother. Talking on the porch late into the night with my brothers, we had the same forty-year-old memories of snapping-turtle soup and black beans around a smoky camp-fire. As we talked of those times, the same ripples of expression flashed across our faces.

Since I was a little girl, I have struggled to make sense of my family, which was noisy, complicated and filled with intense, emotional people. They argued politics and religion and they made diverse decisions about love and work. I tried to figure out how everyone was wired. Why did certain people fall in love? Why was one cousin spoiled and hard to get along with and another wonderfully patient with his younger siblings? Why did one uncle drink so much? Why did one family forbid rock and roll?

When I went to college, I majored in anthropology. I wanted to understand why we do what we do. Why do we value what we value and hate what we hate? How do cultures get organized in certain ways? Who makes the rules? What part of family business is unique to the family and what part is cultural? How does being Irish and Scottish shape our family? How does coming from poor, rural areas such as the Ozark Mountains and eastern Colorado affect our point of view? Later, I went to graduate school in psychology and became a therapist. My adult work is really the continuation of a lifelong quest to figure out "what the deal is."

The answers are complicated, elusive and partial. Honest parents don't always raise honest kids. Abusive parents sometimes have wonderful children. One of the most wholesome girls I know lives with her alcoholic mother in a small apartment. Some of the unhappiest children I know come from the families of sensitive, child-focused parents. Children who are loved and protected sometimes grow up strong and well adjusted and sometimes they grow into hothouse flowers who suffer from "the princess and the pea syndrome."

Children who are ignored sometimes become as strong, beautiful and resilient as sunflowers and sometimes they turn into dangerous psychopaths. Well-meaning families sometimes have extraordinarily bad luck with their children, while slapdash parents may raise highly successful children.

Not all families are healthy and not all parents good at their jobs. I have seen terrible things happen in families. My first client was a young woman who had grown up on a farm and was repeatedly raped by her father and brothers. Another client's mother had murdered her brother. Currently I'm seeing a woman who has a crooked back because her father threw her across a room when she was two years old. I've seen hate-filled, violent families, families with addictions, families in which the parents were not grown-ups and the children had no childhoods and families in which the children were starving for moral nourishment. I know how destructive families can be, how stifling and riddled with pain. But I also know that this is not the whole, or even the most interesting part, of the story.

Families are ancient institutions. Since humans crossed the savannas in search of food, our families have been unique. Human brains are so large that our heads can barely make it through the birth canal. We are born helpless and dependent, and after birth our brains continue to grow. Unlike monkeys, who can run around within hours of birth and are self-sufficient within a few months, it takes humans in even the simplest environments more than a decade to be independent of parents. Homo sapiens needs families to survive.

We need our families but we don't always behave well in them. We love and hate them, yearn for them deep in our bones and feel so disgusted with them that we want to spit. Like all interesting and important phenomena—jazz, Shakespeare or Zen—families are sad and happy, complicated and simple, and full of victories and failures. Families remind me of what Greg Brown wrote about life, that sometimes it seems as if we should be grateful for every breath and other times it's a miracle that we don't all drink ourselves to death. They make me think of lines from a Leonard Cohen song. In "Dance Me to the End of Love" he writes, "Raise the tent of shelter although every thread is torn." Buddhists say that families are filled with ten thousand joys and ten thousand sorrows.

It's impossible to capture the diversity or complexity of families. I'll attempt something considerably less ambitious—to explore how our culture affects the mental health of families that I know. This book tells stories of the families I see in my Midwestern city. My goal is to encourage discussions about what families need. The book isn't a how-to book but is, I hope, a how-to-think book. I discuss fewer solutions than I do problems. I believe the solutions will be found family by family and community by community.

This book will sympathize with families' efforts to survive a difficult era. It is for the vast majority of parents who are trying hard to do the right thing. It will connect family problems to larger cultural forces. My goal is to help readers be anthropologists, who look at the broader culture and ask—How does the culture affect the life of my family? What values does it teach? What behaviors does it influence? How does the culture define the good and important? I want to help families become more conscious of how they are shaped by the culture in which they live.

I write about families because I love them. When I travel alone far from home, I think of my children's faces to calm myself down. I picture them smiling, studying, playing violin or volleyball. I picture my husband's face bent over his guitar or relaxed and fresh, the way it is on the mornings when we drink coffee together on the front porch. Those faces are my mandalas. They comfort and secure me. The faces of those we love are the first, the primal, mandalas for us all.

Part I

THE CRISIS

THE FIRST SECTION of this book examines the loss of old-fashioned communities, the rise of an electronic community and a consumer mentality, and the influence of popular psychology. I want to explore the relationship between this family ecology and family well-being. I tell two main stories, that of my grandparents, who homesteaded on the harsh plains of Colorado in the early part of this century, and that of a family I saw recently in therapy. I'll compare these families on a variety of dimensions—their relationship to the broader culture, their tools, their media exposure, the importance of time and money and the involvement of mental health professionals in their lives.

These are both good families trying to do their best, but the different times present them with different challenges. The Pages had problems of privation, the Copelands the problems of plenty. The Page family had time but no money, the Copelands have money but no time. It is hard to argue that the 1930s were idyllic. They were times of poverty, disease and backbreaking labor. My grandparents told stories of children dying of rattlesnake bites and cholera. An old couple from Kit Carson County was found dead in their bed, an empty box of cereal between them. But I will argue that the Pages knew what the enemy was—tornadoes, droughts, locusts, blizzards. Their worst enemies were external to the family and they could fight against them together. This family had the closeness of people who worked in subzero weather together.

The Copelands were relatively protected from the natural elements, but they had new hostile elements—crime, isolation and a continuous flow of information that was impossible to process. Brian did work he hated at a corporation that was downsizing. Sandi, whose work was more rewarding, came home tired with "second shift" work awaiting her. Their oldest daughter was anorexic, their second daughter was acting up and their son was afraid to go to school. They'd been told they were dysfunctional.

The Copelands were more prosperous and had more choices, but they were thirsty in the rain. They were stressed as individuals and as a unit. They didn't know each other very well and rarely had time together. The Copelands were less clear about who the enemy was and sometimes they blamed each other for their pain.

Chapter Five explores how tools and electronic media have changed communities and families. Chapters Six and Seven examine the role that therapy has played in the lives of families. I outline some of the mistakes that we therapists have made and offer some suggestions for a more family-helping therapy.

Chapter One

═══════════════

Thirsty in the Rain

"Events are in the saddle and ride mankind."
RALPH WALDO EMERSON

We have a six-foot corn plant in our office waiting room. It's not a good environment for a plant. There are no windows, little kids tear off its leaves, and we therapists, who are known for our nurturing abilities, keep forgetting to water it and dust its leaves. Sometime in the late 1980s we gave it plant food. But month after month, as old leaves turn brown and drop off, fresh green leaves sprout from its center. The corn plant is a good metaphor for families—it's plain, not at all exotic or even attractive, and it's in a hostile environment. But it's surviving.

Our culture is at war with families. Families in America have been invaded by technology, mocked or "kitschified" by the media, isolated by demographic changes, pounded by economic forces and hurt by corporate values. They have been frightened by crime in their neighborhoods. Parents worry about their children's physical safety and children are afraid of strangers. When I speak to or smile at children I don't know, I see fear and doubt in their eyes. I know adults who no longer touch or spend time with children they don't know well. (They are afraid of misunderstandings.) A culture in which children fear adults and adults are uneasy around children is an unhealthy and dangerous place.

Until quite recently adults and children trusted each other. When I was a girl, I sold Girl Scout cookies door to door to everyone in my town of 420 people. Now parents do not allow their daughters to knock on strangers' doors. And most neighbors are strangers. Instead the parents sell the cookies to their co-workers. The children miss a chance to meet adults and adults do not know the children who live nearby.

Something is terribly wrong with the culture in which families are expected to function. Parents who would have handled things on their own twenty years ago now call for therapy appointments. Often the parents are decent people with reasonable ideas about parenting. The kids seem well meaning and likable, but something clearly isn't working. The parents are trying harder than parents twenty years ago tried, and yet their children aren't doing as well. In the 1990s, it's harder to be a "good enough" parent. Parents seem desperate and lost and their children are bitter and out of control.

Too often families are blamed for our cultural crisis. They make an easy target. They are screwed up in a variety of ways. People argue or they don't express themselves, they depend on each other too much and then let each other down. Families have secrets and shame, overemotional and underemotional members. Family members are too close or too distant, have too much conflict or too little. Family members ignore, control and perpetually make mistakes. Every family has its Achilles' heel or even its Achilles' torso. We all can tell "family from hell" stories, usually about our own families.

But families are also our shelter from the storm, our oldest and most precious institution and our last great hope. Families were once powerful institutions, strong enough to withstand assaults. But now almost every force in our culture works against families. Parents do not know how to protect their children from crime, media, poverty, alcohol and bad company. They can no longer give their children childhoods. It's a terrible time to undercut families.

The culture of the 1990s is too hard for many families to handle. As a therapist, I see families in which the parents work long hours, in which sick children go to day care or teenagers rebel in ways that terrify their parents. Parents are confused and vulnerable to depression, addictions, violence and mind-numbing cynicism. One in eight adults abuses alcohol, a phenomenon that wreaks havoc in families and in the culture. We have many new tools: fax machines, computers and car phones. We have home entertainment centers, which keep people from neighborhood events; and Nintendo, which keeps kids from playing with each other. We can interact on the Internet with people from all over the world. Now, all these tools have their uses and their good points. I wouldn't argue that any tool is bad and should be eliminated. It's the whole pile that's the problem. The cumulative effect of the pile is to change the way we live in families.

Tools have been added to our lives, one at a time, and we haven't been terribly conscious of the psychological effects of all this technology. We've slowly absorbed each change and been changed in the process. I'm reminded of a story. A frog who is dropped in a beaker of boiling water will jump out and save himself. But if he's in a beaker with water that's slowly heated, he'll stay in and cook to death. We've experienced change slowly and we haven't jumped.

The last decades of this century have produced families stressed about time, money, lack of social supports, addictions and crime. As Jonis Agee wrote: "Every family is trying to figure things out. Maybe not the exact things we are, but everybody's got the same things going on: parents mixed up about their own lives, kids not trusting each other and trying to figure out how to live. Nobody gets a map anymore."

Since my childhood, the world has changed dramatically. When I was a child, my world was about Sunday dinners, relatives, card parties, church, school and farming. Now it's a world about talk shows, cable television, e-mail, nanoseconds, microwave meals, celebrities and other people far away getting rich. Our children are growing up in a consumption-oriented, electronic community that is teaching them very different values from those we say we value.

The role of parents has changed dramatically. Good parents used to introduce their children into the broader culture; now they try to protect their children from the broader culture. Good parents used to instill the values of the broader culture; now they try to teach their children values very different from the ones the world at large teaches.

Because of these changes, all of us are off script. But we sense how different and how much more difficult things are. A father said he could no longer take his seven-year-old daughter to the public pools. She'd been subjected to "filthy taunting" by a group of nine- to eleven-year-old boys. He said ruefully, "I'd like to see public caning for sexual harassment." One mother said, "I wish we could live in a castle with a moat full of alligators. I want to lock my kids up till they're twenty-five, just to keep them safe." Another told me of her fantasy of taking her children to live in the wilderness, "if there are any wild places left anymore."

While I bought gas at a Quick Stop, a young man came in. He bought a pack of cigarettes and a six-pack of beer and paid for his gas. He shyly bought a ticket for Powerball and asked the clerk to explain how it works. He looked so young—nineteen at most—and so eager to learn about life. I wondered if he'd get hooked on gambling. I felt bitter that our voters have made it easy for him to acquire another bad habit.

Gabriella, a pretty girl with long black hair, suffered some social isolation in junior high. She said, "At school I'm nice to my teachers and other kids call me a suck-up." She looked confused. "But that's the real me. I don't want to throw spitballs at the ceiling." She was afraid to go to parties with her friends. She sighed. "Last week at a party, a boy brought 'hot shots.' That's cherry Jell-O made with Everclear. They got drunk and barfed up red Jell-O all over a white carpet. I don't need that in my life." She rubbed her forehead sadly. "But I do want friends."

Micki came in after her son Reuben was picked up for shoplifting. She worked at a demanding job an hour's commute from their small apartment. Many of the neighbor children were poorly supervised and Micki was afraid her son would find bad company. But she hated to have him stay inside and watch TV all the time. She felt her son needed a "father figure." Over the years she had had boyfriends, but they all had abandoned Reuben when they broke up with her. Reuben loved his grandfather, who took him fishing and told him stories about the olden days. Micki said, "There's nothing wrong with my son that his grandfather couldn't cure. But Dad lives a thousand miles away and Reuben has seen him twice in his life."

Anna sobbed through her entire session. Her daughter was having a big wedding with three hundred guests and a country club reception. The daughter hadn't invited Anna and her husband. Anna said, "I know we've made mistakes, but we did many things right. I stayed home with Leslie. I was her Camp Fire girls' troop leader and drove her to dance lessons. Joe and I didn't drink or hit the kids. We paid for a private college. Leslie says I emotionally abused her when she was a girl. I yelled sometimes, when I was really pushed, but I wasn't abusive. Why is our daughter acting this weird?"

Families are old institutions with very new problems. For the first time in two thousand years of Western civilization, families live in houses without walls. That is, they live in a world in which walls offer no protection. Technology has brought the outside world into the living room.

Social scientists have walked in and second-guessed the way parents function. Crime on the nightly news makes all places feel dangerous. Electronic media seeps into the interstices of homes and teaches children ways of thinking, feeling and behaving that are at odds with common sense. Families are reeling under the pressures of a culture they can't control. I worry whether families can keep surviving the way the office corn plant keeps surviving.

MEDIA

The media forms our new community. The electronic village is our hometown. The old community of particular people in particular places and times who knew each other in a variety of ways over decades has been replaced by what Greg Brown calls "one big town." Parents and children are more likely to recognize Bill Cosby or Jerry Seinfeld than they are their next-door neighbors. All of us know O.J., Michael, Newt and Madonna. The gossip is about celebrities—Did Liz spend time at a diet camp? Why did Lyle Lovett and Julia Roberts get a divorce?

Relationships with celebrities feel personal. We are sad when our favorites—Jackie, John Lennon, Roy Orbison or Jessica Tandy—die. We're happy when Christie Brinkley marries on a mountaintop or when Oprah loses weight. We follow the news of the stars' addictions, health problems, business deals and relationships. We know their dogs' and children's names. These relationships feel personal. But they aren't.

We "know" celebrities but they don't know us. The new community is not a reciprocal neighborhood like earlier ones. David Letterman won't be helping out if our car battery dies on a winter morning. Donald Trump won't bring groceries over if Dad loses his job. Jane Fonda won't baby-sit in a pinch. Dan Rather won't coach a local basketball team. Tom Hanks won't scoop the snow off your driveway when you have the flu.

These vicarious relationships create a new kind of loneliness—the loneliness of people whose relationships are with personae instead of persons. Years ago a sociologist postulated that there was a critical number of social contacts that a person needed every week to stay sane. He speculated that unless seven familiar people "interacted" with the person, he or she would be at risk for mental illness. I think about that study as I write this and wonder how many people have fallen below that critical number.

The electronic community is less diverse than real life. The problems it deals with are not the problems that real people must face. Certain situations, such as young starlets being threatened or handsome men fighting crime, are overexplored. Other stories, much more common, such as school board meetings, poetry writing, trips to museums, piano practice or the delivery of Meals on Wheels, are virtually ignored. People who are not visually interesting, which is most of us, are underrepresented. The stories that are selected are those that make money. A richness and complexity of real life disappears.

We are just beginning to grasp the implications for families of our electronic village. Parents have no real community to back up the values that they try to teach their children. Family members may be in the same house, but they are no longer truly interacting. They may be in the same room, but instead of making their own story, they are watching another family's story unfold. Or even more likely, family members are separated, having private experiences with different electronic equipment.

As Bill Moyers put it, "Our children are being raised by appliances." There are televisions in birthing rooms so that literally, from birth on, children are exposed to media. Children see and hear information that is not appropriate to their developmental needs. Before they learn to ride tricycles, they are exposed to sexual and violent materials. Two-year-olds are not ready for sexual scenes or news of the murder of children. Five-year-olds aren't ready for the Power Rangers, and eight-year-olds are not equipped to think through the messages of Snoop Doggy Dog.

We flood children with sexual stimulation. In magazine ads, seminude teens lock in an embrace to sell underpants or jeans. On a talk show, a man describes his sexual interest in feet. On the radio a filmmaker describes his work: "Making a movie is like simultaneously getting a blow job and getting hit on the head with a hammer." Video games often feature scantily clad sexualized women. Home computers connect pedophiles with children learning to type. Children have scant protection from sexual messages that twenty years ago would have been taboo for grown-ups.

We must remember that all television is educational. It teaches values and behavior. Children are manipulated from the time they can sit in front of a television. The average child is exposed to four hundred ads a day, which will add up to more than four million ads in a lifetime. Children are taught to be consumers and sold products—junk foods, overpriced clothes and useless toys. Two-year-olds beg parents for products they've seen advertised on TV. One mother told me that her son's first words were "I want." Another mother brought in her four-year-old's drawings of beer signs.

Children learn these things from ads: that they are the most important person in the universe, that impulses should not be denied, that pain should not be tolerated and that the cure for any kind of pain is a product. They learn a weird mix of dissatisfaction and entitlement. With the messages of ads, we are socializing children to be self-centered, impulsive and addicted. The television, which Leonard Cohen called "that hopeless little screen," teaches values as clearly as any church.

We may try to protect our own children from such nonsense, but they live in a world with children who have been socialized into this value system. Indeed there is corporate colonialism. Children everywhere may be teased if they don't have designer jeans and Barney toys or if they don't know how to power-kick. Their peers will teach them to be consumers even if they do not learn from the primary sources. Recently I was on the west coast of Scotland in a town overlooking the Inner Hebrides, a town of less than a hundred people that was known for its silver sands and steam train. As I hiked beside a loch, I met a girl picking wild blackberries with her mother and grandmother. She wore pink plastic Barbie doll boots.

CULTURE AND PERSONALITY

"Make society do its duty to the individual and the individual will be sure and do his duties to society."—Henry James

On public radio a Native American from Alaska discussed the problems of his Arctic Circle village—child abuse, alcoholism, gambling, malnutrition, insanity and violence. He said, "They took away the people one by one for treatment, but really the disease was in the village. We could only understand what was happening by looking at the community."

Freud said a healthy human is one who can love and work. What is true for individuals can apply to cultures. A healthy culture is one that allows its members to love and work. All cultures are not equal. When a culture is not healthy, individuals become sick as well.

Decent societies produce decent people just as indecent ones produce circumscribed, cruel people. Certain environments allow the human spirit to flower. New England in the middle 1800s comes to mind, especially the Concord, Massachusetts, of Louisa May Alcott, Ralph Waldo Emerson and Henry David Thoreau. The mood of that time and place was optimistic, adventurous and striving. People were encouraged to grow and develop personally and to work hard for the betterment of others. Other cultures, such as China in this century, produced people whose souls were scarred by the adjustments they made to survive.

Now it's time to say something about words, such as "moral" and "values," which I use throughout this book. These are emotionally loaded, under-analyzed words exploited by demagogues, mocked by some people and candy-coated by others. It's almost impossible to use them without falling into one polarized pit or another. But morality is not the property of any one political party, race, religious group or segment of the population. And morality refers not only to sex and violence but also to the use of power, time and money. Broadly defined, morality is about making decent and wise choices about how to be in the universe. It implies purposeful action for the common good.

For a society to flourish, people must have some common moral beliefs. These beliefs determine many things—the kindness of the culture, its work ethic, what it punishes and what it rewards. We're a pluralistic culture struggling to find common beliefs, and unfortunately, our most central belief system is about the importance of money. Many of us reject a value system based on economics—a value system that says that more is better, that money equals happiness and that consumption is the goal of life. But via media and advertising, our children are being educated to believe that products are what matter. This will hurt them, and ultimately it will hurt us all.

America has long been a culture that produced good people. However, our culture has changed rapidly in the last twenty years. Many of the changes—in technology, the media, the economy and values—are making it more difficult for us to be good people. Parents, many of whom are trying harder than their parents tried, are having more trouble with their children. Children growing up in inner cities find they have few options besides joining gangs and selling drugs. Their schools are poor, there are no jobs and college loan moneys have dried up.

Cultures construct reality for their members. Morality, eroticism, work and families are all social constructions. As Neil Postman pointed out in *The Disappearance of Childhood*, childhood is a social construction. In the preliterate culture of the Middle Ages, children had no childhoods. They were viewed as small adults, as we can see from the way they were painted in the pictures of the times. They weren't seen as having special developmental needs and they were used for economic and sexual purposes. They drank, smoked and worked alongside adults.

When people began to read, a two-tiered culture formed—adults could read and children couldn't. Children were viewed as different from adults and as having developmental stages with corresponding needs. They were defined as a protected class and sheltered from certain experiences. They were encouraged to play and learn. From this distinction between readers and non-readers, the walls of childhood were constructed—schools and freedom from wage-earning work. Before books, everyone had access to the same kinds of information. After books, literate adults knew things that children didn't. They knew about such things as theology, history, people in other countries, science and philosophy. They also knew about bad things, such as murders, wars and famines, from which they sheltered children. With print culture, adulthood conveyed both responsibilities and privileges.

In the last decades of our century, for the first time since the 1500s, children have access to the same information that adults have. The walls that protected children and elevated adulthood are coming down. In our electronic village, everyone can watch MTV, Freddie Kreuger and the nightly news. Everyone can play Nintendo and plug into the Internet. Children are not sheltered from what has been considered for hundreds of years to be adult material.

With electronic culture we are deconstructing childhood. Likewise adults are vanishing, if by "adults" we mean people who have special knowledge and who accept special responsibilities. Many adults have no different information than their children have. They watch the same television shows and play the same computer and video games. As Joshua

Meyrowitz wrote: "We are becoming a nation of neither children nor adults. Rather we all exist in some age zone between childhood and adulthood. We're a nation of adolescents—preoccupied with ourselves, sexualized, moody and impulsive, seeking freedom without responsibility."

Culture acts on personalities and vice versa. Good and bad people live in all times and places. Barbara Tuchman's *A Distant Mirror* tells the story of a man, Enguerrand de Coucy VII (1340–1397), who was gentle in a brutal time and civilized in a barbarous culture. The Marquis de Sade and Rousseau were contemporaries, as were Jack the Ripper and Charles Dickens, Miguel de Unamuno and Francisco Franco. The Nebraska culture of the 1950s produced Dick Cavett and Charles Starkweather.

The problems in any given family are not just the result of cultural forces or just the result of family dynamics. Both the culture and the family influence the development of children. When one factor is examined exclusively, the picture is incomplete. Focusing solely on family dynamics, we let the culture off the hook, and focusing exclusively on the culture lets the family off the hook. Somehow we need to attend to the interaction of the cultural and familial factors.

Families have existed in all times and places, but their forms and philosophies vary enormously. Certain eternal questions must be addressed. What is family business vs. the business of the state? What is the balance between family unity and individual independence? What are the relations between parents and children? Who does what work? How are children socialized into the culture? How are values passed from one generation to the next? Who is responsible when a person fails to do his duties? These questions must have answers if families are to know how to behave and raise their children. If children are not properly raised, a culture will not long survive.

The healthier the culture, the more individual and familial factors can be the defining ones. In a healthy, decent society, families have some power to define their members. And individuals have great power to define themselves. Many important variables, such as safety, education, adequate income and freedom, can be taken for granted. Hence, family dynamics and individual choices account for many of the differences between people.

When psychologist Lois Murphy did her research with families, Topeka was a safe, homogenous environment. What mattered most were the individual characteristics of children and their particular parents. But in less safe and secure cultures, society defines individual lives much more than membership in a particular family. In Nazi Germany, during the reign of Pol Pot in Cambodia or in an urban ghetto in the 1990s, the larger culture shapes the lives of its members. I would argue that in America today, the broader culture is increasingly shaping the lives of our children.

Of course, today's families have the old problems that they have had for centuries, the problems described in the Bible, *The Canterbury Tales*, and the work of Shakespeare, Faulkner and Ibsen: ungrateful children, self-involved parents, jealous siblings, insane relatives, unfaithful mates and prodigal sons. I would never argue that families are blissful. In fact, my favorite writers, Raymond Carver, Barbara Kingsolver, Carol Blye, and Alice Munro, write about the humble, sometimes hopeless, efforts to hold things together in the modern family. But I will argue that today, in addition to the problems that families have always had, many new burdens have been added.

We have seen that countries do better when their enemies are external. Think of England during the blitz or the United States right after the bombing of Pearl Harbor. Since the Soviet system has fallen, we Americans are fighting more with each other. When we have a common enemy, such as an earthquake or a war, citizens are more united. The same is often true of families. With external enemies, such as a house fire or a tornado, they rise to their zenith of loyalty.

Families also tend to do better with concrete rather than abstract problems. Parents know what to do when children are thirsty or hungry. They are less sure what to do about children with no motivation. When families are reasonably prosperous and healthy, abstract problems become more important. When people are poor, ill or politically persecuted, the enemy is easy to spot. Family angst comes in times of plenty and relative security. Nobody worries about their mate's neuroses when they are worried about bread for the table or a bear is attacking the tent.

Wealthy parents in this country have a difficult dilemma. They must say no to children for abstract rather than concrete reasons. They can afford to buy what their children want, yet most know that too much consumption is not good. It spoils children. They must explain their decisions to their children, who have been primed to consume. They say,

"You don't really need that" or "That isn't good for you." These explanations engender more arguments and resentment than saying, "We can't afford it."

Here's an example of how a family problem is related to cultural change. Many parents bemoan their teenagers' dependency. Adolescents want parents to do things for them that the parents remember doing for themselves when they were teens. Teens beg for rides and money and act helpless when it's time to plan a school project. One father said, "I don't understand it. We have worked hard to give our kids choices and responsibilities. Why are they so helpless?"

When the father was growing up, his parents allowed him to go places without constantly warning him about dangers. He could develop a sense of competency as he navigated his small world. He learned to structure his own time and he learned that his own behavior determined his successes or failures. Today his children are more fearful. It's harder for them to feel safe, competent and in control. This isn't just a parenting issue, it's a social problem.

In *The Age of Missing Information*, Bill McKibben reported that in the 1950s Americans were the most satisfied with their lives. The 1950s were more prosperous than the 1920s, but less materialistic than the 1990s. By the 1950s most people had indoor plumbing, electricity, telephones, refrigeration, good roads and antibiotics. But they didn't have flowered toilet paper, designer jeans, computer games or vaginal sprays. In the 1950s people were less sexually repressed than in the 1920s, but not as sexually obsessed as in the 1990s. The media was new and unsophisticated. It had not yet become the defining force in the education of children.

Any discussion of the 1950s is immediately emotionally loaded. The left focuses on the problems of the 1950s and the right focuses on the benefits of that era. Any statement about the 1950s sounds political. But in fact, the 1950s were much more complex than either side acknowledges. The 1950s had serious problems. It was a time of Jim Crow laws, anti-Semitism, McCarthyism and the enforced housewifery for women. Many problems were hidden rather than solved and there was a great deal of hypocrisy. Of course, we haven't exactly eliminated those problems by today.

The 1950s was not an era with much tolerance for diversity. For example, I remember Rick, the one gay in our town. He "came out" by trying to kiss another boy, who told all his friends about the incident. Rick was shunned by all the boys and most of the girls and teased mercilessly for the "sin" of being different. He does not come back for high school reunions. Today there is probably more tolerance of diversity and less institutional racism.

But the 1950s also was a time of strong unions and of government and economic policies that supported a strong middle class. Many people were more prosperous than their parents had been. In the fifties, most children and parents were optimistic about the future. Communities existed all over America, including in cities. Even my Afro-American friends, none of whom wants to go back to the 1950s, speak fondly of the black community in those days. Crime rates were low and people were safer. Most parents could be good enough parents. Ordinary people with ordinary skills could raise decent children.

In our era families have the worst of all worlds. In the wilderness a family is a self-contained unit that can protect itself from external forces by building a cabin with strong walls. In a caring community, a family can survive without walls. Family members live among friends who share their values and will help them out. Today families are neither self-contained nor embedded in caring communities. They do not have walls, and yet in many places the wolf is at the door.

BELIEFS ABOUT FAMILIES

When I speak of families, I usually mean biological families. There is a power in blood ties that cannot be denied. But in our fragmented, chaotic culture, many people don't have biological families nearby. For many people, friends become family. Family is a collection of people who pool resources and help each other over the long haul. Families love one another even when that requires sacrifice. Family means that if you disagree, you still stay together.

Families are the people for whom it matters if you have a cold, are feuding with your mate or training a new puppy. Family members use magnets to fasten the newspaper clippings about your bowling team on the refrigerator door. They save your drawings and homemade pottery.

They like to hear stories about when you were young. They'll help you can tomatoes or change the oil in your car. They're the people who will come visit you in the hospital, will talk to you when you call with "a dark night of the soul" and will loan you money to pay the rent if you lose your job. Whether or not they are biologically related to each other, the people who do these things are family.

If you are very lucky, family is the group you were born into. But some are not that lucky. When Janet was in college, her parents were killed in a car wreck. In her early twenties she married, but three years later she lost her husband to leukemia. She has one sister, who calls mainly when she's suicidal or needs money. Janet is a congresswoman in a western state, a hard worker and an idealist. Her family consists of the men, women and children she's grown to depend on in the twenty-five years she's lived in her community. Except for her beloved dog, nobody lives with her. But she brings the cinnamon rolls to one family's Thanksgiving dinner and has a Mexican fiesta for families at her house on New Year's Eve. She attends Bar Mitzvahs, weddings, school concerts and soccer matches. She told me with great pride, "When I sprained my ankle skiing last year, three families brought me meals."

I think of Morgan, a jazz musician who long ago left his small town and rigid, judgmental family. He had many memories of his father whipping him with a belt or making him sleep in the cold. Once he said to me, "I was eighteen years old before anyone ever told me I had something to offer." Indeed he does. He plays the violin beautifully. He teaches improvisation and jazz violin and organizes jazz events for his town. His family is the family of musicians and music lovers that he has built around him over the years.

If you are very unlucky, you come from a nuclear family that didn't care for you. Curtis, who as a boy was regularly beaten by his father, lied about his age so that he could join the Navy at sixteen. Years later he wrote his parents and asked if he could return home for Christmas. They didn't answer his letter. When I saw him in therapy, I encouraged him to look for a new family, among his cousins and friends from the Navy. Sometimes cutoffs, tragic as they are, are unavoidable.

I think of Anita, who never knew her father and whose mother abandoned her when she was seven. Anita was raised by an aunt and uncle, whom she loved very much. As an adult she tracked down her mother and tried to establish a relationship, but her mother wasn't interested. At least Anita was able to find other family members to love her. She had a family in her aunt and uncle.

Family need not be traditional or biological. But what family offers is not easily replicated. Let me share a Sioux word, *tiospaye*, which means the people with whom one lives. The tiospaye is probably closer to a kibbutz than to any other Western institution. The tiospaye gives children multiple parents, aunts, uncles and grandparents. It offers children a corrective factor for problems in their nuclear families. If parents are difficult, there are other adults around to soften and diffuse the situation. Until the 1930s, when the tiospaye began to fall apart with sale of land, migration and alcoholism, there was not much mental illness among the Sioux. When all adults were responsible for all children, people grew up healthy.

What tiospaye offers and what biological family offers is a place that all members can belong to regardless of merit. Everyone is included regardless of health, likability or prestige. What's most valuable about such institutions is that people are in by virtue of being born into the group. People are in even if they've committed a crime, been a difficult person, become physically or mentally disabled or are unemployed and broke. That ascribed status was what Robert Frost valued when he wrote that home "was something you somehow hadn't to deserve."

Many people do not have access to either a supportive biological family or a tiospaye. They make do with a "formed family." Others simply prefer a community of friends to their biological families. The problem with formed families is they often have less staying power. They might not take you in, give you money if you lose a job or visit you in a rest home if you are paralyzed in a car crash. My father had a stroke and lost most of his sight and speech. Family members were the people who invited him to visit and helped him through the long tough years after his stroke. Of course, there are formed families who do this. With the AIDS crisis, many gays have supported their friends through terrible times. Often immigrants will help each other in this new country. And there are families who don't stick together in crisis. But generally blood is thicker than water. Families come through when they must.

Another problem with formed families is that not everyone has the skills to be included in that kind of family. Friendship isn't a product that can be obtained for cash. People need friends today more than ever, but friends are harder to make in a world where people are busy, moving and isolated. Some people don't have the skills. They are shy, abrasive or dull. Crack babies have a hard time making friends, as do people with Alzheimer's. Formed families can leave many people out.

From my point of view the issue isn't biology. Rather the issues are commitment and inclusiveness. I don't think for most of us it has to be either/or. A person can have both a strong network of friends and a strong family. It is important to define family broadly so that all kinds of families, such as single-parent families, multigenerational families, foster families and the families of gays are included. But I agree with David Blankenberg's conclusion in his book *Rebuilding the Nest*: "Even with all the problems of nuclear families, I will support it as an institution until something better comes along."

Americans hold two parallel versions of the family—the idealized version and the dysfunctional version. The idealized version portrays families as wellsprings of love and happiness, loyal, wholesome and true. This is the version we see in *Leave It to Beaver* or *Father Knows Best*. The dysfunctional version depicts families as disturbed and disturbing, and suggests that salvation lies in extricating oneself from all the ties that bind. Both versions have had their eras. In the 1950s the idealized version was at its zenith. Extolling family was in response to the Depression and war, which separated families. People who had been wrenched away from home missed their families and thought of them with great longing. They idealized how close and warm they had been.

In the 1990s the dysfunctional version of family seems the most influential. This belief system goes along with the culture of narcissism, which sells people the idea that families get in the way of individual fulfillment. Currently, many Americans are deeply mistrustful of their own and other people's families. Pop psychology presents families as pathology-producing. Talk shows make families look like hotbeds of sin and sickness. Day after day people testify about the diverse forms of emotional abuse that they suffered in their families. Movies and television often portray families as useless impediments.

In our culture, after a certain age, children no longer have permission to love their parents. We define adulthood as breaking away, disagreeing and making up new rules. Just when teenagers most need their parents, they are encouraged to distance from them. A friend told me of walking with her son in a shopping mall. They passed some of his friends and she noticed that suddenly he was ten feet behind, trying hard not to be seen with her. She said, "I felt like I was drooling and wearing purple plaid polyester." Later her son told her that he enjoyed being with her, but that his friends all hated their parents and he would be teased if anyone knew he loved her. He said, "I'm confused about this. Am I supposed to hate you?"

This socialized antipathy toward families is unusual. Most cultures revere and respect family. In Vietnam, for example, the tender word for lover is "sibling." In the Kuma tribe of Papua New Guinea, family members are valued above all others. Siblings are seen as alter egos, essential parts of the self. The Kuma believe that mates can be replaced, but not family members. Many Native American tribes regard family members as connected to the self. To be without family is to be dead.

From the Greeks, to Descartes, to Freud and Ayn Rand, Westerners have valued the independent ego. But Americans are the most extreme. Our founders were rebels who couldn't tolerate oppression. When they formed a new government they emphasized rights and freedoms. Laws protected private property and individual rights. Responsibility for the common good was not mandated.

American values concerning independence may have worked better when we lived in small communities surrounded by endless space. But we have run out of space and our outlaws live among us. At one time the outlaw mentality was mitigated by a strong sense of community. Now the values of community have been superseded by other values.

We have pushed the concept of individual rights to the limits. Our laws let adults sell children harmful products. But laws are not our main problem. People have always been governed more by community values than by laws. Ethics, rather than laws, determine most of our behavior. Unwritten rules of civility—for taking turns, not cutting in lines, holding doors open for others and lowering our voices in theaters—organize civic life. Unfortunately, those rules of civility seem to be crumbling in America. We are becoming a nation of people who get angry when anyone gets in our way.

Rudeness is everywhere in our culture. Howard Stern, G. Gordon Liddy and Newt Gingrich are rude. It's not surprising our children copy them. Phil Donahue and Jay Leno interrupt and children learn to interrupt. A young man I know was recently injured on a volleyball court. The player who hurt him didn't apologize or offer to help him get to an emergency room. An official told him to get off the floor because he was messing it up with his blood and holding up the game. I recently saw an old man hesitate at a busy intersection. Behind him drivers swore and honked. He looked scared and confused as he turned into traffic and almost wrecked his car. At a festival a man stood in front of the stage, refusing to sit down when people yelled out that they couldn't see. Finally another man wrestled him to the ground. All around were the omnipresent calls of "Fuck you." Over coffee a local politician told me she would no longer attend town meetings. She said, "People get out of control and insult me and each other. There's no dialogue, it's all insults and accusations."

We have a crisis in meaning in our culture. The crisis comes from our isolation from each other, from the values we learn in a culture of consumption and from the fuzzy, self-help message that the only commitment is to the self and the only important question is—Am I happy? We learn that we are number one and that our own immediate needs are the most important ones. The crisis comes from the message that products satisfy and that happiness can be purchased.

We live in a money-driven culture. But the bottom line is not the only line, or even the best line for us to hold. A culture organized around profits instead of people is not user friendly to families. We all suffer from existential flu, as we search for meaning in a culture that values money, not meaning. Everyone I know wants to do good work. But right now we have an enormous gap between doing what's meaningful and doing what is reimbursed.

THE FAMILY AND THERAPY

Long ago, the Greeks pounded on the walls of Troy, a city-state with which they were at war. The walls around the city held, and the Greeks' blockade wasn't working. Enough food entered the city to stave off starvation. Finally the Greeks built an enormous horse and filled it with soldiers and left it as a gift to the Trojans. Then they hid in the hills and waited to see what happened. The Trojans awoke one morning to find the Greeks gone and the gigantic horse outside their gates. They pulled it into their city and had a day-long party. That night when all the Trojans passed out, the Greeks emerged from the belly of the horse. They opened the gates to the city for the other soldiers and took over the town from within. We therapists have sometimes been like the Trojan horse. Under the guise of friendship and gift giving, we have sometimes invaded families and done great harm.

Therapists have enormous power to do good or ill in families. We are called upon to explain behavior and to say why something is happening. When a delinquent adolescent boy comes in, we can ask about his parents' relationship, his friends, the music he listens to or the school he attends. When a woman comes in depressed, we can ask questions about her exercise, diet and use of chemicals, her health, her marriage, her work or her childhood. Our questions suggest causes and lead clients toward solutions. We can ask questions that pull for pathology or questions that bring out strengths. We can ask questions that increase distancing and scapegoating of family members. Or we can ask questions that begin the healing.

Therapists have a mixed record of helping families. I have known therapists who saved the lives of families, who gave them hope, a sense of direction and the skills they needed to work their way out of crises. I have known therapists who, with caring and competence, helped families fight addictions, heal from trauma and stop being violent. But therapists enter the family as guests and sometimes our manners are not what they should be. I've seen families hurt by therapy—families who ran amok following simplistic advice, families whose members were hospitalized for the wrong reasons and grew sicker with "treatment" and families who lost confidence in themselves after being labeled dysfunctional.

I know of an old woman who died alone in a hospital far from her only daughter. In her last weeks, the old woman begged her daughter to come home. The daughter's therapist, who had never met the mother, told her client this request was manipulation and that she should refuse to go. The nurses who saw the mother's breathing change and her body waste away and who heard her call out for her daughter had a very different perspective than the faraway therapist.

A neighbor's husband of twenty years was diagnosed with terminal prostate cancer. She was anxious and depressed, unsure she could cope. She visited a therapist who encouraged her to "take care of herself" in this situation. In the short term she did "take care of herself" and left her husband with his pain and pills. But now, years later, she dreams of her husband calling out to her in the night.

Recently I talked with a student therapist. Matt told me about a young mother he worked with who was alcoholic, poor and alone. I asked about resources, especially those within her family. He said, "I've encouraged her to stay away from them. They're pathological." I thought to myself, If she's estranged from her family, who will help this young woman? Matt's training has left him feeling proud that he identified a "pathological" family. Yet he won't be baby-sitting for his client or teaching her child to ride a bike. Nobody calls out for their therapist on their deathbed.

Therapy has helped many families, but it has hurt many others. Because we are trained to look for pathology within the family, we spot failure quickly. For the last hundred years, many experts have focused on the negative role that families play in the development of individuals. Therapists and pop psychologists have explored how families diminish, manipulate and abuse their members. Our focus has scared people, especially mothers, who tend to bear the brunt of the criticism. My women friends joke about how they are traumatizing their kids with no pets or forced violin practice, but that joke is not really so funny. They worry about their children's future therapy. They fear their efforts to parent will be framed by a later therapist as abusive.

Especially in the last two decades, the family has been the unit of analysis to explain pathology. Bookstores are loaded with books on individual improvement via analysis of childhood experiences. Their messages have added pressure to already beleaguered families and encouraged self-absorption, not social action.

Freud let the culture alone. By explaining pathology purely in terms of family experiences, he kept people from questioning the broader culture. By treating problems one person at a time, he abdicated responsibility for making society more accountable to its members. In 1995, the family pathology approach needs rethinking. It's even worse than useless; it can destroy the family from within.

THEORIES ARE LIMITED BY TIME AND PLACE

Recently I previewed a training film for parents in which a black mother approached her teenage son about his long hair. First she asked him to cut it for his own good and he reacted angrily to her interference. Then after coaching on communication techniques by a male therapist, the mother asked him to cut it because it made her feel uncomfortable. He smilingly agreed.

I had several reactions to the film. First, I've never known a teen to smilingly agree to wear his hair the way his mother wanted, no matter how he was approached. Second, the film suggested that by speaking correctly the mother had the power to make her son well behaved. The film ignored drugs, gangs, poverty, gender role stereotypes and racism. Instead it suggested that the mother was responsible for everything. This film was based on the theory that parental communication is the critical influence on adolescent behavior. At one time that might have been true. But that was before gang wars, heavy metal music and crack houses.

Theories have zones of applicability and work best for particular places and times. Freud knew middle-class Vienna in the late 1800s and Perls knew German families of the 1940s and 1950s. The dysfunctional family theory worked best for the families for which it was invented, those of longtime alcoholics. The humanists understood American families in the 1960s. Most children had two parents, one of whom was a stay-at-home mother. Parents had more control, communities existed and families had walls. Certain kinds of therapy made sense. But psychological theories have a short shelf life. Our old ideas about how to help are useless in the face of new realities. We attempt to solve problems with theories developed for a world that no longer exists.

In *An Enemy of the People*, Ibsen writes: "There is no established truth that can remain true for more than 17, 18 or at most 20 years." Most of our theories are much older than that. They predate television, personal computers and the downsizing of America's businesses. Many theories are as out of place and time as dinosaurs in a shopping mall. How do we discuss sexual repression in the world of MTV? How would Alice Miller handle date rape? How would Fritz Perls help a family who lost their income in a corporate takeover? Each of these therapists was helpful in his or her time. But in a war zone, it's crazy to ask people if they were breast fed as babies or to analyze their dreams.

My own theories have a zone of applicability that's limited by my time, place, occupation, gender and income. I'm a middle-aged Midwestern feminist. I'm well educated and I have enough money. Also my own personal quirks enter in: I'm allergic to machinery, fascinated by humans and in love with the natural world and books. As a therapist, I mostly see Midwestern, white, middle-class people. Most of the parents I see are doing their best. Most of the children have escaped the violence of poverty. My ideas about families best fit these kinds of families. We need other therapists with different experiences to write about their ideas concerning families.

People have culturally determined stories about why they are in pain. The Chinese story has to do with the temperature of the body, with the blend of yin and yang. The medical story is that unhappy people suffer from a biochemical imbalance. Probably the two most powerful American stories today are that unhappy people come from dysfunctional families or that they do not have enough consumer goods.

I would argue that much of our modern unhappiness involves a crisis of meaning and values. We all feel vulnerable and alone, uncertain how to behave. Today there are no safe houses. Children know about Susan Smith and Rwanda. They see the faces of kidnapped children on milk cartons. Teenagers consume designer shoes and designer alcohol. One-third of all teens have had sex by eighth grade. Almost half of all college students get drunk weekly. Teenage girls in Texas report that to be initiated into a gang they must have unprotected sex with HIV-positive gang members. What would Freud say to these clients? How would Otto Rank respond?

Issues cannot be handled the way they were in the past. For example, a father came in to discuss his son's situation. The boy, who had a slight harelip, was attacked at his junior high. The dad said, "My father would have told me to fight back, but now it's dangerous. I want my son to stand up for himself, but the other boys might have handguns."

A mother called to say that her daughter at a small private college in Iowa was lonely on weekends. All the students got stoned on alcohol and drugs. The daughter, who didn't use chemicals, had no place to go and nothing to do. Saturday night at her school, the students had "purity parties," where they got drunk and quizzed each other about sexual experiences. If a student hadn't done something on the quiz, he/she did it right then. The daughter was sickened by all the sexual assaults, fights and out-of-control students. The mother asked, "What's the right thing to do? Should I encourage her to stay or to come home, where it's more civilized?"

Sometimes therapy seems as antiquated as corsets or icehouses. Two loving parents worry about small details in the home. Do they divide the work equally and make sure that the mother does some yard work and that the father does dishes? Meanwhile the teenager listens to Mötley Crüe and hangs out with racist kids who sniff glue. Of course the parents may be vaguely worried about the media their children consume and the peer pressures they encounter. But they probably underestimate the impact of these forces on their families.

In the past when therapists saw troubled teenagers, they could generally assume that the parents had problems. That's because most teenagers were fine. Troubled teens were an exception and required some explaining. Today most teenagers are not fine. At one time we helped kids differentiate from enmeshed families. Now we need to help families differentiate from the culture. Today's families are rarely well organized hierarchies with rigid boundaries. Rather they are often falling apart at the seams. Some parents are frightened of or besieged by their children. Others debate when to let their children leave home and enter a world where they may be hurt. The anxiety that parents feel for their children is not neurotic, it is realistic. In our current world, it's almost impossible to be an overanxious parent.

Twenty years ago teenagers often needed help emancipating themselves from families. Often teens were rebellious and wanted to break free of stifling parental constraints. Now it is much more complex. Today the real problem is helping teens reject what is hurtful and select what is helpful from the world around them.

Many teenagers sense it is a dangerous world and are not all that eager to grow up. It is harder to label any parents as overprotective in a country where 1.3 million people were assaulted by handguns in one year. Furthermore, it's less clear that it is in teenagers' best interests to emancipate them. Parents often provide healthier environments than the alternatives. Our old rules don't always apply. We need to reconceptualize much of our developmental theory.

Americans face an enemy within—a crisis of meaning and technology. Our familiar world is topsy-turvy and the old categories of meaning no longer help us. Liberals now speak lovingly of the past, while conservatives are the futurists. Newt Gingrich is photographed with the Power Rangers, while free-speech defenders like myself argue that we need to monitor our media, especially as it affects children.

Therapists need new approaches because it is a new world. Families need to be supported, affirmed, protected and validated. Therapists can work to disconnect families from forces and systems that will harm them and to connect families to people and places that will help them. The therapist's job becomes connecting people—parents and children, families and extended families, parents and other parents and families to schools and communities.

Today therapists can help families build rituals, beliefs and values. We can help families define right and wrong. The values most children learn as they grow up are junk values no more nourishing than Diet Pepsi and as bad for their souls as Moon Pies are for their teeth. Important things—compassion, self-sacrifice, humor, tolerance and resiliency—are not being taught. There hasn't been a drop in the moral IQ of newborns, but we're letting this generation of children down.

President Clinton said that "governments don't raise children, parents raise children." But, especially with adolescents, communities raise children and electronic communities are doing a horrible job. Our culture of consumption has thoroughly confused most people about how to live in families. We live in the United States of Advertising and many therapists have inadvertently played a part in the spread of existential flu. Advertisers and pop psychology dovetail to produce a certain kind of adult—one who is shallow, self-absorbed, concerned about inadequacies.

Popular psychology has implied that if one's intimate relationships are in order, life will be fine. But the situation is more complex than that. People cannot be whole and healthy unless they connect their lives to something larger than their own personal happiness. Freud postulated a great need for sex; I say our greatest human need is for love. We need to be reconnected one with another.

Therapists can train families to look at their culture with the eyes of anthropologists. We can help them to examine the effects of technology on the lives of their family and to make conscious choices about what technology to keep and what to reject. Psychologists can be what Donald Meichenbaum called "purveyors of hope." And we can encourage people to form a "tiospaye" for the families around them. The new millennium will be about restoring community and rebuilding the infrastructure of families. We need to take back our streets and our living rooms.

Chapter Two

THE PAGE FAMILY

My grandfather, Fred Page, was born in 1885 in southern Nebraska within sight of the Missouri River. When he was fifteen, his mother died of cancer and he was left to work his way through high school and later two years of college. I have a picture of him as a young man, dressed in a stiff suit. He's slender with a cleft in his chin, soulful eyes and a big nose. He joked that it was a Roman nose, it roamed all over his face.

My grandmother, Agnes Blank, was also born in 1885. As a teenager, Agnes had an appendectomy and a long convalescence. Forever afterward, her health was fragile. But she worked and saved to go to college. In her college picture, she wears a high-necked white blouse with a brooch. Her hair is pulled back in a stylish chignon, her eyes are large, her mouth stern.

My grandparents attended the Nebraska State Normal College. Agnes and Fred met in a graveyard. He was funny, she was serious. Their courtship was romantic—they liked long walks and buggy rides and read poetry aloud atop a knoll that overlooked the Missouri.

After graduation, Fred rode a horse to eastern Colorado and "proved up" his homestead. Back in Nebraska Agnes taught high school for four years while she waited for Fred to get settled. In 1913, Agnes Blank married Fred Page.

Their homestead was near a town built along the railroad in Kit Carson County, Colorado, fifty miles north of the site of the Sand Creek Massacre. Flat yellow land rests under an enormous sky. Then as now it was ranch land, although fields of wheat and corn crisscrossed the county.

It was a place of sagebrush, tumbleweeds and dry creek beds sprinkled with snakes and bones. The wind blew storms in from the west. The air smelled of prairie grasses, dust, wheat and sometimes rain or ozone. It's a merciless place with all kinds of bad weather—droughts, tornadoes, dust storms, blizzards, floods and hail. Temperatures varied by sixty degrees in the course of a day and caused sunstroke in July and hypothermia in January. The wind blew all the time.

There were almost no trees. My grandmother brought an elm seedling with her from Nebraska and nursed it along for years. Water was so scarce that she carried the rinse water from dishes and laundry to the tree. She talked to that tree and coaxed it into growing the way one would a sickly baby.

Fred built a simple, functional house. Downstairs was a kitchen, living room and two small bedrooms, upstairs an attic. There was a dinner bell, loud enough to be heard in the fields, a smokehouse, an outdoor privy, a windmill, a chicken coop and a barn far enough away from the house to keep manure smells down.

In 1914, Betty was born. It was a hard delivery and Agnes almost died of eclampsia. But Betty was a healthy, sturdy girl who grew up to be Fred's helpmate outside. She was a typical oldest child, hardworking and responsible. Margaret was next; delicate and fair-haired, she worked mostly in the house. She was the intellectual who hoped someday to be a professional violinist. Avis, my mother, was third. As a girl, she was shy and clumsy and outsiders often thought she was mentally slow. After my mother came Agnes, or Babe, the happiest one. Much later came Donald, the long-awaited son.

There's a picture of the girls taken when Betty was six, Margaret five, Avis three and Babe still a toddler. They are dressed in starchy white dresses, staring unsmilingly at the camera. Betty has a dimple in her chin and a topknot. Margaret has long curls and a floppy bow in her hair. Avis has a boy's cut, but wears white stockings and silk slippers. Babe, bald in a tucked white dress, sits regally in a chair surrounded by her three standing sisters.

In the summer, a child was stationed by the front door to keep out flies. In winter snow blew through the walls of the attic and ice formed in the washbasin. The children who slept up there kept their feet from freezing by heating irons on the kitchen stove, wrapping them in towels and slipping them to the bottom of their beds.

Once Fred made up his mind, it was forever closed to new information or rethinking. As he aged, he was given to pontificating, which irritated some family members and amused others. He repeated himself on certain topics, such as the way the railroads cheated the farmers or the evils of alcohol. My grandmother was the only person who could soften his opinions or convince him to back down from an inflexible position. When upset, Fred shouted and blustered, but he didn't swear. He and my grandmother didn't permit themselves that kind of latitude. Generally Fred was steady and easygoing. He sang and whistled as he worked. Fred hated to be alone and wouldn't walk into the house if it was empty. He called in through the front door, and if no one answered he found work outdoors until someone showed up.

The sun never set without his telling Agnes he loved her. Before a meal, Fred looked proudly around the table and said, "Now, aren't I a lucky man." His affection embarrassed my grandmother and caused him to be teased, but he never wavered in his outspoken devotion to "the mother of his babies." He also loved his mother-in law and once wrote a poem to her that began:

> *When I need a friend that's loyal and true*
> *I don't think of the butcher, the banker or you.*
> *I don't think of the swindlers that treated me raw,*
> *I just stop and think of my mother-in-law.*

Fred had a prodigious memory for stories, riddles, jokes, puzzles and limericks, which he could recite at gatherings for hours. He was probably not as bright as his wife, but then few people were. He was bright enough to know how lucky he was to be married to Agnes and confident enough not to be threatened by her intelligence and will.

Fred was a prolific poet who published a volume of work for his family and friends. His poetry exudes an optimism and happiness that's as antiquated as two-seater buggies. Even his political poems are touching in their gentleness.

> *When I'm in reverse I like to go slow.*
> *I'm rather concerned as to where I might go.*
> *I'd rather be shipwrecked adrift on a raft,*
> *Than sailing straight backward with Senator Taft.*

He wrote many poems about his family. I'll include only one, entitled "The Mother of My Babies."

I have known some wondrous ladies
in the springtime and the fall,
but the Mother of my babies
is the finest of them all.

Some were just a little speedy,
some were just a little slow,
But the Mother of my babies
knew just the pace to go.

Some were fat and fine and funny
and they wobble as they go,
Some were lank and lean and loony
not a shadow could they throw.

But the Mother of my babies
not too fat and not too slim,
Not too tall and not too stubby,
Hangs our washing on a limb.

Her hair is getting lighter now
in fact, it's almost gray,
I would not have her dye it blue,
I like it best that way.

The changes wrought upon her brow
are not from lack of fun,
but from the trials she endures . . .
It's possible I'm one.

The springtime of my life is past
the summertime is here,
yet I won't dread the coming fall
so long as she is near.

To be near one so fair and fine
is heaven to my soul.
I'll cherish more years of it
Till countless ages roll.

And when the winter storm is past
and I'm beneath the sod,
I'd have her with me once again
in the paradise of God.

Agnes, a fan of Dickinson, Browning and Emerson, proudly accepted his poems for what they were—love poems from an honest heart. If she was embarrassed by their amateurish qualities, she never showed it. She knew Fred was not T.S. Eliot, but he had some good qualities that Eliot may have lacked.

Dignified and morally impeccable, my grandmother ruled by example. No one, especially her husband and children, ever questioned her moral authority. "Mother wouldn't approve of this" meant this shouldn't happen. Her children feared her disapproval and they worked hard for her praise. She had high expectations of her family and herself, but was generous and forgiving. When neighbors spoke badly of others, she changed the subject. Once several women were criticizing a local woman's sexual behavior and Agnes was asked her opinion. She said, "I don't know how the world looks from her shoes. So I couldn't judge."

In the family, there was always a feeling that my grandmother was a lady and unsuited for the rough life on the plains. Partly it was her delicate physique and frail health. Partly it was her idealistic and intellectual nature. She loved libraries, plays and concerts, all things that were in short supply on the prairie. Sometimes, stuck five miles out of town on a ranch with a pigheaded husband, she must have missed the company of someone who could talk to her about books.

Fred had her on a pedestal, where she remained all her life, and whenever he could, he encouraged her to be a proper lady. She didn't do fieldwork like the girls did. Agnes had enjoyed oyster stew as a girl, and so even though they had to be special-ordered, fresh oysters were served on Christmas Eve. Agnes was on the library board and once a year traveled into Denver to the symphony, taking one lucky daughter along with her. But of course Agnes, like all farm wives, had her share of work, dirt, blood and pain.

I suspect Agnes was one of those women who had been admonished to regard sex as a marital duty, something mildly unpleasant but necessary if the species were to continue. There's a story about the instructions that Queen Victoria gave her married daughters regarding sex: "Close your eyes, grit your teeth and pray for the Empire." That sounds like my grandmother. Even her pregnancies were kept secret. Sexuality was rarely discussed, even by married adults. Avis said, "What we learned we learned from watching the animals." In that household, a risqué remark or smutty joke was unthinkable.

———

It's hard to explain to modern children what an unsexualized world most people lived in. This was before blue movies, *Playboy* magazine or the Kinsey Report. The most risqué literature around was Captain Billy's *Whiz Bang*. There were no ads showing half-naked teens embracing or scantily clad women on their knees with their mouths open and eyes shut. Teenagers' exposure to sexual materials involved reading *The Scarlet Letter* or *Romeo and Juliet* in school, and looking at underwear ads in Sears catalogs or the bare-breasted natives in *National Geographic*. Poetry, literature and music were about love, not sex.

Religion was more a topic of conversation than sex. Grace was said at every meal and speech was sprinkled with Bible stories and metaphors. Children were taught to say their prayers at bedtime. The Pages disliked the prayer that began "Now I lay me down to sleep, I pray the Lord my soul to keep. . . ." and instead they taught the children to pray their own words. By the time children started school, they could recite the Lord's Prayer, the Twenty-third Psalm, John 3:16 and the books of the Bible in order. Everyone knew Bible stories—Job's suffering, Daniel in the lions' den, Noah's flood and Cain and Abel. These stories gave the family and their neighbors a common language with which to discuss a moral universe.

People generally agreed on right and wrong behavior. They shared a unified value system that included the Golden Rule and the Ten Commandments. Not everyone followed the rules, but at least everyone understood them. Suffering, seen as necessary and inevitable, was ennobled by the belief that it built character and happened for a reason. The purpose of life was to be good, which meant to do one's Christian duties. Life made sense because, whatever happened on earth, the good would be rewarded after death and the evil punished.

Almost everyone was Christian. No Jews or members of minority groups lived in town. Some Native American families lived in the county, but they rarely came into town. Gypsies came through every summer, but they only mixed with the locals to sell them things. The community's values were reinforced at church, school and home. Probably the main division in the community was between Catholics and Protestants. The few Catholic families had to travel thirty miles to church. The Pages belonged to the Congregational church that was built to include all the town's Protestants.

The family was the source of everything. Anything that needed to be done was done by the family—fixing equipment, curing meat, treating illnesses in people or animals, mending harnesses and building furniture. There was always work—gathering eggs, gardening, fixing fences, cleaning, planting, harvesting and washing. Water was pumped and carried by hand. Butchering was in the fall, when the weather was cold enough to cool the meat. The family was up before dawn to milk the cows. In the winter they hauled snow and buried it deep in the ground so that it would last into the summer.

Everyone had his/her favorite chores and the work he/she dreaded. Margaret loved haying the most, while Fred relished making silage. Avis hated Thanksgiving, when the girls walked the fields picking up corn until their fingers were frozen. But mostly she and all the others had a positive attitude about the work that was a necessary part of living. Fred and Agnes made it fun whenever they could. For example, after dinner the dish tub was filled with hot soapy water and then Agnes yelled "Fire." The girls hurried over to the tub, or "hospital," with the "people," the silverware, and later "the furniture," the dishes.

The family lived and worked in the natural world. Weather, seasons, sunrises and sunsets affected them directly. There was no air-conditioning, no central heating. The work was physical. It involved mud, grain, cows and water. At the end of the day muscles hurt, hands and faces were wind-chapped, arms mosquito-bitten. All the work was "good work," to use Wendell Berry's phrase; that is, it was connected to real benefits for the people involved. The work made sense and produced concrete results—calves branded, kraut chopped and put in jars, gardens weeded and hogs butchered.

Company came often and stayed a long time. Everyone's favorite visitors were my great-grandparents—the Scottish grandmother who called her grandchildren "wee bairns." When she was well into her seventies, her Irish husband would remark on her lovely complexion: "She had skin like a peach when I married her and she still does today." In fact, she was wrinkled as a prune, but no one contradicted him. Great-Grandmother was nearly blind, but Great-Grandfather maintained that only she could cook his eggs properly. Because she couldn't see well, she often poured pepper in the eggs, which he dutifully ate, his eyes reddening and filling with tears. Once she served the family wormy home-canned applesauce, which they swallowed rather than embarrass her.

Most of family land was unfenced prairie that Fred and the girls patrolled by horseback. Cattle were raised mainly for beef, but some were kept for milking twice a day. Each girl was assigned five or six cows. My mother described dark mornings in the cold barn, milking cows that swished dirty tails in her face.

Every spring Agnes ordered four hundred baby chicks to be picked up around Easter. She placed them in a brooder, heated by a kerosene burner, and fed them ground meal. The males were eaten, the females saved for next year's eggs. Fred bought pigs to fatten and butcher even though my grandmother thought they were dirty. Their fat was rendered into lard and the residue was made into lye soap.

The horses—Felix, Dolly, Boots and Blaze—were family members. Once lightning struck a fence that some horses were standing near and several horses died. The family regarded it as a great tragedy, not for financial reasons but because so many friends were lost at once. In the 1930s and 1940s, when tractors replaced horses and many ranchers sold their horses for dog food, my grandparents held out. They worked with horses till they retired. My grandfather couldn't understand a man who preferred a tractor to a living animal.

The word "media" wasn't in the language. By the time of Roosevelt's fireside chats, the family had a radio. Major news, such as the kidnapping of the Lindbergh baby and later the war and the New Deal, reached town via newspaper. Generally, the news that was most important was local news—whose corn was hailed out, who had twins or bought a Model T, how the football team was doing or who would be the new choir director.

Many residents were immigrants who spoke with German or Scottish accents. Children often attended country schools with only one or two other neighbor families. Many families came to town only on Saturdays. Some people, especially women and children, almost never made it. Winter storms could keep people trapped in their homes for weeks at a time. The isolation created more "characters" than we have today and these characters made for funny and sad stories.

Telephones had no numbers on them. Rather, the caller gave the operator a two-digit number. The Pages were on a party line and all their neighbors could listen in. One lonely lady called them frequently. Mrs. McPherson had no children and was married to a taciturn, humorless man who seldom left the farm. She would say hello and then wait for the Pages to talk. They would take turns, one after another, telling her about their lives and the news from town and then, after half an hour or so, when the last person finished, Mrs. McPherson softly said good-bye.

The biggest topic of conversation was the weather. Storms killed people on a regular basis. Much more than today, weather determined schedules and income. A sunny day meant work in the fields. A hailstorm meant no wheat crop, which meant no school clothes in the fall. Almost everyone had a story. For example, once Fred and Betty were caught in a hailstorm. Fred headed for a haystack and burrowed a hole for Betty. She jumped in and he used his body as a shield to protect her from the baseball-size hail. Before they made it home that dark night, they both al most died from hypothermia.

Medical care was primitive. Doctors were comforters more than healers and no one assumed they could protect people from death. The word "cancer" was not even spoken aloud. Instead people who had cancer were told to put their affairs in order. This was before polio vaccine, antibiotics or even most painkillers. A doctor's bag contained bandages, a stethoscope, morphine, a blood pressure cuff and digitalis to stimulate the heart. Doctors set bones, delivered babies and sat with the dying. People got better or died, and generally they died at home.

Agnes had a "doctor book" that she used to treat her family. The most common remedy was castor ill chased by sour pickle, which didn't help

much but discouraged malingering. Burns were treated with mentho-
ladum. Ben-Gay was for sore muscles. People were quarantined and fu-
migated to prevent infectious illnesses. Agnes worked to keep things
clean, no small job on a ranch in a house without running water. All of
her children survived measles, pneumonia and diphtheria and she attributed their longevity to her scrupulous cleanliness.

Sick children often died. Their graves decorate the cemeteries on the
edges of prairie towns. One of the saddest stories was of two Bottinger
girls playing outside on a hot August day. Their mother was busy in the
kitchen and they got thirsty. They were too young to know any better
and drank from the water put out for the chickens. Both had big gulps
of the warm, fetid water, and a day later both were dead of dysentery.

Health problems led to gruesome experiences that people had little
choice but to tough out. While Margaret was rounding up cows, she was
thrown by her horse and splintered her elbow and upper arm. She lay
for hours pushed into the dirt by her saddle. Betty found her and rode
for help. Eventually Margaret was lifted into a truck bed and banged over
hilly fields to the bumpy road that went into town. Betty tried to cushion her arm on her lap, but with each jolt the bone jutted out farther.

The local doctor, who didn't have an X-ray machine, knew she must
go to Denver. The mortician whose hearse doubled as an ambulance was
out of town. So the doctor removed the passenger seat from his two-door
Ford and placed an ironing board there for a bed. By the time Margaret
arrived in Denver her arm was infected. This was before sulfa drugs, let
alone antibiotics. She was given a tetanus shot and her arm was packed
in ice for a week. She was lucky to avoid an amputation or death from
blood poisoning. Margaret's arm never healed properly and her days as
a violinist were over.

Mental health care was nonexistent. Many schizophrenics spent their
lives in a state hospital that was really a warehouse for those whose mental problems were untreatable. Others were kept at home out of sight.
Depressed people often committed suicide without ever talking over
their problems. There weren't many alcoholics, but those who were
around kept their problems secret and often drank themselves to death.
Drinking too much was a sin, not a disease, and the remedy was willpower.

Women with abusive husbands had no recourse except to suffer. Starla
was the prettiest girl in Avis's class. She was blond, winsome and high-

spirited, and she was snapped up right after high school by a farmer south of town. He turned out to be jealous and controlling. Since her husband rarely allowed her to come to town, Starla was essentially invisible in the community. During the Depression, things got worse. One Saturday Avis saw her at the grocer's and eagerly went over to talk. Starla was much aged and weather-beaten with a baby in her arms and two toddlers clinging to her legs. She plunked down a dime on the counter and asked for five cents' worth of flour and five cents' worth of tobacco. Gritting her teeth, she said, "I'll resent that five cents' worth of tobacco till I die of old age."

People were less psychologically minded than they are today. Parents worried about their children's character more than their psyches. Peevish or upset children were joked or scolded out of their moods or left alone till they recovered themselves. Margaret, at eight, had her tonsils out without general anesthetic. Teeth were pulled with pliers. Both mental and physical suffering were expected and not regarded as special events that needed explanation.

Food was close at hand, and most of the time no one went hungry. Diet was simple and delicious—garden vegetables, milk, eggs, cream, beef, chicken, homemade bread, and jams. The family cut cabbage for kraut, made pickles and canned beef. Food was stored in a cellar in jars that sparkled like jewels. Pies were a staple of the diet, like milk and eggs. Every good housewife had her no-fail piecrust recipe and her specialty pie. Agnes's was gooseberry. Meals were taken together, three times a day, usually around a table that could seat twelve.

Food preparation was from scratch. Cooking meals took all day by the time chickens were killed and dressed, rolls baked, peas shelled and butter churned. After the water boiled, corn was picked, rapidly husked and dropped in the pot. Tomatoes and strawberries tasted of summer and sun. My mother tells of playing with her brother, Donald, in the watermelon patch. They split a melon on a rock and ate the warm red fruit with their hands. When she was dying seventy years later, she described how delicious the watermelon juice was as it dribbled down her fingers.

For a treat children were given penny candy. The family's favorite dish was stewed chicken with homemade noodles. My aunts were adults before they realized that noodles could be those hard dry strips sold in stores. The family kept a can of store-bought peas for surprise guests.

Agnes and Avis did the sewing for the family. A few things, such as brassieres, stockings and overalls, were ordered from what Fred called Monkey Ward's. But most everything else was handmade. The fabric for underwear came from the cotton of flour sacks. Sheeting was bought by the bolt and used to make nightgowns and nightshirts. Underwear more different than that from Victoria's Secret can scarcely be imagined. It was plain, functional and deliberately nonsexual.

The nearest neighbors were a half mile away, so mostly the siblings played with each other. The girls dressed up in old clothes from a trunk in the attic. On winter evenings the family played rook or dominoes or looked at slides on a stereopticon machine. The creek through their land made a great natural sandbox. The barns and granaries were playgrounds. Children loved outdoor games, of which there were many—Run Sheep Run, hide-and-seek, statues and "Mother may I."

After dinner the family read aloud—*Little Women, Ben Hur, Pilgrim's Progress, Silas Marner, War and Peace* or *Les Miserables.* Agnes carefully selected the books and banned trashy romances. She admonished, "Choose your books as carefully as you choose your friends."

Fred and Agnes belonged to a "country club" for fifty years. This was a group of couples who met for a monthly potluck dinner. There were community celebrations and religious holidays. On Christmas Eve, Fred bought a tree for the family to decorate. The family went to the children's holiday programs at church and school. At Christmas, the children received one practical gift, such as a coat or wool stockings, and an orange and hard candy. On Easter there was a sunrise service followed by a church-sponsored Easter egg hunt.

The family traveled, which was unusual in those times. They visited the mountains, relatives in Kansas and Nebraska, and one memorable summer when the crops were hailed out, they drove across country to Niagara Falls. The Pages were good at having fun. Many a workday in the summer Fred would come in from the fields and say, "Pack dinner. We have time for a swim before we eat." They'd drive to Crystal Springs, with kids riding on the running boards and fenders, for a special treat.

The community was financially homogenous. Some people had a little more money than others, but nobody had much. Those who had more kept quiet about it. Shopping was called trading. Farmers traded eggs for flour, cream for coffee. There really weren't all that many products to buy. Consumption was regarded as an affliction, not a lifestyle.

During the 1920s the family was prosperous, but in the 1930s they lost their savings. During the Depression years, the family burned cow chips for fuel. They didn't feel ashamed and deprived the way poor people do today. Their expectations were lower, and as my mother put it, "Everyone was in the same boat."

There were close relationships between neighbors, who often needed each other in life-and-death ways. For example, once a blizzard hit when the children were coming home on the school bus. After the bus stalled, the driver unloaded the children for a walk to the nearest farm. He had them hold onto a rope with the big kids alternating with the smaller ones. Then he led them to the house. They were there for several days with all the girls piled on one bed and the boys on another. They ate feed corn ground into coarse meal and topped with milk from the one dairy cow.

Agnes and Fred took their civic duties seriously. Once they drove through a blizzard to vote, even though they canceled each other out— she was a Republican and he a Democrat. Fred ran for state senate and Agnes helped organize a library and was president of Ladies Aid and PTA. Agnes was in Eastern Star and Fred was a Freemason and proud of it.

People were busy, but not hurried. Farmers scheduled their lives according to weather and the needs of the day. Generally there was time to sit, drink strong black coffee and tell stories. On the main street old men sat on benches in the sun and pulled pennies from their pockets for the children who walked by.

The school was an important and beloved part of the life of the family and the community. Classes were small and everyone knew everyone. Teachers often boarded with local families. Sports, music, debate and the popular oratory contests were followed closely. The next day the events would be discussed at the pool hall and in the café over pie.

Country kids were at a disadvantage. Many had to be home for chores and missed extracurricular activities. Girls' basketball was important. Avis desperately wanted to play on the school team, and her senior year her parents let her miss the evening milking. Sometimes she walked the long miles home in the dark and cold.

With twenty-three students, Avis's graduating class in 1935 was the largest in the history of the town. That time is captured by her high school yearbook with its worn brown cover. The yearbook was financed by bake sales and carnivals during the worst of the Depression. Later my mother told me that she felt guilty that her class had asked the impoverished community for money.

The class motto in 1935 was "To my school I owe my best. I can give no more, I should offer no less." All the students had nicknames: June Kliewer was "Angel," Eileen Goetschel was "Irish." Each student had a motto above his/her picture. Lester Robb's was "The girl who gets me will be lucky." Gordon Parrott's was "I almost never pet, nor chew, nor swear, nor drink." Jud Baxtor's asked "Why wasn't I born rich instead of handsome?" Serious Irene Loutzenhizer's read "Diligence hath its rewards."

Beside the picture was a list of the student's activities. Avis's reads: Glee Club 1, Annual staff 1, Literary Society 1234, Debate 234 and class officer 1. Avis and Irene wrote the class poem. Its earnestness and idealism are as dated as horses and wagons.

Now the close of high school days has come,
They're now but memories of the past;
But we know wherever we may roam
Our loyalty to FHS will last.

Dear school to thee, dear school to thee,
Our hearts forever beat in accents true,
And we will hope that through the days to come
We may bring honor to you.

Dear classmates, friends and teachers too,
Wherever we go no matter what we do,
We'll think of the happy times we've had
In FHS with you.

The other classes had group photos, the boys mostly in overalls and the girls in homemade gingham dresses. The students stare straight into the camera, unsmiling yet unself-conscious. Their faces signal "We are more than we look." The sophomore class motto was "Climb through the rocks, be rugged." The eighth-graders' motto was *"Nil sine labore,"* or "Nothing without work."

All the children except Babe left town after high school. The 1930s and 1940s were the years the school was filled with children and the main street teemed with wagons and Model Ts. Those were the years when young people found work on the farms or in the stores. But after the war, the town began to die. The hospital and theater closed. Many of the young who left didn't return. There was no work, no money in farming. All over the country the lights were going out in little prairie towns.

The years when their town was dying were not unhappy for Agnes and Fred. They sold their farm in the 1950s and moved into town. They bought a small stucco house with maple and ash trees in the front and fruit trees in the back. They planted a big garden and visited with their neighbors. Every morning after his oatmeal, Fred put on his felt hat and walked downtown to get the mail and have a root beer at the pool hall. Agnes did housework or baking and called her friends. In the afternoon they napped or read under the ash trees. At night they had couples in for canasta or dominoes.

Sometime in the 1960s the children bought them a television set. They liked the news and occasionally they watched a Billy Graham special or a holiday service. But mostly the television sat covered with handmade doilies and planters in the corner.

The Pages stayed active in church and school activities. As many of the women became widows, Fred busied himself with household repairs and chauffeuring. After a lifetime of hard work, they enjoyed leisure immensely. Although they had almost no money, they managed to do everything they wanted.

When I was a student at Berkeley and quite full of myself I visited my grandparents. I asked my grandmother if she'd had a happy life and she brushed off the question. I repeated it. Agnes put down her mending and said, "I don't think of my life in those terms. I ask myself—Have I done the right things, have I been useful? What's important isn't happiness, but that I spent my time properly."

Fred's favorite song from the early part of the century was "When You and I Were Young, Maggie." He sang it all his married life and had it sung at the fiftieth wedding anniversary party, which was a church service followed by a potluck dinner and open house. Fred bought Agnes a blue silk dress for the occasion. A few years later she wore that dress to his funeral, and two years after that, she was buried in it.

Fred died at home. Two days before Thanksgiving he carried the left-overs out to the garden to bury. While digging, he had a heart attack. Both of them had hoped he'd die first and be spared having to walk alone into an empty house.

Agnes died more slowly and painfully, of multiple myeloma. She stayed at home and resisted pain pills because she didn't want to get addicted and didn't like feeling "fuzzy." She had toughed out many things in her long life and she toughed out this too. One by one the children came and stayed with her, to help her bathe and make her soup and tea. She didn't complain. The last book she read was William Shirer's *Rise and Fall of the Third Reich*. During her last month, when she was too ill to read, Margaret read her the Bible, King James Version.

After Agnes died, Margaret, who had cared for her near the end, had several dreams in which Agnes appeared and Margaret called out, "Mother, Mother, how can I help you?" Twice she dreamed this and woke in despair. The third time she dreamed this Agnes answered her, "Margaret, you can't help me anymore. Now you must help other people."

Fred and Agnes were reunited at the cemetery. They are buried beside each other under modest stones, near the two girls who died from drinking the chickens' water. Their friends surround them. The cemetery is on a gravel road outside of town. Storms come from the west and pass over them. The wind is always blowing.

Chapter Three

THE COPELAND FAMILY

Session One

Late Wednesday afternoon, Brian, a balding man dressed in a rumpled three-piece suit, sank into my couch and flashed me a weary smile. His wife, Sandi, dressed in a silk suit and Italian shoes, dumped her briefcase and papers and dropped into the chair by the window. She looked even more frazzled than Brian and announced dramatically, "My life is great if you like avalanches."

Sandi and Brian had come in separate cars from separate parts of the city. Brian had been out of town for several days and Sandi hadn't seen him since Monday morning. Before we began, she mentioned their son's concert and their oldest daughter's phone call. Sarah needed help filling out college aid applications. Brian made notes in his personal planner, but said sadly, "I can't get off work in time for the concert."

He turned to me and said, "My corporation is downsizing. I have no time."

"He's missing everything," Sandi said. "We all live in our own little worlds. Lately I don't want to go home. It feels too lonely."

I asked some general questions about their lives. Brian was the production manager at a manufacturing plant. He'd worked for his company for years and moved around the country as was necessary for career advancement. Recently his company had been sold to a French conglomerate that was turning the plant into a "lean, mean corporate machine."

All of a sudden, history and loyalty no longer mattered. As Brian put it, "For the bosses, greed is good. For the employees, the work ethic no longer pays off. The reward for jumping through hoops is more hoops."

Brian said that his new boss, who was making a six-figure salary, relished the thought that employees lay awake nights worrying about losing their jobs. Brian had been forced to lay off some long-term employees and cut back on the others. Brian said, "The boss tells me to look at the position, not the person. But I don't see positions, I see friends. I know their families. These are good people."

As people were fired, those who remained did the work of three people. Everyone was exhausted and irritable, but dared not complain for fear they would be canned. Brian was working ten-hour days, six days a week. Suddenly going to work was unpleasant. The anxiety created by layoffs was infectious. As workers passed in the halls, they no longer joked and chatted. When Brian asked how people were doing, they no longer said they were fine. Instead they said grimly, "I'm here." Many jokes were circulating. One was "An optimist is someone who brings his lunch to work." Brian hated what his job had become, but he was terrified of losing it. As he put it, "Companies are unforgiving. You lose a few steps and you're out of the parade."

Even with both of them working, money was tight. Mental health and medical bills had piled up over the years. Sarah's inpatient treatment for anorexia had cost $22,000 and now she wanted to attend an expensive modeling school. Their son's violin lessons and computer were expensive. They were a three-car family and their home was nicer than they could really afford. "But we have two teenage daughters and we wanted a safe neighborhood," Sandi explained.

"I'm here because I'm losing my sense of who I am. I always thought I didn't care much about money, but lately I think about money all the time," Brian said. He reached out for Sandi's hand. "People used to describe me as happy-go-lucky. I didn't sweat the small stuff. But too much is happening at once. There isn't any small stuff."

Brian enjoyed the children until Sarah, who is eighteen, got so thin and Jennifer, fourteen, turned into "a teenager from hell." He said simply, "With me, family is physiological." He felt particularly close to ten-year-old Tyler, whom he described as "a kinder and gentler person than I am." Before the work crunch, Brian and Tyler had played computer games and watched videos together. Now he choked up when he talked about missing his son.

I thought that Brian had good instincts—to love his family and do good work. But right now he was having trouble handling his complex situation. At work he was rewarded for cutthroat behavior and punished for loyalty. He had little time or energy left for his family.

Sandi worked as the personnel director at a local care facility. Her boss was a cranky person who timed Sandi when she went to the bathroom and called her at home when Sandi was sick to make sure that she wasn't malingering. Sandi described her job as high pressure and low pay. She spent her days comforting people and handling crises. She had lots of responsibility and not much authority. "I come home shelled," Sandi said. "I have the least to give to the people I love the most."

Sandi struggled with PMS and depression and was currently on Prozac. Like most people with master's degrees in counseling, she was full of insights about herself and her family. She felt she was still "differentiating from her family of origin" and "had old issues that kept her from being the best parent she could be." She felt Brian had difficulty expressing his feelings and that, like most men, he insisted on fixing things. To this statement, Brian commented rather heatedly that he wished like hell he could fix things.

Sandi had read every self-help book written for families, couples and women. Her sophistication was a mixed blessing. Her reading on codependency had totally confused her. She was apologetic because she had expectations of others and cared about what happened to them. She was unsure when she was being controlling. Was it controlling to ask Brian to limit his computer time or to quit smoking? Was it manipulative to want her kids to make good grades? Sandi labeled much of her own behavior as pathological. She was so paralyzed at the thought of being dysfunctional that sometimes she stopped functioning.

On the other hand, self-help books had comforted and supported Sandi through some tough times. The books on grieving had helped her through her father's death. Sandi appreciated the knowledge she gained from books about working women. She knew that she needed to take care of herself and not take responsibility for everyone's feelings. But she was vague on specifics. Was going to Tyler's concert when she was tired being a good mother or overfunctioning? Was crying about her dad's death daily facing her grief or giving in to her depression? Was bugging Brian to quit smoking being assertive or overinvolved? Was she giving unconditional love or being a chump?

Like so many women, Sandi was trying hard to be good at everything—mothering, work, housekeeping, personal development and exercise. She said, "I am utterly failing to be supermom. No matter where I am I feel guilty that I'm not somewhere else. When I'm at the health fair at Tyler's school, I can see work piling up at the office. When I'm at work, I picture Tyler in front of the television eating potato chips for dinner. Brian says I'm a saint, but I am an exhausted saint."

Sandi was a Lutheran and attended church most Sundays. She tried to talk Brian and the kids into going to church, but only Sarah would go with her and Sarah usually worked Sunday mornings. Brian said that Sundays were the only time he had for himself. Sandi wished she could attend the women's group, but it met on the night she worked late. In other churches and neighborhoods, she'd made good friends. But she said, "I kept moving away from them. This last move I gave up. I can't take another set of good-byes."

She looked guiltily at Brian. "I hate to complain about you. You work hard and deserve some alone time. But when you're home, you're always on the computer. I know this sounds paranoid, but I feel jealous. It's like you're having an affair with the Internet."

Brian said, "It's work. I've got to keep my job. We're hemorrhaging money."

In spite of their pressures, Brian and Sandi obviously loved each other. Sandi referred to him as "my knight in shining seersucker." Brian said, "Sandi does more in one day than most people do in a week. I couldn't have made it without her."

I asked how long since they'd had a date; they looked at each other blankly. Sandi finally answered, "Was it on our anniversary?"

"No," said Brian. "We had to cancel that because Jen was missing."

Sandi looked at me. "We tried for a while to have a date/sex night on Fridays, but I kept falling asleep before the kids went to bed."

I asked about the kids. Brian laughed. "Raising teenagers is not for the faint of heart." He took a deep breath and continued. "Sarah developed anorexia her sophomore year. Jennifer and Tyler are going down the tubes at the speed of light." Sandi sighed. "Saturday Jen stayed out late with God knows who. Tyler meanwhile won't leave the house."

Jennifer, the middle child, was a handful. As a child, she had had asthma and scoliosis and she had been teased about her back brace and her chubbiness. Sandi thought this gave her chronic low self-esteem. But in elementary school, Jennifer had muddled through things. She made friends, her grades were fine and, now and then, she had a nice time with her parents. Her serious trouble started with the move to our town.

Too many things happened at once. Brian and Sandi tackled new jobs and weren't around as much as they had been in Georgia. Sarah lost weight dramatically and was hospitalized at the point she began wearing size 0 shorts. Sandi's dad died. Meanwhile, Jennifer began a large junior high with some gang and drug problems. She became self-conscious about her body, which attracted all the wrong kinds of attention. The previous summer when she had gone to the pool, guys had leered and made crude remarks. Another summer afternoon she was followed home from the library by a man who exposed himself. After those incidents, she stayed indoors and read magazines.

Jennifer refused to do anything with the family, which she nevertheless kept in a state of chaos and uproar. She called Sandi a bitch and said Brian needed a personality-ectomy. Sandi worried about Jennifer's depression and anger and felt that she was "expressing her inner pain and low self-esteem." Brian put it differently. "She considers us pond scum."

Both parents were concerned about the possibility that Jen was using alcohol and drugs. They knew she was skipping school and hanging out with hard-core kids. Sandi said, "I try not to be overly protective but I don't want her to get hurt." Brian said, "Jen and her friends are accidents about to happen."

They tried to set limits, but found it exhausting to keep track of Jen. Both of them were away from home all day and needed their sleep at night. Jen was clever at sneaking out. Sandi said, "We need to chain her to the bed or hire a guard."

They were also concerned about Jen's sexual behavior. They didn't think that Jen was sexually active yet, but two girls Jen knew were pregnant. Sandi had heard her ask guys if they had been laid the night before. Jen listened to music by Love Acid and Nine Inch Nails and she watched MTV whenever she could sneak it by them. Sandi said, "Jen's a media junkie. She can't study, talk on the phone or fall asleep without rock music."

Sandi worried about Jen's poor planning skills. She said, "She lives to-

tally in the present. She burns her bridges before she crosses them."
Brian was more worried about her choice of peers. Brian said, "Jen is set
on self-destruct. I wish we could send her to some safe town until she's
out of high school." He looked at me. "Are there any towns like that left?"

Tyler presented them with an opposite set of problems. Sandi said,
"Tyler's been an A student. He's good-hearted and well behaved. He's a
great violin player, which is a cardinal sin at his school, and the other
boys won't leave him alone."

"Tyler's the clumsiest kid this side of the Mississippi." Brian sighed.
"He doesn't have a mean bone in his body. It drives me nuts to hear about
kids picking on him. He'd be the first to defend another kid who was in
trouble."

Sandi interrupted. "He's not standing up for himself, though. He's
afraid of getting beaten up."

Brian said, "He pretends he's sick so he can stay home. Except for musical events, he won't leave the house. Mostly he lies around and watches
TV."

Sandi said, "We restrict his TV, which he considers a major rights vi-
olation."

She asked if I'd seen *Beavis and Butthead* and I confessed that I had not.
She said, "In last week's episode Beavis and Butthead were on a runway
at an airport. An airline stewardess was clearly trapped in the plane. You
could read her lips as she begged Beavis and Butthead to help her and
the other passengers out. They wouldn't do it. Later that night Beavis and
Butthead were back home, laughing as they listened to the news story
about the plane exploding and all these people dying."

She looked at me wide-eyed. "I won't let him watch a show where
punks let people burn to death just for the fun of it."

I asked about Sarah. Sandi said, "She's a senior this year and a people
pleaser like me. She's had a real battle with anorexia, but she's better now.
She has too many social obligations, she works twenty hours a week and
she's applying to colleges."

Brian said, "Sarah's the perfect one, never a hair out of place, the A-
plus student, the hard worker." He laughed. "We worry about her, too."

Like most families in the 1990s, the Copelands didn't have enough
time. Brian was up by five-thirty, on the computer for a while and off to
work by seven. Sandi exercised with a television show at six. Later she

showered, had coffee and woke the kids. Both Brian and Sandi worked jobs with no lunch hours and no personal time. Sandi arrived home around six, "shelled" from rush-hour traffic. Brian had West Coast calls coming in until seven.

At home, Sandi wished she could watch the news or read the paper, but usually the phone was ringing and the kids had requests or errands. Generally she brought home pizza, TV dinners or sandwiches. Even though Sandi was tired, she would have fixed meals, but no one wanted to eat. Sarah was often at work or a social activity and Tyler was on the computer. Jennifer hated home-cooked meals. As far as Sandi could tell, Jennifer ate only food that came from convenience stores or machines. As Brian put it, "Her basic food groups are Pepsi, chips and candy bars." In a good week the family had a meal together, but this was more likely to happen if the parents bribed the kids with a restaurant meal.

Brian and Sandi split their work the way most couples do—Sandi did inside work while Brian managed the cars and yard. Sandi said, "It's more work to get the kids to help than to do it ourselves."

"I agree," Brian said. "But the kids aren't learning to pull their share of the load and to do a job right."

Usually Sandi fell into bed around ten, while Brian stayed on-line until after midnight. Both parents tried to have time with their kids daily. Sandi usually managed an argument over rules with Jennifer and a look at Tyler's homework. Brian played computer games with Tyler and made sure Jen was in for the night. Even though they'd been told not to at the treatment center, both bugged Sarah about her eating.

Sandi tensed as we discussed schedules. "I rush all the time and I have nothing to show for it. Brian and I spend more time worrying about our kids than our parents did. Mom played cards every afternoon with her friends."

Brian said, "That's another thing Sandi feels bad about. She wishes her mother were closer."

Sandi said, "I worry about her. Most of her friends have moved to retirement villages." She reached for the tissues. "I think of Mom every day. She's the only person left who takes care of me."

By the time they reached my office, Brian and Sandi had seen many mental health workers. Sandi had been in individual therapy to help her with depression. Brian had been hypnotized to quit smoking, but I could see a pack of smokes in his pocket. As a couple, they'd been in therapy twice, once when Sandi's father was dying of cancer and later when Sarah was in treatment. They trusted counselors and I wondered if we deserved their trust.

Previous therapists had cited parental inadequacies as the main cause of Sarah's anorexia. When Sarah had inpatient treatment, Sandi was diagnosed as "overinvolved and controlling" and Brian as a workaholic. He said wryly, "Yeah, I'm addicted to feeding my family." They had made changes, and Sarah had improved some, but now Jennifer was in trouble. Tyler looked like he was on his way to being a social isolate. Brian said, "Our kids aren't as happy as we were. What are we doing wrong?"

I suspected that for them, like for many parents in the 1990s, parenting was a tough task. They had few familial or community supports, limited time and a media culture that taught their kids all the wrong things. The children had heard via commercials that they should indulge every whim, meet every need and buy every product. Everyone was overstimulated and disconnected from themselves, each other and the natural world. The parents were exhausted from their efforts to do the right thing in a world where the right thing was increasingly less clear. I wanted to help the family understand the stresses that the culture inflicted on families.

This family needed shelter. They needed protected time and space and they needed to be reconnected to each other and other people. For starters, I recommended that these parents have a date night and that they pick a family night when everyone had to be home doing an activity together. I said, "Next time, have everyone come in and talk things over."

Session Two

The first family session was chaotic. Brian had a flight to catch right after the session and before he even sat down, his beeper went off. Sandi was jangled with PMS and announced that she felt like an ATM machine with everyone withdrawing from her account. Sarah was unhappy that she wasn't at her telemarketing job. Jennifer hated shrinks and worried someone might see her in our building. Tyler's eyes widened with anxiety as he insisted he had no problems.

I asked Brian and Sandi about assignments. Brian reported that they managed to go to the movies. Sandi laughed. "I enjoyed Brian, but not the movie. It was too violent for me." Jen sneered, *"Bambi* is too violent for you, Mom." I asked about family night and Sandi said, "We can't find a night that works for everyone."

"Besides," said Jennifer. "What would we do?"

"Yeah," said Sarah. "We don't have much in common."

Sarah was casually but impeccably dressed. Her blond hair was short and shiny, cut in a stylish way, and she had obviously spent time putting on makeup. Even her toenails were carefully manicured. She spoke about her anorexia immediately. "I've been hospitalized, but I'm okay now. I haven't lost any weight in over a year. I go to group."

I asked what she learned from her hospital time. "I learned that I'm a parental child and that Mom and I are both codependents. I need to express my anger more, which I still don't do, but I know I should."

Sandi said, "Sarah is still at the bottom of the weight charts, but she's less obsessed with her looks."

"I relapse if I get stressed out," Sarah said. "But I don't run to Weight Watchers when swimsuit season hits."

"She was homecoming queen this year and she makes straight A's." Jennifer interrupted in a tone that suggested these feats were the equivalent of contracting leprosy.

Sarah continued, "I'm hoping for a modeling scholarship."

Jennifer scowled. She was a chubby girl with fine dark eyes. She wore torn jeans, green boots and a Smashing Pumpkins T-shirt. When I asked her about herself, she said, "I'm the family screw-off."

"Why do you say that?"

"I'm not a good little girl like Sarah."

"Yeah," said Tyler. "She yells at us all the time."

"Shut up, brat," Jennifer said. "I'm so over your interruptions."

Sandi looked sadly at me. "She has these outbursts of anger frequently."

Jennifer shouted, "Why can't you be like normal parents and let me handle my own life?"

"We love you, Jennifer, even though we disapprove of your behavior," Sandi said.

Jennifer rolled her eyes. "I wish you would just beat me and get it over with."

"Why are you having trouble?" I asked Jennifer.

She thought for a moment. "I'm fat. Only losers will hang out with me."

Sarah said, "That's not true. There are plenty of kids who would like you if you gave them a chance. If you dressed up and were friendlier."

Jennifer yelled, "I don't like those snobs you hang out with. They're big phonies and you know it."

"Jennifer is very conscious of peers," Sandi interrupted. "Her friends are nice people, but they drink and smoke. Most of them are flunking out. Sarah's right, there are alternatives."

Jennifer sneered. "You don't understand anything about my school."

We talked some about her junior high. It was a school of two thousand kids. Because of budget cuts, there weren't many clubs or supervised activities and Jennifer was too shy to talk to the kids she met as she moved through eight classrooms a day. She'd gone to one school dance, but kids either hung around awkwardly in the gym or vomited up their wine coolers in the restroom. Even most of her teachers didn't know her name and she'd met her counselor only once, when he called her in to talk about truancies.

Sandi said, "Jen missed so much school. We've tried to be positive about the kids' education, but maybe unconsciously we're doing something wrong. We're worried she'll have trouble getting into college."

"I hate your foreboding futuristic bullshit," Jen said.

"Settle down," Brian said wearily. Jen folded her arms across her chest and snorted angrily.

Jen was experimenting with drugs, alcohol and rebellion and Sarah was a perfectionistic, people-pleasing young woman with an eating disorder. Both girls hurt themselves as they tried to fit into the world of their friends. They faced the dilemmas all young women face in our culture— how to be independent and explore the world and yet stay safe.

I turned to Tyler. "How's your life going?"

"Okay." He shrugged self-consciously and looked to his father for support.

Brian said, "Tyler, tell her the truth. You're unhappy at school."

"There's nothing to tell. "Tyler kicked at the carpet.

Jennifer said adamantly, "He's a wimp and he's getting creamed."

Brian said, "Tyler told me that he's afraid of being beaten up by bullies or kidnapped by strangers." He shook his head. "When I was Tyler's age, my biggest worry was if the coach would let me pitch the next game."

I asked about friends and Tyler said, "I had a friend who studied violin with my teacher. But his parents got divorced and he moved."

Sandi touched Tyler's hand. "He could use a new best bud."

I asked about goals for the family. Brian wanted more family harmony and fun. Sandi wanted more conversations. Everyone wanted Jennifer to stop being obnoxious. Sarah said that between work and school, she almost never had time alone. Tyler wanted more time with his father and a family trip to Disney World and the MGM studios. Jennifer wanted everyone off her back, but she also said that she thought her parents worked too hard and that Tyler needed more of a life.

I asked about chores and the kids all groaned. Sarah felt she was doing quite enough already. Tyler, whose one job was to mow the lawn, complained it made his allergies act up. Jennifer said she hated dishes and besides, no other girls had to do them. She agreed her room was a mess, but insisted that she liked it that way. She said that if her parents minded, all they had to do was shut her door. Her last comment was "I'm not really into helping out at home."

Everyone looked discouraged by this topic. I had made a mistake in bringing it up that day. Chores were not this family's biggest problem. Really the heart of the family was being damaged. When families get too busy, the first things that go are their rituals. Perhaps I could help them build in some rituals. This family needed more nourishing activities. As adults, people remember three kinds of family events with great pleasure—meals, vacations and time outdoors. I wanted this family to have some memories.

"I'm going to make a couple of radical suggestions here," I said. "One is that you turn off the television and computer for at least a couple nights a week, and two, that the family do something out of doors every week. Watch a sunset, go for a walk or take a trip to a wilderness area."

These were standard suggestions for me. I think the natural world has great power to heal and restore broken families. Children need contact with the natural world. It's an antidote to advertising and gives them a different perspective on the universe. Looking at the Milky Way makes most of us feel small and yet a part of something vast. Television, with its emphasis on meeting every need, makes people feel self-important and yet unconnected to anything greater than themselves.

After my suggestions everyone looked at Sandi, who said rather ruefully, "I like my feet to be on man-made surfaces at all times. I like pavement."

Brian chuckled. "Sandi's idea of an outdoor event is a Holiday Inn fun dome."

"No television or computers will be easy for me though," Sandi said. "That's where the rest of you will suffer."

Session Five

Sarah was at work and Brian was out of town on business so only Jennifer, Tyler and Sandi came to this session. Sandi seemed less ruffled and tense as she slipped off her high heels and curled her legs under her on the couch. Jennifer wore a shirt that said, "Drain bamaged" and had what I hoped were temporary tattoos on her arms and hands. Tyler looked uncomfortable, but he smiled gamely at me when he sat down by his mother.

I checked on old assignments. Sandi said that she and Brian were getting their Friday night dates and also ten minutes a day alone to talk. Sandi said, "It isn't enough, but it helps." She said the kids were helping more with chores, especially if she or Brian worked with them. The television and computer were now off three nights a week. Sandi said, "That's made a big difference. We have more time. People are talking to each other. Tyler and Jen actually read books for a change. We've played Scrabble and Pictionary. One night Jen and I made galaxy cookies and mailed them to Mom."

"We took a walk on a prairie," Tyler interrupted. "It was hot. There were ticks and chiggers. Everyone hated it but Jen."

"We saw a deer," Jen said. "And flowers were blooming, all colors."

Jen talked about the prairie and I lent her my book on flower identification. Then I asked about her summer. She said sarcastically, "I'm snorting cocaine and selling my body to guys who are HIV positive." I shook my head at her joke. Sandi said, "Jen's joking, but she is cruising main street and hanging out in an area that has drug busts."

Jennifer interrupted. "Like I'm never supposed to see my friends."

"Why don't you invite your friends to our house?" Sandi asked.

"Yippee," she said in a voice dripping with sarcasm. "Would you serve us milk and cookies?" Sandi looked helplessly my way. Jen said, "I'm so over your worrying about me."

"There's room for compromise between cruising and milk and cookies in the living room," I said. We talked for a while about what that compromise might be and Jen agreed reluctantly to give her mother's suggestions a try.

I asked Tyler how he was doing. He screwed up his face. "Mom made Dad take all the video games off the computer."

Sandi said, "We wanted him outside—riding his bike or playing with other kids. We want him to go swimming."

"No way," Tyler said. "That's where the gangs hang out."

"I won't go there either. The guys at the pool are animals," Jennifer said. "They call Tyler a fag and me a big butt. I look like a sea cow in my swimsuit."

Tyler jumped in. "I want to take steroids or growth hormones, whatever would make me bigger."

Sandi said softly, "I didn't know you were worried about your size."

Tyler scrunched into his seat miserably. "How do you know if you're gay?"

Jen said, "Beat the hell out of anybody who calls you a fag. Or tell me and I'll take care of it for you."

"Maybe you should tell your dad," Sandi said.

Tyler said, "Dad's never been in a fight in his life. These guys have weapons. I'm not messing with them."

"I taught Tyler to respect women, but that gets him in trouble," Sandi said. "He won't tease girls the way other boys do."

"Hell, playing the violin gets him in trouble," Jennifer interrupted.

Tyler jumped in with stories about the things boys said to girls. His friends had goaded him to touch girls' breasts and hips. They called girls sluts and bitches. If he talked to a girl, guys asked if he'd done it with her. At home, he'd learned that sexual remarks were insulting and wrong, just like saying "nigger" was wrong. He knew his sisters didn't like taunts and touches, but he was confused about the right thing to do. The guys his age claimed that girls liked it. Also, he knew girls who harassed boys. This one girl in fourth grade was always asking guys if they wanted to have blow jobs.

Sandi looked shocked that Tyler even knew what a blow job was, but he said, "This is 1995, Mom. Get real."

Jennifer said, "Kids tease me all the time about my body, just to make themselves feel better. Everyone has to suffer."

These revelations led to a discussion of body types. I said that in my experience, small boys and well-developed girls had the most trouble. Boys are penalized for any physical weakness and girls are targeted as sexual objects. Jen said, "I am fed up with guys making cracks about my breasts. Someday I'm gonna hurt somebody." Tyler worried most about getting beat up. He knew one of the easiest ways for guys to look macho was to pick on small guys like himself.

Jennifer said, "Just beat the shit out of them."

"Easy for you to say," Tyler said. He started to cry. "I wish we lived in a different town."

"Every town in America is hard for kids right now," I said.

We talked some about the confusing messages boys receive about manhood. The media suggests that cool guys are loners who do whatever they want. The message is that real men are sexually voracious and avoid emotional commitments. Heroes are guys who can kill dozens of people and not lose a night's sleep. Yet real boys get in trouble if they act like these heroes. Boys are encouraged by the media to be wild and free, even to break laws, but if they are caught, they are harshly judged.

I noted that many boys believe that to be popular they must harass girls. Gentle boys who respect girls are at best ignored and at worst brutalized. Eventually their altruistic behavior drops out of their repertoire because it's not reinforced by anyone except mothers, which at this age is worse than no reinforcement at all.

I said that Tyler and Jennifer were caught between the lessons they learned from parents and from peers. To be accepted they must do things that are wrong and harmful. Jennifer was doing her best to increase her coolness quotient and getting in a lot of trouble. Tyler was staying away from peers and feeling bad about himself. Sandi was sympathetic with both kids, but at a loss about how to be helpful.

I asked if Tyler had made any new friends. Sandi said, "He's been trying, but it's tough. He had a boy over recently who wouldn't take no for an answer. When I asked this kid to put toys away, he called me a bitch." She sighed. "We won't be asking him back."

"He was bad news," agreed Tyler. "But he was new in town and hadn't learned I was a nerd."

I complimented Tyler for trying to make new friends and sympathized that not all good effort is immediately rewarded. I praised both kids for talking honestly about problems. We ended the hour with a brief review of assignments. Jennifer would go back to the prairie. Tyler would continue his friend search. I suggested that Sandi and Brian discuss a cheap vacation—maybe a camping trip. She groaned, but seeing Tyler's eager face, she agreed to discuss it.

Session Seven

In the late afternoon on a hot Friday in July, Sarah, Sandi and a stony-faced Jennifer sat before me. Today Sarah was a walking ad for designer jeans. Jennifer was dressed in green boots, tights and a sundress. She carried a book called *Shampoo Planet*. Tyler was at computer camp and Brian was at an out-of-town meeting. "I had a hard time getting Jennifer to come today," Sandi began. "She's into denial about her behavior. After last weekend she didn't want to face you."

"Is that true, Jen?"

Jen stiffened and looked out the window while Sandi continued. "I hate to tell on her, but Saturday night Jennifer came home drunk. She was stumbling around the house bumping into things. Brian couldn't understand her. He woke me to ask if we should take her to the hospital."

"I just went out with some friends. What's the big deal?" But Jennifer's face belied her words.

Sarah said, "They were drinking this new kind of alcohol that tastes like pop. The first time I had some I turned into a zombie. It's get-you-there-quick booze."

Sandi's eyes filled with tears. "Jennifer could have been killed from alcohol poisoning. She could have walked in front of a car or been raped."

Jennifer rolled her eyes and said, "Mom, I'm so over your hysteria."

I suspected that Jen was using alcohol to fit in with peers and to handle the stress of adolescence. I wanted to help her learn a different way of dealing with pain, one that was a good precedent for handling all the pain that comes with life. I suggested that she should come alone. "You are running from your feelings and that's not working too well." Jen grimaced, but after we made the appointment she visibly relaxed.

I brought up a less personal issue. "It's weird that to be considered grown up, teens have to do things that are dangerous. I've known many girls who fought with their mothers because they felt they should. It's different in other cultures, you know. In Asia and Europe, kids aren't expected to rebel the way they are here."

Sarah said, "I know what you mean. When I've turned down drugs, I've been teased about being a prude and a baby and not wanting to make my parents mad, like it's a bad thing."

"My friends don't pressure me," said Jen.

"We don't give teens permission to love their parents," I continued. "We teach them there's something sick about being close."

We talked about cigarette and alcohol companies that are masterful at associating smoking and drinking with adulthood. Movies and music teach that sophisticated people are sexual and violent without thinking about consequences. Sarah remembered being offered drugs and alcohol for the first time in the sixth grade. Jennifer said, "Sex is a big deal then too. Most girls do it the first time in seventh grade. Usually they're drunk at a party. After that it's easier."

Sandi said, "Brian and I want our kids to fit in, but we don't want them out of control."

Sarah said, "My best friend doesn't drink, but almost everyone else I know does. Preppy kids are in just as much trouble as metalheads. They are just more sneaky about it."

I asked Sarah about her college search. She said, "I haven't heard yet from the modeling school. But I am not sure about going, even if I get the money. I filled out an application for the university."

I asked why she was wavering. She said, "I don't want to build a life around looking good. Someday I'll get old and wrinkled like everyone else."

Jennifer wrinkled her nose. "She's going to be a business major."

I asked Jen about herself. She said, "I rode my bike to the prairie. It's kind of hard to identify flowers. They look different in the book, but I think I figured out a few—leadplant, purple poppy mallow, yarrow and butterfly milkweed. That's what is on the prairie now."

"Good job," I said. "Why don't you call the nature center and volunteer? You could learn more about plants." For the first time that hour, Jennifer smiled. "Maybe."

Session Ten

Brian and Sandi showed up together for a Saturday session. Both looked more relaxed than at earlier sessions—Brian wore golfing clothes. Sandi was dressed in jeans and a sweatshirt that said, "A Woman's Place Is in the House and in the Senate." She reported that she'd joined the women's spirituality group at her church. She also said that she was setting better limits. "I'm less of a giving machine at work. I'm saving more of myself for the family."

I asked about the marriage. Sandi said, "I felt distant from Brian when we first came here. He woke up and turned the computer on. He was online when I fell asleep at night. Except for family business, we hardly spoke."

"I had a hard time sympathizing with Sandi. I was working twelve-hour days. I wasn't having an affair. But from her point of view, I might as well have been. Finally I decided no more computer work at home," Brian said. "If it costs me my job, so be it."

Sandi gave him a noogie. "Things are better. We talk to each other after dinner. Friday nights we order pizza and play games. Sunday we take a morning walk."

"The best thing that's happened from my point of view is our time outdoors." Brian looked ruefully at Sandi. "Sandi isn't a fan yet, but the kids love it. Jen is into flower identification in a big way. Tyler likes anything that we do as a family. We've taken more bike rides and hikes in the last two months than in our entire life. We're going camping soon."

Sandi wagged a finger at Brian. "This was Brian and Jen's idea. When I ask about hot showers, Brian just snickers."

Brian continued, "With less television, the kids talk more. They are reading. Heck, I'm reading."

"We've had good conversations," said Sandi. "One day Jen asked me if I would do a striptease for a million dollars. I said to her, 'Money isn't a great motivator to me. Let's talk about if I would strip for world peace or a cure for AIDS.' That launched a conversation about what our family values are. We wouldn't have had this talk six months ago."

"These days kids know everything," Sandi said. "When Tyler was five, he heard that Magic Johnson had AIDS. He's upset about the woman who drowned her sons."

"That kind of stuff is hard for kids to handle," I said.

"It's hard for me to handle," Sandi exclaimed. "If Tyler disappears for a few minutes, my first thought is he's been kidnapped. I keep close tabs on where he is. Mom didn't do that with me. She rang a bell when she wanted us home."

Brian said, "When I was a boy, my parents played canasta with another couple every Saturday night. We kids goofed around and listened to our parents talk. Now the parents go out and leave their children with a sitter."

Sandi added, "My dad was an attorney and his office was on the town square about three blocks from our house. He walked home for lunch, then napped on the living room couch. He and Mom drank coffee and talked every morning in the kitchen and most evenings on their porch."

"My parents took us with them to dances at the armory and to church dinners. They took us fishing and on picnics." Brian shook his head in puzzlement. "They never read a book on relationships in their lives. They didn't try as hard or worry as much as we do. My dad coached Little League but he didn't do it to enhance my self-esteem; he did it because he liked baseball."

Sandi said, "I know some kids did, but I never mouthed off to my parents. I've never called my mom a bitch."

Sandi sighed. "That's another thing I feel guilty about. Mom needs me and I can't be there for her. The kids miss her. Calling isn't that hard, but getting to Georgia is impossible."

"Have you thought of bringing her here, maybe finding her an apartment near you?"

"It would be good for me. And Jen could use her grandmother nearby after school," Sandi said. "But I don't know if Mother would like it."

Brian said, "Your mom's young enough to make friends and a life for herself."

"What if we end up moving again?" Sandi asked.

"We won't move. I won't do that again to you or the kids. We just aren't that portable anymore. The job will go before we move," Brian said.

He looked at Sandi. "I'm thinking of quitting. Life is too short for me to spend it being this unhappy."

"We can work the money problems out," Sandi said. "All of us need to curtail our spending. Sarah can work while she goes to the university."

Brian said, "Jen loves her grandmother. She could help her with errands and chores. Tyler could use an older person in his life too."

Sandi said softly, "I need her too."

I asked about Jennifer and Tyler. Brian answered, "Jen's better. She's been less hostile around home. It helped her to talk to you about stress.

She still hangs out with kids we don't like, but she is going to the nature center. There are some good kids there."

Sandi made a face. "Last week she cared for their snakes. Ugh. Jen got a real kick telling me about chopping up worms for snake food."

I laughed. "That's a good way for her to horrify and alarm her mother."

"We're still worried about her, especially when school starts," Brian said. "But we see a glimmer of hope."

"Tyler still hasn't made any friends," Sandi said. "But he's going out with us."

Brian added, "He's been joking around more. He likes family night and the walks. He's psyched for this camping trip."

I said that Tyler's distance from peers wasn't all bad. Maybe we could work to connect him with older and younger people, people who are less judgmental about violin players and less into being macho. I congratulated this couple on their good work and wished them well on their first camping trip.

Session Twelve

It was now mid-August and school would be starting soon. Early in the morning, the Copelands showed up for a session. Brian had made pancakes for the family and they were all in a well-fed, joking mood. The girls looked more alike; Sarah wore no makeup and Jen had no tattoos.

Right away I asked about the camping trip. Sandi said wryly that she liked it except for the outdoor toilets. Sarah asked, "Do you know of any campgrounds without mosquitoes?" We all laughed as she showed us her bites. "I'm not much of a Camp Fire girl, but I liked seeing Tyler and Jen happy."

I checked on other issues. Sandi still was moody, but she had discontinued her Prozac. She said, "When I first came here, I felt like those dogs in psychology experiments that got shocked whichever way they jumped. Eventually they stopped jumping and just felt depressed. Now I've found ways to jump that aren't punishing."

She felt more optimistic that she and Brian could survive their children's adolescence. She attended the church group for women and was making friends. She said, "I'd forgotten how much I need relationships with women."

Brian continued to be stressed at work. Since he was saying no to extra tasks, he suspected the ax could fall any day. But he seemed ready for the consequences of his actions. As he put it, "I don't have any choice really. I'm not going to become an automaton."

I suspected Jen might still use drugs occasionally with her school friends, but probably less now than when we first met. At the nature center she had made friends with two girls who were slightly older than she but "straight edge," which meant they'd decided to be chemically free.

Tyler had a good experience at the neighborhood block party. He'd played "America the Beautiful" on the violin and received many compliments from the neighbors. One older lady told him how much she enjoyed hearing him practice. She often sat on her porch, just to hear his morning session. He'd met a boy down the block who was into computers. The boy was younger, but he played an instrument too. Tyler had talked to Brian at length about homosexuality. He was still worried about being called gay, but he was no longer worried about being homosexual. He dreaded school in the fall.

Sarah was starting college at the state university in two weeks. She'd heard the classes were big, the dorms rowdy and that many girls had been sexually assaulted on campus. She was fearful of leaving the family, but right now she was doing all right. Her weight was up to 115, and at my suggestion she had been taking "imperfection lessons" from Jen. She seemed to be mellowing a little and often left the house looking less like a *Vogue* model and more like an ordinary person.

Brian and Sandi seemed reconnected as a couple. The family continued to limit their television and spend Friday nights together. Jen was reading *Catcher in the Rye* and Tyler was into the Hardy Boys mysteries. The kids still weren't doing their chores. Sandi's mother was coming to live near them and they were working together to find her an apartment. Sandi said, "We won't move again unless we're starving. We've cut back on spending and Brian's looking for other jobs."

We talked about the therapy. Sandi said, "We are blaming ourselves less and looking at the culture more."

Brian said, "In the past when we saw therapists we left feeling that we were a uniquely weird group. This time, we feel like we are a good family who has run into problems. We realize that we have some control now. We can make choices about what we'll accept and reject."

Jennifer gestured toward Sarah. "I don't hate everybody anymore."

Sarah said, "My last therapist thought I cared too much what my family thinks. But my family doesn't care how I look. Mom and Dad want me to be happy."

Brian gave her a hug. "Thank you for saying that."

Sandi said, "I'm pleased about more time with the family. I really appreciate Brian being with me instead of on-line. All the TV was rotting the kids' brains."

"I'd like to quit smoking," Brian said. "I should do it now, but I'm under too much work stress."

"Just say no, Dad," quipped Jen.

"This school year will be tough on the family," I said. "I'm glad you've gotten stronger so that you are ready for it."

Brian said, "We've slowed things down and found some time for each other. We feel like a functional family. How many families who have seen a therapist can say that?"

Chapter Four

═══════════

Then and Now

In *Grass Roots: The Universe of Home,* Paul Gruchow wrote that it's in fashion to disparage nostalgia as a "cheap emotion." He wrote: "In its Greek roots it means literally, the return of home. Nostalgia is the clinical term for homesickness, for the desire to be rooted in a place, to know clearly, that is, what time it is."

"Nostalgic" is often a derogatory term applied to those who suggest the past was in some ways superior to the present. But if we define nostalgia that way, Thomas Jefferson was nostalgic when, as an old man, he wrote of the early days of democracy. Black Elk was nostalgic when he talked about the era when the Sioux roamed freely over a buffalo-studded plain. Wendell Berry was nostalgic when he described a Kentucky where neighbors helped each other with the planting and harvest. Must we doubt everyone who speaks positively of the past?

There are dangers in romanticizing the past. Forgetting bad things could make them more likely to happen again. Pining for the past can lead to negativism and inaction. But to be fair, we need a comparable word for those who are overly optimistic about progress. Our consumer culture teaches us that more is better and that new is always improved. Futurists can gloss over problems and be naively optimistic. As Paul Gruchow asks, "Why is it delusional to regret what has been lost, but sanity to trust what has not yet happened?"

To accuse all who speak well of the past of being nostalgic is to deny that environments can be discussed rationally. If we don't compare, then we can't make sense of difficult times. If we claim that all eras are essentially the same, we have established a rationale for passivity.

All times and places are not equal. Particular communities produce certain kinds of families. To say that in the past families had more connection to their communities and to each other is not necessarily to lie. One can be clear-thinking, as opposed to sentimental, and reach this conclusion. Furthermore, respect for the past doesn't necessarily lead to reactionary thinking. Rather, a healthy appreciation for what worked in previous eras can inspire action. We can examine what worked well and what didn't and use this knowledge in planning for a better world.

Of course some things have changed for the better and some for the worse. Although the proportions vary across decades, there have always been happy and unhappy families and well and poorly adjusted individuals. The fortunes of families rise and fall. Human nature may be a constant, but the conditions under which humans develop change tremendously. The interesting question is, Under what conditions do families and their members flourish?

Since the 1920s, expectations about what families need to be happy have changed. At one time, most families were content with small homes that kept out the rain and snow. People with a high school diploma could make a living. People felt reasonably prosperous if they could have chicken on Sundays and take their kids into town on Saturday night. Virtually no one expected to travel to Europe, eat in elegant restaurants or own two vehicles.

The satisfactions of daily life came from solving concrete problems. Men felt satisfaction when they chopped wood to keep their families warm. Women took pride in offering their families fresh bread and homemade soup. Families rejoiced with the harvest. Today most of us do more abstract work. The problems we encounter are more nebulous and less easily solved. It's less clear that we are doing something useful.

In the 1930s people worried about physical survival—food, shelter and warmth. People had bad teeth and scars from injuries poorly treated. Hands were knobby from hard labor and frostbite. Now most Americans have their survival needs satisfied, but this doesn't necessarily make life easier or better. In some ways it's easier to worry about harvesting wheat than self-actualizing, or about making sauerkraut than networking with the right people. In some ways it's more rewarding to milk a cow or to bake a pie for hungry children than it is to fill out paperwork for an insurance company, supervise disgruntled employees or sell fancy underwear to strangers via telephone.

To survive in the country in the 1920s people required certain skills. As Bill McKibben pointed out, to eat a hamburger a person needed to know how to clear land, raise cattle, grow feed, kill and preserve meat, build a barn and talk his neighbor into helping him. These weren't easy skills to acquire, but the average person could do it and feel pride in his/her self-sufficiency. Now it's harder to know what we need to survive. Success requires different skills—coping skills, such as anger control, stress management and communication skills, such as assertiveness and empathic listening. The demands of the modern world are too hard for many people to meet. Many turn to therapists or to chemicals to help them cope.

In my grandparents' town, people were careful about relationships. A small-town custom was to clearly identify people in terms of kin and location before any discussion about them could occur. A conversation about Joe Smith would begin this way. One person would say, "You know Joe, he lives three miles north of town on the old Creed place. He's married to Hal Jones's youngest daughter, Marie. His mother teaches school in Burlington. His cousin Tom is the mailman." The other person would answer, "Yes, isn't he John Smith's son? Didn't he play fullback for Seibert when he was in high school?"

There was a basic civility between neighbors. Word of rudeness or impropriety got around. In fact, the big complaint was lack of privacy. Whatever you did was discussed. If you offended the sensibilities of others, you were judged harshly. The Copelands do not know their neighbors. As long as their behavior doesn't cause problems for others, no one cares what they do. That makes for more privacy but less accountability. Of course, the judgmental communities of the 1920s created pain. Divorced people were often shunned by their neighbors, for example. But by today, we're noting the problems that occur when people are not accountable to each other. The close monitoring that occurred in the past sometimes fostered hypocritical behavior, but in many cases it also fostered proper behavior. People didn't do things they didn't want their neighbors to know about.

In my grandparents' community, families worked and played together.

Big families were possible, even financially sensible. Relatives of all ages were nearby. Sick people were tended at home. Children looked after aging parents, not because they were more moral than children today, but because it was both possible and necessary that they do so. This mixing of the ages allowed children to learn from adults, adults to supervise children and both ages to know each other as people. Older relatives often had time for games and stories. Children learned from them family history and other kinds of history as well.

In the 1920s most families had a hierarchical structure. Parents were definitely in charge. There was a sharp line between children and adults. Only children were addressed by first names. Among adults, even close friends referred to each other as Mrs. and Mr. Adults had both privileges and responsibilities. They were entitled to respect, which they earned by teaching skills and values to their children. Many things, such as money or family problems, were not discussed when children were present.

Children were taught how to behave. There were literally hundreds of rules that all adults tended to enforce with all children—take off your hat when you enter a building (for boys only), stand up when a lady enters the room, don't chew gum with your mouth open, wear white gloves in church (for girls only), don't interrupt and don't sit down if grownups are standing. These rules could be silly, but also comforting in their clarity and concreteness.

Basically everyone learned the same rules. Most people felt that their actions had significance, that there was a God evaluating their behaviors and intentions. Much of social life was organized around churches. There was no competing value system that kept families and communities from agreeing about rules. Today it's difficult to obtain agreement even within families about right and wrong and what the rules should be. It's even more difficult to mesh these rules with the outside world.

The Page children rode the bus to high school. They played basketball and joined the debate team and drama club. Margaret played the violin. They all loved books. There was neither time nor money to get in much trouble. In fact, trouble was hard to find.

In contrast, I think of the girls I met at a junior-high camp in Kansas. During the school year, they communicated via e-mail with their science professors and each other. During the summer they did research and studied together at the university. We met in the lounge on their dorm floor—sixty-five of us in a windowless room filled with beanbag chairs. The girls were yelling at each other, giggling, wrestling and talking nonstop. But when I talked about my work as a therapist, they quieted down.

I asked how many of them argued with their mothers. Every hand shot up. I told them about the Asian girls I interviewed who were devoted to their mothers, who organized their days so that they could cook for their mothers or spend time playing cards with them. I quoted a Vietnamese girl who asked me, "Why would I fight with my mother? She gave me the gift of life." As I talked, several girls began to cry.

Afterward the girls all wanted to talk at once. A girl from Salina said, "I had to hurt my mother; we were too close." A girl from Russell said, "I got mad when Mom tried to stop me from getting in trouble. But what else could she do? She didn't want me to be destroyed." A minister's daughter said, "I hurt my parents badly. I lied to them, called them names, told them they were awful parents."

The girls talked about drugs and alcohol. A girl with braces and a sweatshirt that said, "My boss is a Jewish carpenter" announced, "In my class, it's socially unacceptable not to get drunk." Girls from towns of five hundred people told me about kids dropping acid, smoking pot and eating hallucinogenic mushrooms. Two girls were hooked on diet pills. Three eighth-graders announced they were alcoholics. Two were in AA and one wasn't. One of the girls who was in AA spoke in a voice laden with experience: "Don't do what I have done." She was fourteen years old.

In their eagerness to share war stories, the girls interrupted each other. A girl with a ponytail and lots of bracelets said that three kids from her school were killed last summer. Driving up and down main street, they'd gotten smashed on wine coolers and the driver had plowed into a bridge abutment. A fresh-faced girl said, "There's nothing to do but drink in my town."

"In fifth grade, my friends and I decided we would have sex with boys. Now we can't get our reputations back," a girl from western Kansas said. "Now we are the sluts of the school." A girl from Mulvane said, "It's confusing. You're pressured to have sex, but when you do, you're a whore."

Other girls talked about friends who had babies or eating disorders, who had herpes, genital warts or crabs. One of the alcoholics had a friend who dropped out of school because she couldn't take the teasing. Girls told of boys who grabbed their breasts or who teased them about the guys they'd had sex with. One self-contained girl said that she couldn't relate to the stories she was hearing. She was from a town of sixty-seven people with only eleven kids in the school.

As I drove home, I thought about my evening. These girls looked like they should be showing horses at the fair or playing jacks, not attending AA meetings or the funerals of their friends. If this group of girls from Kansas was in trouble, there was no safe place left in America.

Teachers everywhere agree that children are having a tougher time and so are teachers. As one teacher put it, "Kids have changed, parents have changed and what families expect of schools has changed." But it is eerie how many teachers say that something has happened to children in the last five years. Then they mention that children have different attention spans and they interact differently with each other.

There are many theories. Families are more on the go and kids stay up late watching TV. There are more unsupervised kids. Parents have mental health problems or addictions. One teacher told me about a mother who smoked pot in front of her first-grader "because she didn't want to be a hypocrite and sneak her dope." Because of divorce, many children live in two places. Children don't get much exercise and many never eat meals. One teacher said that children don't know common vegetables, such as carrots, celery and cucumbers. They eat only fast foods and snacks.

Teachers agree that children are less polite and innocent Kindergartners use the "F word." Teachers believe that children are learning how to interact from TV, not people. As one teacher said, "Manners are not in the culture. Beavis insults, so my students insult."

Another teacher said, "Kids today are missing some essential social skills for relating to each other. They don't know how to introduce themselves to other kids. They don't know how to negotiate or sustain a conversation. They relate to each other via put-downs. They've learned this from TV sitcoms. We can tell kids to be quiet and they just keep talking."

Teachers agreed that they spend more time disciplining kids now, that kids have more serious problems and that nice, well-behaved kids are overwhelmed by the system. One teacher said, "I wake up in the night feeling sorry for the well-mannered kids who want to learn. I am letting them down."

Many teachers commented on a vicious cycle that has developed. Teachers have unruly students, so they structure more, but that allows children even less interaction time. Students don't learn the interaction skills they need so they remain unruly. Then the teachers must structure more.

On the other hand, many teachers said that schools do a better job with problems today. They mentioned anger-control and stress-management groups and meetings for gays, children of divorce and girls with eating disorders. Schools actively fight racism and sexism. Special-needs children, such as those with learning disorders, get more attention. Schools now offer parenting classes and day care for student mothers. Problems are faced rather than brushed under the rug.

The speed at which families live their lives has accelerated. If I had a video of an ordinary day in the life of the Page family, I suspect it would look like a slow-motion film. No one was in a hurry. The Copeland family is always rushing. In their family, as in most modern families, time is a major problem. Life is increasingly unstable, inconsistent and hectic. There's too much information and not enough meaning, too much happening and not enough time to process it.

Jack Levin wrote in the *Baltimore Sun* about family life in the 1930s. He asked how he could communicate with middle-class kids about what it meant to scrimp and save for years and often never get what one wanted. He wrote of a world where people walked five miles to save five cents' car fare, skipped meals and wore clothing to shreds and shoes until holes appeared on the soles. He talked of the despair of a time when a fourth of the civilian labor force was out of work. But he wrote about the bonding that came from interdependence and shared sacrifice.

Many old folks have stories of that shared sacrifice. In my father's home, they ate bread and gravy every day, but they gave it different names each day of the week. Mother spoke lovingly of the one orange she got each year on Christmas morning. People from cities also have good memories of earlier days. One New York friend said his family was poor as church mice, but the public schools were good, the streets were safe and, in the summer, his family slept in Central Park. Over and over, people of the Depression era say, "We were poor, but we didn't know it. So was everyone else" or "We were poor, but we were happy" or "There was no crime. People shared what little they had."

Certainly poverty created problems. Families went to sleep hungry and cold. Many children left school to work for bread. The stories of farmers fleeing the dust bowl tell of a merciless time. Families were often separated for economic reasons. This kind of poverty leaves its scars. For example, many people of the Depression era never totally lost their fear of hunger. My parents' generation often built elaborate pantries that they filled with bagsful of food, bought supposedly because it was on sale but actually to reassure themselves that there will always be enough peanut butter, sugar, syrup or coffee. Adults who came of age during the Depression tend to be security oriented and many have worked at bad jobs all their lives because of their memories of unemployment and hunger.

But ironically, money was less important in the 1920s than it is today. Garrison Keillor talks about a "Ralph's Pretty Good Grocery," where "if they don't have it, you probably don't need it anyway." That's how my grandparents' town was. The kids all wore the same kinds of clothes, had the same meager toy collections and mostly played with each other and their animals. The Pages would have considered it ludicrous to buy things that they didn't really need. Money had little to do with the quality of anyone's life.

In contrast money is important to the Copelands. Money is necessary for health insurance, lessons and educational opportunities. Because the community is stratified, money is necessary to keep the family in the middle class. It's necessary to buy the right clothes and bikes so that the kids won't be ostracized at school. Money is necessary to buy the violins, computers and dance lessons so that the children can have the right friends. Money is now necessary to keep families safe. And Brian and Sandi are both worried that their children will be poorer than they are.

Sex was not discussed by polite people in the 1920s. It was an intensely mysterious and personal act that was to occur between married people. Of course, many people had sex outside marriage. But especially for children, sex was not part of their daily lives. Sexual innuendoes didn't flood the language.

Of course there were serious costs. Sexual ignorance created needless fear and misery. Girls were frightened by, and even ashamed of, their periods. Many people were ashamed of natural sexual urges. Teenagers who masturbated worried about hell, warts and blindness. Girls who were sexually active were isolated and scorned. Unwanted pregnancies traumatized the married and unmarried. People "had to get married," sometimes to people they didn't even like. Women died from repeated childbirth because they had no birth control or contraceptive information. Victims of incest or assault had no way even to report their experiences.

On the other hand, our modern environment has become so sexualized that we now have problems with boys barely in puberty harassing girls on school buses. New York City considered separate swimming pools for boys and girls because there are so many sexual problems when children swim together. Sexual information is available now, but so is a great deal of sexual misinformation. Children learn to have Mcsex, to just do it and not to worry about babies or sexually transmitted diseases.

Sex has been demystified, which may be a good thing, but it's also been marketed, which is not a good thing. We have moved from sex that is forbidden and terrifying to sex that is as accessible and interesting as a breakfast burrito. The din of sexual stimulation that surrounds children now leaves many of them jaded by the time they are through high school. College students often report sexual histories that would make a libertine blush. And as teenagers talk about sex, what is most noteworthy is their lack of joy.

In my grandparents' community, there was almost no crime. Especially during the Depression years, poor strangers showed up regularly and were given work and food. Houses didn't have locks, and keys were left in the ignition. Natural dangers—rattlesnakes, bulls, hailstorms and blizzards—not other humans, were what scared children. One summer after the hail took the crops, the family had a vacation. They drove an old car around the country and camped. If they saw hitchhikers they gave them a lift. Ordinary people hitchhiked and were safe doing it. In contrast, the Copelands are all too aware of crime. The house is locked at all times and has both Neighborhood Watch and an elaborate security system.

Not everything in the 1920s was better. Racism was much worse. We were a segregated society with Jim Crow laws and lynchings. Native American children were sent to Indian schools far from their families and forbidden their own languages. In the 1920s people starved, and died awful deaths from diseases or exposure to the elements. Children died for lack of antibiotics or even aspirin to bring down fever. Farm work with primitive equipment led to grisly farm accidents. Factory work was brutal and dull. There were many orphans and families separated by poverty. The isolation, especially in winter, drove people crazy.

Isolated families could be nightmares. In every community, there were men who beat their families in frustration and abused their powers simply because they could. Divorce was rare and scandalous. Women and children had almost no legal or economic rights. If the father was a petty tyrant, if he was physically or sexually abusive, family members had nowhere to go, no recourse but to endure. Many of the people who lived through the Depression era prefer today with all its problems. A friend's father will never wear blue jeans because that is all he had during the Depression era. My mother never wanted to live on a farm again and said, "Anyone who is romantic about farming just hasn't done it."

The stories of poverty and plenty point out an important difference in the times. Families in all eras face both internal and external problems. But in the 1920s, internal problems were minimized as families defined most of their problems as external. Families were clear that their biggest enemy was low cattle prices, dust or hailstorms and farm foreclosures. These outside problems united Depression-era families. Fighting them together built up family loyalty.

Today families are much more confused about who the enemy is. They tend to focus on internal problems, such as family tensions and the individual flaws of family members. They are less clear about their external enemies, such as an unfair economic system, an alcohol- and drug-soaked society, crime and the fear that comes with it, junk media and the pressures of consumerism. It's harder to fight an enemy that isn't properly identified. When the external enemy is confusing, the family doesn't unite but rather blames itself, and falls apart from within.

While external enemies often unite and strengthen families, internal enemies corrode family strengths. External enemies, such as the Great Depression or the Holocaust, often engender fierce loyalties. Absence makes the heart grow fonder. We love what we care for, sacrifice for. We love what costs us a great deal.

Family members feel intense yearning for each other when they have been separated by disasters. The irony is that when families have easy access to each other they often choose to stay apart. Family members who live near each other are often strangers. Rather than being the deepest love of their lives, family is perceived as a bother and a chore. When family is just a telephone call away, many people do not pick up the phone. In countries where citizens can get killed by voting, the voter turnout is higher than in America, where it's safe and easy to vote. That which is difficult to obtain is often valued highly.

When people have money, work and good health and still things go wrong, they blame themselves for their misery. It's the same with nations as with families. America had less internal strife when we could unite against the Nazis or the communists. Now that we have no common adversary, we fight amongst ourselves.

Families who identify an external enemy do better. Racism and illness are examples of external enemies. Many black families grow strong as they organize around protecting their children from the racism in the broader culture. A young couple with a Down's syndrome son told a reporter that his birth redefined the meaning of their family and taught them about love and commitment. From their son, the parents have learned that family is more important than anything. The mother said, "Pettiness has no place in our lives anymore."

I remember a family with a terrible external enemy. The wife, Rose, worked at Hardee's and the husband, Eldon, had Huntington's chorea, an inherited disease that causes paralysis, brain damage and eventually death. When we met, Eldon had only the beginning problems—his balance was poor and his hands and feet shook. But he knew what was coming. Rose and Eldon came in to discuss what and how to tell their daughter about Eldon's future.

The parents were fiercely protective of Chloe. They bought her a violin and paid for Suzuki lessons. At dinner they listened to the Book One tapes. They wanted her to have the experiences of more prosperous children. Rose described how she cried hearing Chloe play a Christmas concert with other young violinists. The music released all her sadness about the future. I thought of a poem with the line "Music unlocks the frozen rivers of the heart."

The family had a limited income and a tragedy awaiting them. But they loved each other fiercely. Eldon said, "We are all we have got." As Rose put it, "We don't have time to fight." I thought of them often when I saw much "luckier" families in therapy who were arguing about allowances or begging a family member to come home for dinner once a week.

There is a lesson for modern families in this business of external vs. internal enemies. Families fail when they attack each other from within. Families do better if they can unite against outside forces. We are all immigrants today living in a culture whose stories are not our stories and whose values are not our values. Families are stronger when they acknowledge this and unite to resist the messages and influences that would harm them.

In the 1930s we had an enormous economic crisis. Today we have the poverty of consumerism, which means never having enough. We're impoverished in a different way—we are, to quote Peter Rowan, "thirsty in the rain." Many of us do work that we neither feel proud of nor enjoy. We are too rushed to do the things we really value. In the 1990s ironies abound. With more entertainment we are more bored. With more sexual information and stimulation, we experience less sexual pleasure. In a culture focused on feelings, people grow emotionally numb. With more time-saving devices we have less time. With more books, we have fewer readers. With more mental health professionals, we have worse mental health. Today we're in a more elusive crisis, a crisis of meaning, with emotional, spiritual and social aspects. We hunger for values, community and something greater than ourselves to dedicate our lives to. We wake in the night sorry for ourselves and our planet.

Chapter Five

ONE BIG TOWN

As a child I stole lilacs from Mrs. Williams. She must have been watching from the window because immediately after I picked them, she was by my side in her robe and slippers. She made me return the flowers and called me a thief. She said that my parents hadn't raised me properly and that I should be ashamed of myself. Then she waddled off to call my mother at work and tell her about my crime. That's the point really—she knew my name and how to find my parents. When I arrived home, my parents lectured me and made me write a letter of apology. To this day I think Mrs. Williams was crabby and overreacted, but I have never stolen anything, not even a lilac, since our encounter.

In contrast, I was on a radio show in which a man called to complain about the junior-high kids who smoked in his front yard during lunch hour. They were trampling his flowers and bushes. The first time he went out to talk to them, they swore at him. The second time they threatened to burn his house down. He didn't know the children's names and he was afraid of them. When he talked on the radio, he sounded both angry and defeated. He couldn't protect his own yard. I thought to myself, This man will never vote for another school bond issue. And the children also missed something. They were not held accountable for their behavior. They didn't learn a lesson about respect.

As I drive along a busy highway I see a girl, who looks about five, with her yellow raincoat and school bag, at the edge of the road. Her face is streaked with muddy tears. As the traffic whizzes by she puts her foot into the street and then pulls back as if she were testing water. I want to help her but I hesitate. Surely she's been warned not to talk to strangers. Will I frighten her more if I stop? Will she report me to the police as someone who tried to pick her up? Will she be so scared she'll run into traffic? Yet what if I don't stop? Will she get hit by one of the trucks roaring by? The man ahead of me pulls over to help her and I am relieved of the decision. But then as I drive on, I worry about his motives.

ONE BIG TOWN

In the past forty years the United States has undergone enormous demographic changes. All over the prairie, the lights have gone out as young adults have traveled to cities and never returned. Farmers have moved to the suburbs, and little towns have dried up like tumbleweeds. Downtown cafés have closed and the locals now drink coffee at the Arby's on the highway. As we travel the interstates, which Paul Gruchow called "tunnels without walls," we see the same stores, cafés and hotels everywhere. It makes life convenient, but dull.

McKibben defined a working community as one in which it would be difficult for outsiders to fit in. That's because the information in the community would be specific, related to that time and place and grounded in the history of its inhabitants. Songwriter Greg Brown said, "Your hometown is where you know what the deal is. You may not like it, but you understand it. You know the rules and who is breaking them."

When I think of a working community, I think of my father's Ozark town. Cousins lived near each other and everyone knew everyone. Outsiders had a tough time getting information about locals because, for most of this century, the only outsiders were salespeople or IRS agents and FBI employees looking for moonshine stills. On the other hand, sixty years after my father left the Ozarks, I can still go there, explain who my family was and extract special privileges—a campground on private property and advice on where to fish and pick berries.

Our country has moved from small, isolated communities to one big company town. Wal-Marts have replaced the small stores and Pizza Hut and Taco Bell have replaced the city cafés. We are united by our media and by what we consume. All over America, regional dialects and ethnic accents disappear as children learn generic language from television.

Civic organizations such as the Elks, Lions and Moose—what we call the "animal clubs"—are being replaced by mailing-list organizations. Shopping channels and televised auctions, even for cattle, keep local folks from gathering. Televised college classes allow students to get degrees without interacting with professors or other students. Our phone book offers numbers to call to discuss personal problems, hear weather reports and celebrity trivia, find new recipes and hear consumer information and jokes. These calls mimic the kinds of things real people used to discuss when they met on street corners and in cafés. The need for connection is there, but it's filled via tape-recorded messages.

We've changed from a nation of primary relationships to one of secondary relationships. Primary relationships are ones in which people know each other in a multiplicity of roles—as neighbor, co-worker, in-law and schoolmate. Secondary relationships are ones in which people are strangers. We don't know their parents, their religion, where they live or if they have a dog. We know only about their role at a particular moment.

By 1990, 72 percent of Americans didn't know their neighbors. The number of people who say they never spend time with their neighbors has doubled in the last twenty years. More people do what John Prine called "live in their heads." They fantasize affairs with people they will never meet. Our children move among strangers.

It's not yet clear what it means that so much of our experience is vicarious. Sociologist James House reviewed relevant literature and concluded that social isolation is just as dangerous as smoking, high blood pressure or high cholesterol. A companion, any real-life companion, is a buffer against stress. I wonder if children learn different lessons from vicarious relationships than they do from real ones.

Real communities give people a sense that they are all in this place together. People who live together have something that is fragile and easily destroyed by a lack of civility. Everything you do matters. Protocol is important. Relationships are not disposable. People are careful what they say in real communities because they will live with their words until they die of old age. Accountability is different in the electronic community. Over the Internet, people can be deleted the second they become annoying or tiresome. Names aren't necessarily even real names. One never needs to see or talk to anyone again.

Parenthetically, demographic shifts explain much of our obsession with looking good. As we've moved from primary to secondary relationships, appearance has become much more important to us. In an earlier time, we had various kinds of information about the people we encountered. We knew their families, their house, their work habits, religion and amiability. Now often appearance is all we have to go on.

Electronic villages are not located in particular places. Cable channels from all over the world blare into our living rooms. Midwesterners hear the weather in Florida. New Yorkers hear the crime statistics from Austin. Domestic-relations court is filmed so viewers can watch other people's lives unravel. We work crossword puzzles to the unwinding of the Rwanda massacres. We hear of the rape of Bosnian women as we sweep our kitchens.

Nonstop data blurs many boundaries that hold our lives in place. As Stoll says, "Data isn't information any more than fifty thousand tons of cement is a skyscraper." Boundaries are blurred between places and times, between sexual and violent material, between funny and sad, trivial and important, news and entertainment and fact and fiction. Public and private behaviors are blurred and the boundaries between childhood and adulthood disappear.

Time is a boundary that's been blurred. Shops used to be closed on Sundays and after six at night. Town whistles signaled when to rise, eat and go home for lunch and dinner. News and weather were broadcast in the morning, at six and again at ten. Everyone's life had more or less the same structure. Now television channels broadcast nonstop and every small town has an all-night convenience store. Banks have twenty-four-hour-a-day, seven-days-a-week automatic teller machines.

As Joshua Meyrowitz noted in *No Sense of Place*, backstage and frontstage have blurred into a twilight-zone middle stage where all of us operate all of the time. With videocameras everywhere, all of us are potentially on frontstage. Our private behaviors can be made public. We see ordinary citizens in their most private moments. The prayers of parents whose daughter was murdered are gobbled up for video. While being filmed on a camcorder, a man commits suicide.

From the point of view of this book, by far the most important lost boundary is that between children and adults. George W. S. Trow wrote: "We are becoming more childish. We're falling out of the world of history into the world of demographics where we count everything and value nothing." Often in the media, parents are portrayed as adult survivors, as lost as children and as unsure of what is right or important. Age no longer implies wisdom.

When we erase lines kids have no protection and adults have no dignity or obligations. Thus, we see children defined as consumers and sold sugary alcoholic drinks and chocolate chewing tobacco. The cover of a Nirvana album showed a baby swimming toward a fishhook holding a dollar bill. When kids are defined as consumers they have no protected space in which to grow. Everyone becomes the same—a stressed victim of forces larger than themselves, i.e., a consumer or prey.

In the *Geography of Childhood*, Gary Nabhan writes that in 1900, 10 percent of our people lived in big cities. By 1992, 38 percent of Americans lived in cities. Most children gain their knowledge of the natural world vicariously. In the history of the world, this distance from the natural world is a new phenomenon. The natural world teaches many lessons, but fewer children have access to its lessons. Even a generation ago most Americans were related to country people. Families visited farms on a regular basis. Children saw cows being milked, pigs fed, chickens plucked, grain planted, corn harvested and apples picked from family orchards.

Public space has disappeared as well. I thought of this recently at a Dairy Queen. I watched tired, stressed teens who barely knew each other waiting on lines of customers whom they didn't know. The customers didn't know each other and were clearly in a hurry to get their cones and be out of there. I contrasted these teens' experience with my own as a carhop at the A & W root beer stand in my hometown. The other employees were my classmates. We knew the customers; they were our friends, teachers and parents. The customers knew each other and visited car to car while they waited for their pork tenderloin sandwiches and root beer floats. Work was connected to the rest of our lives. We worked hard because adults we knew were watching. But we had fun, too. We were at the center of our town's social scene.

Children are more frightened in electronic communities. They do not know the adults around them and have been taught that strangers may be dangerous. Most children think they are in danger. A study of children in Ohio found that 43 percent of them thought they were likely to be kidnapped. In the last few years, basic facts have escaped us. We've emphasized the perils of "bad touch" and forgotten the importance to children of "good touch." We've focused on the dangers of strange adults and ignored the danger to children of not having loving adults involved in their lives.

With our warnings, we probably have protected some kids, but at a considerable expense. The children have lost opportunities to interact with interesting adults and genuine characters. I think of the Yo-Yo King from Detroit as I write this. He was my cabdriver in from the Detroit airport. We talked about his long career. For three years in a row he was the winner of the Detroit yo-yo championship. A yo-yo company sponsored his tours in this country and abroad. He performed yo-yo tricks in stadiums. Mostly, though, he went from school yard to school yard, teaching kids tricks and selling yo-yos. Now school policies don't allow him on school yards. He was bitter and said, "Perverts ruined everything for me and the kids." I felt sad as I listened. I knew that the policies were probably necessary, but much had been lost.

Children need to believe that the world is an interesting and safe place. They need a tiospaye. Without it, they cannot grow and explore. When we rear our children to fear other adults we truncate their growth. Lev S. Vygotsky, the great developmental psychologist, taught us that learning is fundamentally social. The relationship between children and their teachers isn't incidental, but rather is the central component of their learning. Human development occurs within the context of real relationships. We learn from whom we love.

NEW TOOLS

"There is no direct connection between convenience and happiness."
—Dr. Suzuki

I remember a story from my undergraduate days in anthropology. Missionaries who settled near a tribal culture gave the native women metal knives. Prior to this the men had made knives from stone and this had been an important source of their power and wisdom. But these new knives in the hands of the women were far superior. This upset the gender balance of the villagers, and ultimately the society was disrupted. Men's rituals were rendered meaningless and the women's place, while elevated, changed in ways that unsettled relationships with their families. Unwittingly, the missionaries had overturned a culture. If that can happen with a few metal knives, what about a culture in which we all are bombarded with hundreds of new "tools" every decade?

The electronic revolution is as significant as the invention of the printing press. It has changed our world as dramatically and much more quickly. The important elements have changed; where they once were snow and rain, they are now car phones and fax machines. We are not yet ready psychologically. We are just beginning to consider how human communities are affected by the new tools. We have no protection from the elements.

New products often erode our sense of community in unpredictable ways. For example, air-conditioning has changed neighborhoods. Adults no longer sit on their front porches to cool down in the evenings. Streets have become more dangerous without the supervision of neighbors. New tools have sped up the pace of our lives. Everyone seems stressed about time. When people communicate by e-mail and fax, the nature of human interaction changes. While some people use computers to communicate with those they know and love, many users communicate with people whose names and faces they do not know, in places they've never been, about people they've never met. I just read that soon we will be able to shop for food via computers. People will be able to pick out strawberries from their own home. When this happens we will be even less connected to those around us.

All the technology of our times has its good uses. The computer, for example, helped find the families of people killed in the Oklahoma City bombing and it helped coordinate medical and relief efforts. But the computer also has made it possible for militia groups to teach each other how to make bombs. Any one invention probably wouldn't do that much damage. The problem is the whole pile. It's the cumulative effect of all this equipment that has changed the very ways we live in families. Eventually quantity becomes quality and the integrity of our lives is altered.

As Clifford Stoll said in *Silicon Snake Oil,* "We program computers but they also program us." I don't think we should throw our machines into the sea, but we must analyze the effects of our technology and choose our tools carefully. We need to ask—Do we like the ways we are changing? How will this new technology affect humans? We need to be in charge of technology, not vice versa.

The speed of change is as dizzying as our lack of reflection on its consequences. To argue that change is inevitable is to say that planning is impossible. But there are precedents for making conscious choices about what tools to accept and reject. The Amish make conscious choices about technology. When the Japanese saw the havoc that guns wreaked on their samurai society, they threw their guns away and lived for hundreds of years without Western weapons.

Before the Seneca tribe made changes, the elders would ask, "How will this affect the next seven generations?" No new tools or customs were introduced without a thoughtful conversation about the future. We are not even asking how our explosion in technology and media is affecting the current generations.

TV

In a college class I asked, "What would it be like to grow up in a world without media?" A student from the Tonga Islands answered, "I never saw television or heard rock and roll until I came to the United States in high school." She paused and looked around the room. "I had a happy childhood. I felt safe all the time. I didn't know I was poor. Or that parents hurt their children or that children hated their parents. I thought I was pretty."

Television has probably been the most powerful medium in shaping the new community. The electronic community gives us our mutual friends, our significant events and our daily chats. The "produced" relationships of television families become our models for intimacy. We know media stars better than we know our neighbors. Most of us can discuss their lives better than we can discuss those of our relatives. We confuse personas and persons. That is, we think a man who plays a doctor on TV actually knows something about medicine. We think a chatty talk show host is truly good-natured. This confusion is especially common with young children, who are developmentally incapable of distinguishing between reality and fantasy. But even adults get mixed up about this.

Most real life is rather quiet and routine. Most pleasures are small pleasures—a hot shower, a sunset, a bowl of good soup or a good book. Television suggests that life is high drama, love and sex. TV families are radically different from real families. Things happen much faster to them. On television things that are not visually interesting, such as thinking, reading and talking, are ignored. Activities such as housework, fundraising and teaching children to read are vastly underreported. Instead of ennobling our ordinary experiences, television suggests that they are not of sufficient interest to document.

These generalizations even fit the way TV portrays the animal kingdom. Specials on animals feature sex, births and killing. Dangerous or cuddly-looking animals are favored. But in reality, most animals are neither dangerous nor cute. Sharks and panda bears are not the main species on the planet. Most animals, like most people, spend most of their time in rather simple ways. They forage and sleep.

TV isolates people in their leisure time. People spend more time watching music videos but less time making music with each other. People in small towns now watch international cable networks instead of driving to their neighbor's house for cards. Women watch soaps instead of attending church circles or book clubs. When company comes, the kids are sent to the TV room with videos. Television is on during meals and kids study to television or radio.

Parents are not the main influences in the lives of their children. Some of the first voices children hear are from the television; the first street they know is Sesame Street. A child playing Nintendo is learning different lessons than a child playing along a creek or playing dominoes with a grandfather. Many children have been conditioned via the media into having highly dysfunctional attention spans.

Adults too have diminished concentration. Neil Postman in *Amusing Ourselves to Death* writes of the 1858 Lincoln/Douglas debates. The average citizen sat for up to seven hours in the heat and listened to these two men discuss issues. People grasped the legal and constitutional issues, moral nuances and political implications. In addition, they could listen to and appreciate intricate and complex sentences. Today the press and the public decry President Clinton's speeches if they last more than an hour. To an audience socialized to information via sound bite, an hour seems like a long time.

The time devoted to violence on TV in no way reflects its importance in real life. In real life, most of us exercise, work, visit our friends, read, cook and eat and shop. Few of us spend any significant amount of our time solving murders or fleeing psychotic killers. On television there are many more detectives and murderers than exist in the real world. A rule of thumb about violence is "If it bleeds, it leads." Violence captures viewer attention. Our movies have become increasingly violent, and as James Wolcott wrote in *The New Yorker*, "Violence is the real sex now."

Some might argue that there is nothing new under the sun. Of course, in a narrow sense, they are correct. There have always been murderers and rapists, and stories about violence have been themes of literature and song. But things are different now. Children, including toddlers, are exposed to hundreds of examples of violence every day. The frequency and intensity of these images is unprecedented in the history of humanity. We have ample documentation that this exposure desensitizes children, makes it more likely they will be violent and increases their fear levels about potential violence.

Another difference is in the attitudes about violence. *Romeo and Juliet*, for example, was a tragedy. The deaths in the play were presented as a cause of enormous suffering to friends and families and as a terrible waste. When Juliet and Romeo died, something momentous happened in the universe. The very gods were upset. Often today, death is a minor event, of no more consequence than, say, the kicking of a flat tire. It's even presented as a joke.

It is one thing to read Shakespeare, which at least requires that the person can read. It's another to, day after day, see blood splattered across a screen by "action heroes." It is one thing to show, as Shakespeare did, that violence can be the tragic consequence of misunderstandings, and another to show violence as a thrill, as a solution to human problems or merely as something that happens when people are slightly frustrated or men need to prove they are men.

Of course, one could argue that parents can keep televisions out of their homes. This is extremely hard for the average parent to do. Even if they succeed, their children go from these "protected environments" to play with children who have watched lots of TV and who behave accordingly.

I don't often go to violent movies, but I do have a stake in them. I don't like living in a world where thousands of teenage boys, some of whom own guns, have been reared on them. Walking city streets, I may be accosted by a youth who has spent most of his life watching violent media. Unfortunately, needy children are the ones most affected. Children with the least available parents watch the most TV. Violent television is like secondhand smoke; it affects all of us.

Heavy viewers develop the "mean world syndrome." This leads to a vicious-circle phenomenon. Because children are afraid and the streets are not safe, they come home right after school and stay indoors. They watch more TV, which makes them more afraid and thus more likely to stay indoors. With everyone indoors the streets are less safe. Families watch more TV and are more fearful and so on.

Television and electronic media have created a new community with entirely different rules and structures than the kinds of communities that have existed for millions of years. Families gather around the glow of the TV as the Lakota once gathered around the glow of a fire on the Great Plains or as the Vikings huddled around fires in the caves of Scandinavia. They gather as New England families gathered in the 1800s around a fireplace that kept them warm and safe. But our TVs do not keep us warm, safe and together. Rapidly our technology is creating a new kind of human being, one who is plugged into machines instead of relationships, one who lives in a virtual reality rather than a family.

ADVERTISING

In therapy a young couple argue about what to buy their six-year-old daughter. Whenever they go out, Caitlan whines and begs for toys and gum. Dad says, "We can afford it, why not? It keeps her from fussing." Mom worries that she'll be spoiled. As we talk, it's clear that no one in the family is enjoying outings anymore. Caitlan begs, the parents argue, the father gives in and the mother gets mad. This reinforces Caitlan's whining and teaches her that products are the point of outings. A day will come when she begs for things the parents do not approve of and cannot afford.

I talk to my neighbor about her daughter, who has just started junior high. Mona says, "All of a sudden she's so money conscious. She wants to know how much we make. She keeps talking about who is rich and who isn't. And she wants expensive things that she doesn't need and we can't afford." Mona sighs. "We didn't teach her to think like this."

Since the 1950s, advertising has increased in amount and in sophistication. Much of what modern psychology knows about suggestion and influence has been usurped to sell products. We have t-groups and marketing polls. The general philosophy of ads—create a feeling of longing about a deeply human need, then suggest a product that will satisfy that yearning—works very well. Wishes are induced with the skill of a nightclub hypnosis, then elevated into needs. Your wish is your command. Ads elevate feelings over thinking and impulses over common sense. It's hard for parental calls for prudence to compete. The science of marketing is much more precise and focused than the science of parenting.

Ads manipulate us into being dissatisfied. As businessman B. E. Puckett said, "It's our job to make people unhappy with what they have." We are encouraged to feel anxious or sorry for ourselves. Advertising teaches us to live on the level of the pleasure principle. This leads to impulse-control problems and to feelings of entitlement. "I am the center of the universe and I want what I want now." This thinking creates citizens who are vulnerable to quick fixes. It leads to citizens filled with self-pity, which is the flip side of entitlement.

Advertising teaches that people shouldn't have to suffer, that pain is unnatural and can be cured. They say that effort is bad and convenience is good and that products solve complex human problems. Over and over people hear that their needs for love, security and variety can be met with products. They may reject the message of any particular ad, but over time many buy the big message—buying products is important.

Advertising trivializes the important and elevates the trivial. Crotch itch gets more attention than the famine in Ethiopia. Soft drink commercials receive more airtime than global warming. We are taught to buy products to fill emotional voids. We hear weird messages about what we deserve.

The propaganda that life is made happier by purchases encourages adults and children to make bad decisions about their time and money. Parents may take second jobs to pay for things. Teenagers work at minimum-wage jobs for designer jeans. Children want things that parents know are not good for them. Children alternate between the belief that products will make them happy and a deep cynicism about the promises of the adult world. They develop a lack of trust and respect for adults. They know that adults lie to them to make money.

We are even encouraged that it's patriotic to spend. Our economy depends on massive consumer spending on nonessentials. We must buy to keep America afloat whether we can afford to or not. This attitude is not fashionable in the 1990s. It is not perceived as good for the nation.

Philosopher Eileen Moody wrote that "the American dream has been re-written in the language of advertisers." Advertising is our national religion, with parables that teach "Buy this product and you will be saved." Children recite jingles instead of poetry and they know brand names instead of the names of presidents. More students can identify Mr. Peanut and Joe Camel than can identify Abe Lincoln or Eleanor Roosevelt. They can identify twenty kinds of cold cereal but not the trees and birds in their neighborhoods.

MONEY

"Rather than earn money, it was Thoreau's idea to reduce his wants so that he would not need to buy anything. As he went around preaching this ingenious idea, the shopkeepers of Concord hoped he would drop dead."—Richard Armour

Sitting Bull traveled with Buffalo Bill and saw the poverty and wealth of American cities. He said, "The white man knows how to make everything but he doesn't know how to distribute it."

Richard Ford: "A market economy is not even remotely premised on anybody getting what he wants."

Our land of opportunity has become a land of opportunists. Our most organized religion is capitalism, which at its meanest turns virtue upside down. Predators become heroes, selfishness is smart and compassion is softheaded. Capitalism favors what's called survival of the fittest, but really it's survival of the greediest, most driven and most ruthless. We have cared more about selling things to our neighbors than we've cared for our neighbors. The deck is stacked all wrong and ultimately we will all lose.

Kale had a job as a telemarketer. Over the phone he pitched junk to people in other states. The company he worked for was owned by people far away who knew neither Kale nor their customers. It was work that benefited only the stockholders. One day Kale was selling travel coupons in Florida. He talked to an old woman with a thick Spanish accent who was lonely and trusting. She was also hearing impaired and about to buy a worthless product. Kale warned her, "Don't do it." He was being monitored by his supervisor, and of course he was fired.

It's easier to hurt people we don't know. By now, our society isn't organized in a way that promotes accountability. In fact, people often must act against their better natures to do their jobs. The business of America is business. Parents are good to their own kids, but in the name of business parents will hurt other people's children. Children are seen as consumers, as a market to be manipulated for money.

Someone said that if you want to know what a culture values, look at its tallest buildings. In the Middle Ages, the churches were the tallest buildings; in the 1800s the schools and institutions of government were the tallest. Today, in America, it is the banks and corporate buildings.

Our current value system emphasizes profit over human well-being. It is, as the French say, *"le capitalisme sauvage,"* savage capitalism. Rats live by the laws of supply and demand; humans should be allowed to live by higher laws, ones that include the concepts of justice, mercy and truth. Economic laws are not the only laws of the universe. The bottom line is not the only line. Most of us are better than this belief system. We want a life organized around something besides money. Most of us do not believe that "the boy with the most toys wins in the end." Rather we hope that what will survive of us is love.

VALUES

Over Christmas vacation I watched some talk shows. First I watched a show hosted by Gordon Elliot, a good-looking middle-aged man in a gray suit. He had an English accent and a smarmy manner. With his handheld microphone he moved with ease between the panelists and the audience.

The topic was "Dealing with My Cheapskate Mate." Onstage were two working-class couples with large wives and scrawny, weather-beaten husbands. Tracy, with dyed hair and blue eye shadow, complained about her Gary. When he took her out to eat, he lied that it was her birthday to get a free dessert. Or he complained about the food or said he was an employee, just to get a free meal. Gary, a balding man with bad teeth and bad grammar, sat sullenly beside her. The audience booed when Tracy described Gary's tightness and cheered when Tracy put him down.

Loretta was a younger version of Tracy—also with dyed hair and heavy makeup. She spoke with a lisp and had a scar, probably from surgery to correct a harelip. As she spoke, she looked nervously at Earl, who sat stiffly beside her. She claimed she was in therapy because of Earl's tightness. She was depressed because she couldn't go shopping with her friends. Earl defended himself by saying that they were maxed out on their Visa and that Loretta was a big spender. A friend of Loretta's stood up to testify that Earl was a cheapskate. The women in the audience booed.

Gordon urged the home audience to call his toll free number, if they had a cheapskate mate. Then he broke for a commercial. "I don't know why I love you like I do" played behind a message about spaghetti sauce. There was an ad for an upcoming show with guests who had sexually transmitted diseases. An ad for appliances featured free financing with no payments for three months. A beautiful actress sold tampons with ultrasmooth applicators. The product motto was "trust." There was an ad for antacid and for Publishers Clearing House, "The House Where Dreams Come True."

We returned to Gordon and the couples sitting stiffly onstage. With their cheap clothes and clown smiles, they looked vulnerable and exposed. Underneath the couples the news flashed: "Thirty-one percent of women surveyed say they prefer money to sex."

Rita and Dennis walked onstage. Rita was heavy, with platinum-blond hair. Dennis limped and spoke English poorly. Rita showed the audience the $29.99 tag on her dress and said Dennis wouldn't let her cut that tag off because he wanted to return the dress after the show. The audience booed and Gordon gallantly offered to pay for Rita's dress. Rita's chin wobbled with emotion as she thanked him. Dennis looked scared and confused. He didn't seem to understand why he was being booed. He said that he gave Rita money whenever she asked—that is, if he had any money. More boos.

The audience crowded toward the mikes for their thirty-second spot on national television. The women in the audience looked like Rita, Tracy and Loretta. They had stingy husbands too. One woman advised Rita to leave Dennis. Dennis tried to explain that he'd been fired from his job at the railroad, that he wasn't really a cheapskate, just broke. But since that point didn't fit with the day's topic, Gordon cut him off.

In a subtle but effective way Gordon encouraged tension, conflict and drama. He said, "I'm really concerned about Rita. Should she leave Dennis?" Many in the audience shouted, "Yes, yes." Soon Rita had a tear running down her cheek and the cameras zoomed in. Without waiting to hear if Rita would leave Dennis, I turned to another channel.

I watched an adult diaper commercial with the slogan "When you're comfortable, everything feels right." Then Sally Jesse Raphael explored the topic of daughters who had never met their fathers. Angela was onstage with her mother, Maxine. They held hands as Angela explained that Maxine wouldn't talk about her ex-husband, Angela's father. Maxine, her voice quivering with emotion, said that it was because she was ashamed. However, with the coaxing of Sally, Maxine told Angela about her father in front of the television audience. She said she'd been physically and emotionally abused by him. As she spoke, her voice cracked with emotion and both mother and daughter wept.

Angela's father came onstage. He was a large, red-faced man who cried as he hugged his newfound daughter. Angela cried too and looked rather sheepishly at her mother, who stood nearby. Millions watched this family's most dramatic moment.

Sally held up the microphone. In a soft, coaxing voice she encouraged a fight. The father denied any abuse in the marriage and said he wouldn't have left if he'd known he had such a beautiful daughter. Maxine said that the reason he didn't know his daughter was that he'd skipped town and she couldn't find him.

I switched to another channel, where Maury Povitch interviewed people who had killed or had a family member killed by a drunk driver. Onstage sat six traumatized parents who had lost their children and a girl who sobbed as she told of maiming her boyfriend. She wailed, "He was an athlete in high school and now, because of me, he's in a wheelchair for life."

Povitch walked into the audience, put his arms around guests and glibly encouraged them to tell their stories. One woman's husband was in jail after killing their six-year-old daughter. She'd forgiven him. Another woman, whose son had been killed, hated drunk drivers. With Povitch's encouragement, she attacked the more forgiving woman. Meanwhile, the parents onstage looked shell-shocked, unsure where they were.

I was struck by how wrong these shows felt. Poor and needy people were manipulated into revealing personal information. People were selling their souls and their most private pain for a few minutes' celebrity. Their grief and tragedy were our momentary entertainment. People talked about their deepest traumas, their worst habits, their arguments and sex lives. For a refrigerator or a trip to Los Angeles, they were encouraged to betray their parents or lifetime companions.

I wondered what happens to these people after they leave. Do they show the videos? Do the men beat up their wives? Do they divorce or pretend the betrayals never happened? What is left for people after they have shared their most private secrets with a television audience?

The shows reminded me of the Russian show trials of the Stalin era. In those trials, people betrayed their families and friends in front of cameras. Their motives were different. The Russians did it to save their own lives while Americans do it for their fifteen seconds of celebrity. But I'm struck with the similarities. Both talk-show culture and Soviet society foster the betrayal of family. By these public exposures of family secrets both cultures teach that families are neither private nor sacred.

In an article entitled "The Loss of Moral Turf" in *Rebuilding the Nest*, Cofer and Jacobsen wrote of the daytime talk shows: "If for some reason a new federal law required television networks to do everything possible to cheapen the social value of the medium, to violate society's traditional understanding of childhood and to inflict gratuitous harm on the family as an institution, the networks could do no better than simply to beam these programs each day into millions of American homes."

A capitalistic country, just like a communist country, has reason to view families as the enemy. In a communist system where people are defined as units of production, families often interfere with production. Parents want their children to go to school and play, to rest and to attend family events. Most parents care much more about the happiness of their children than the production quotas of the government. The Soviet system worked best when there was no intermediary between the individual and the state.

In a capitalistic system where people are units of consumption, families often interfere with sales quotas. Parents intervene between their children and the marketplace. Parents don't want their children to drink alcohol, use tobacco or have sugar diets, even if the consumption of those products is good for the economy. Parents don't necessarily want to buy designer jeans or expensive toys. They have different values and different goals for their children than corporate society does.

Families are about love, relationships and time. Of course parents make mistakes. But even at their worst most parents are not trying to make money off their children. They are not interested in exploiting their children for personal gain.

In their concern for children, parents are both deeply conservative and deeply subversive. Families are a buffer between individuals and the state, and all totalitarian states attack families. In many such states young children are taken from their families for education. Often the values taught are contrary to what the parents believe and contrary to the interests of the children themselves.

In the former Soviet Union, children were trained to work as informers and to betray their own parents. They were to listen to their parents' talk and report it to authorities if it was seditious or even disgruntled. Children who "informed" on their parents were publicly revered. By this process children learned the supremacy of the collective over the family.

In America today people betray their families. As a member of Megadeth put it, "Parents are dickheads." All adult problems of whatever ilk are attributed to poor parenting. The message is that if people are having trouble or in pain, their parents must have failed. Both nations produce houses with no walls. Children turn to the broader culture for guidelines on how to live. In the former Soviet Union, children were encouraged to produce, while in America children are encouraged to consume. Both the Soviets and the talk shows demonize intellectuals, who are, by definition, people who might actually think about what is happening in the culture and argue articulately against certain activities.

In both cultures children grow into deeply cynical adults. Hedrick

Smith wrote that Russians believe in their friends and little else. Alcohol then becomes a way to kill the pain of helplessness. This description fits young adults in the United States as well. And like the Russians, this generation uses chemicals to deal with their lack of influence. Many have been drinking heavily since junior high. They use alcohol to deal with all their emotions—bitterness, anger, insecurity and despair.

Neither the communist state nor the money-driven corporate culture supports communities. Communities are for families. They teach proper behavior and good values. They give families a sense of history, of place, and they offer them a complex weave of people from whom to learn how to be more fully human. Communities provide children with good stories, with cautionary tales and moral fables. Communities give families a tiospaye.

Families need communities the way my corn plant needs soil. Since the beginning of time, humans have shared their lives with those around them. Families shared their fish from the sea, gathered reeds for thatched roofs and looked at the stars. We have watched out for each other. Now for the first time in human history many of us feel alone and unconnected to groups. The world has changed but we have not. We all want love, respect, good work and interesting pastimes. We want a safe, stimulating world for our children and friends and a planet that will survive. We humans are all more alike than we are different.

I want to end this chapter with a story of a family who has been judicious in its use of tools. They have made careful decisions about what they will and will not take from the broader culture and have connected their family to many good resources. The Millers are both lucky and thoughtful. They are almost too perfect. I suspect that the reader may feel a bit inadequate and envious, as I did when I visited them. But I learned from the Millers and I want to give readers that opportunity as well.

The Millers include Jim and Jane and their children—Karl, age fifteen; Matthew, age thirteen; Cora, age nine; Grace, age four; and Ruby, age thirteen months.

Early on a July morning I visited the Millers' acreage. The modern house had a big porch that overlooked the Blue River valley. Jim answered the door with Ruby in his arms. Ruby, dressed in a pink sunsuit and cowboy boots, reached out her arms for an embrace. Jane and Grace joined us in a comfortable living room filled with books. Jim was a soft-spoken man who taught at the university. Jane was small and round with soft brown eyes and a wry smile. She was a certified schoolteacher, although she hasn't taught outside the home since Karl was born.

I asked if all the children were home-schooled. Jane said, "Karl's the only one of the children who ever attended public school. He went to a progressive kindergarten, but we had a sense that we could do more creative things in less time. We felt Karl would have more time to learn and play at home."

Jane caught Ruby as she tumbled toward the edge of the couch. "We don't like the term 'home school.' It implies an artificial division between life and learning. Every day is an opportunity to learn and the world is full of interesting things. We'd rather talk about learning based on the needs and interests of our kids."

Grace walked over to the piano and played some Suzuki songs. Ruby scrambled over to watch her. I was struck by how well behaved and calm these kids were. I asked about Karl.

Jim said, "He loves books. He'd read twenty-four hours a day if we allowed him to. This summer one of our goals is to have him doing things besides reading."

"He's read everything in the house except Jim's textbooks," Jane said. "He loves Arthur Conan Doyle and has about five versions of his work. He likes C.S. Lewis and Ray Bradbury."

"Karl read early," Jim said. "Matthew was different. He didn't show any interest in reading until the last couple of years. Now he and Cora are reading the Bobbsey Twins and Hardy Boys mysteries. He reads everything he can about poultry and horses."

While Ruby pounded happily on the piano bench, Grace played her "Twinkles." Ruby "sang" along with the notes. Jane said, "We don't have to force our kids to fit into any system. They learn to read when they want to learn to read.

"We've taken school a year at a time. For a while we asked Karl every year if he wanted to go public. Finally we realized that none of us want to enter a big system again."

Jim suggested that Grace play a piece over and continued. "Next year Karl's taking some university classes and also a class on electrical wiring at the community college. It will be interesting to see what he thinks of those classes."

I asked how they structured things. "Some home-schoolers have regular classes, a curriculum and tests. Others are totally loose," Jane said. "We're somewhere in between. We have study time almost every day. We do more indoor stuff in winter and stay out of doors in the summer. We're more project-oriented than lesson-oriented. Our next project is to build a barn."

Jim added, "We try not to turn school on and off. Life is learning. But mornings are more organized and we loosen up as the day goes on. We require the kids to work on math, which is something none of them enjoy. We don't do grades or tests because they focus on mistakes. We want our kids to understand that learning is achieved by making mistakes."

Jane said, "So many parents have told me that they couldn't stand to be home with their kids every day. I hope their children don't hear them talk that way. Most kids in self-directed learning environments end up calm and easy to live around."

Ruby returned to her mom and began to breast-feed. The older three kids tromped in from outdoors and introduced themselves. They all had 4H cards to fill out and they spread across the floor, working on their cards.

Jane said, "The children are close to each other. Because they learn at home, they are not separated like most siblings are. Karl and Matthew really know Ruby and vice versa. Particularly Matthew and Cora spend lots of time together. They do their chores jointly. Lately, Karl has wanted more time to himself. He wanders out under a tree and disappears for hours. But he also reads to Ruby and Grace. We all work together on the horses and poultry."

As I listened to the parents talk in a leisurely way for over an hour, I felt myself becoming anxious about time. I kept glancing nervously at the kids to see if they were bored or restless. Would they leave before I could interview them? Would they feel left out? When I really looked at them, I realized they were fine. They were enjoying listening to their parents and me. They didn't have television-age attention spans nor had they been socialized to think their parents were stupid and ridiculous. They weren't addicted to being the center of attention.

Jim said, "We often get asked if the kids have enough social experiences. They have plenty of time with other kids—in 4H, on soccer teams, at their church. But they're not isolated with only their age mates.

Our kids spend time with people of all ages who share their interests. For example, Karl hangs out at the university. Cora is friends with an older neighbor who is teaching her to garden."

Karl said, "I get mad when I'm asked about social life. Going to public school doesn't mean that you'll have good friends. I know kids who were lonely in the public system."

Cora walked into the kitchen to make limeades. Ruby stopped nursing and padded into the kitchen to watch her sister.

"Most of my close friends are home schooled," Karl continued. "My best friend lives in a cabin in Colorado and we communicate mainly by modem. Every year we take a long bike trip together."

Karl looked both older and younger than most kids his age. His face reminded me of faces from my childhood, faces I'd forgotten could exist. I asked him how he fit in with kids from the neighborhood.

"They probably think I'm weird because I'm so interested in horses and poultry. My favorite musical group is Simon and Garfunkel. I prefer soccer to football. In Nebraska, that's not cool." He laughed. "I handle stuff differently than kids who go to the public schools. On my soccer team, some of the guys goof off when they come to practice. Then if they play poorly at games, they blame the other team. They'll do stuff like spit on their palms before they shake hands with the other team. I don't care about winning or losing, just learning to play. I don't hate the guys on the other team."

He looked at his dad. "Another way I'm different is that I love my family. One guy asked me if I'd been brainwashed. I think it's spooky that liking my family is considered crazy."

Matthew went to help Cora carry in our drinks. Grace came back from the piano and snuggled in beside her dad. Jane said, "Tell about when you watched MTV."

Karl shook his head. "I was on a trip to Mexico with some kids from church and we watched it in a hotel room. I thought it was boring and strange. I didn't like it."

Matthew handed me a drink. He was a calm, quiet boy with enormous eyes. He spoke shyly to me. "Last week my duck had six ducklings. The mother is a Black East Indies duck. In the sun her feathers are iridescent green."

Cora said, "Matthew's got a new quarter horse. He's been winning awards for his riding." Matthew discussed his horse as if she were the miracle of the universe.

When the subject was animals all the kids chimed in. Grace ran out and found two kittens to show me. She presented them proudly. Cora's horse was a hackney pony fourteen years old who, Cora said, "mainly sleeps and eats anymore." Karl had a lazy Appaloosa. They all worked with the chickens and ducks. In fact, they had an incubator and a variety of breeds. Matthew said, "We get all colors of eggs: pink, green, even blue."

Grace gently placed the black kitten on my lap. I patted the kitten and asked if I could see the poultry later. Jane said, "We try to spend a lot of time at home. We don't like to hurry. We like long days out here when we can work and play at our own pace. We let each child play one musical instrument and one sport. All the kids but Karl play piano. He plays trumpet. They all like soccer."

Jim nodded. "If an activity interferes with our schedule, we don't do it. We don't like too much commotion. Our other rule is that if we can't do an activity as a family we're unlikely to do it. We all go to the games and recitals. We all clean the chicken house and go to the fair."

Jane said, "I don't own a watch. The kids do and they keep me on schedule on the days we go into town." She helped Matthew with a card and then continued. "There's a limit to how many people our family can see and still keep its integrity. We're close friends with another home-school family that has seven kids who roughly match our kids in age. The children do theater and Spanish together. Our two families put out a monthly newsletter on the computer."

Karl complimented Cora on the limeade and turned to me. "We can take long trips whenever we feel like it. Last fall we went to our grandparents' farm in Wisconsin for a month."

Cora said, "This fall we're going to go to our other grandfather's house in Pennsylvania and learn woodworking. He has a shop in his garage and promised to teach us how to use power tools."

Matthew said, "Next summer he's coming here to help us build the barn."

Jim said, "I like teaching because I can take the time off to do things like build a barn with the kids. Most dads aren't that lucky. Recently I had a job offer to work in New York City, but I turned it down. It was an exciting job, but it wouldn't have worked for our family."

I asked about television. Jane answered, "We didn't have a television for years. But we wanted to watch the Olympics. We couldn't find one to rent so we bought one." She laughed. "We keep it in the closet, except for special occasions."

Karl said, "Right now it's out because we're watching World Cup soccer."

Cora chimed in, "And we watched *Sarah Plain and Tall.*"

Jim said, "We saw *The Way West* and took an ETV course in sign language."

I asked when the family had last seen a movie. Jane said, "Jim and I haven't been to a movie in years. We're too busy."

"Movies can be a problem," Jim said. "The kids aren't desensitized like most American kids. Cora and Grace get upset when animals suffer in Disney movies. Even 'safe' movies cause nightmares."

Grace nodded. "I didn't like *Homeward Bound,* did I, Mom?"

Jane ruffled her hair and agreed.

I asked about magazines. The family didn't get a daily paper, but they listened to the weather and news on public radio. They subscribed to some magazines about poultry, *National Geographic, The New Yorker* and *The Atlantic Monthly.*

Cora moved over to the piano and began to play her lessons. Matthew sat beside her on the bench and waited for a turn. Cora played a Bach minuet. I asked about religion. Jim said, "I wouldn't say we're religious in a traditional way. But we do believe that our family needs a spiritual center. We believe that we are here to glorify God and to use the abilities He's given us in a productive way. We believe in helping other people."

Jane said, "We don't use a Bible-based curriculum but our focus is becoming the person who God wants you to be. We are grateful that our school gives us a chance to teach good values."

It was Matthew's turn to play piano. He played a soothing sonata. I asked about discipline. Jim seemed puzzled by the question, and indeed, discipline didn't look like an issue in this family. But living as I did in a different world, I thought, How could it not be?

"We teach self-discipline," Jim said. "You can do your math now or before bed, whichever you prefer. We try to help the kids set priorities and schedule their time wisely. Caring for animals is a good way to learn to work. If you don't do your job, something bad happens."

Jane looked around the room. "We have a nice life, with the horses and farm. We teach that we have this life because we made good choices for a long time. We want the kids to think in terms of long-term goals."

Jim added, "Right now Karl wants a driver's license and we've told him fine, as soon as he gets money to pay for his insurance. He's already taken a driver's education class and passed the test."

"Our main rule is you help whoever is working," Jane said. "We do most of our work together and that makes it easier."

We'd been talking for over two hours. In that time, no child had cried, begged for attention or interrupted. Ruby had toddled between family members, sitting on whatever lap was handy. The three middle kids had played some piano. They'd all filled out their 4H cards and joined in the conversation. Grace had showed me the kittens and Karl had dug out some issues of their newsletter, *Family Times*. Except for me, nobody had looked at a watch.

We went outside to see the poultry. It was noon, but the roosters were still crowing. There was an amazing variety of fowl—ducks, bantam hens and white-bearded silkies. The children crowded around me, eager to show me their birds. Even Grace could pick up a big rooster and spread out a wing for proper viewing.

Matthew proudly carried over a baby duck. I held the wiggly creature carefully so that he wouldn't jump out of my hands. Matthew said, "These ducks could swim within hours after their birth. They hatched naturally and were able to stay with their mothers. They get oil from rubbing against her body, so they can float. Ducks hatched in incubators have no oil on their feathers and sink if they try to swim."

I write about this family in some detail because I think in many ways they combine the best of the 1930s and the 1990s. They have made careful decisions about what aspects of the larger culture they will accept and reject. They use many modern tools, but they use them judiciously. They have the best of the 1990s—modern medicine, word processors, public radio and good transportation. But the children are protected from the world of consumerism and the mass media. They aren't avalanched with material that is overwhelming and inappropriate for children.

They have plenty of what they need and not too much of what they don't need. The Millers have a great deal of contact with the natural world and animals. The parents are tolerant and low-key and they allow their children to be individuals. But they also have high expectations and a clear code of values. The children have good manners and they know how to work.

The family is fortunate. They live in a serene country setting in a safe, beautiful house. The parents are smart, well educated, healthy and well adjusted. They have ample financial resources. In addition the parents have devoted a great deal of time and energy to raising their kids in the best possible way. What happened with the Millers can be done, but requires exceptional resources. Most of us can't do it. But we can learn from them.

This interview reminded me of *Brigadoon*, a trip back in time. Calm, happy children and relaxed, confident parents are so rare today. Probably most notable were the long attention spans of the children and their willingness to sit and listen to grown-ups talk. The family had a manageable amount of information to deal with. They weren't stressed by more information than they could assimilate. The kids weren't overstimulated and edgy. Nor were they sexualized in the way most kids now are. The parents weren't overwhelmed or in a hurry.

These parents would have done quite well under any circumstances, but I think home school played an important role in this family's adjustment. The challenges the kids faced—showing chickens, caring for horses, making limeades and playing piano—were challenges they could meet. These kids hadn't been age-segregated and hadn't been pressured by their peers into a variety of self-destructive behaviors and attitudes. They had been allowed to develop slowly at their own pace, following their interests and abilities. They had spent time with people who shared common interests—not a common age. They hadn't learned from peers to avoid younger children and adults.

They weren't big consumers. They'd learned to be responsible for themselves and had some ability to delay gratification and think of long-term goals. The family has strong beliefs about the purpose of life that combine elements from the 1930s and the 1990s. Their life is about doing one's duty and helping others, a 1930s value, as well as growing and becoming all you can be, a more 1990s value. I am sure this family, like all families, has its bad days. I'm sure the parents have arguments and that the kids sometimes sulk. But I am also sure that this family has a focus and belief system that help it through our troubled times.

Chapter Six

THERAPY, THE TROJAN HORSE

HISTORY

Sigmund Freud, the inventor of talk therapy, had good ideas about defenses, dreams and somatic symptoms. He defined the role of a therapist in ways that are useful today: "Where there was id, there shall ego be." He recognized the power of two people alone in a room, one of them paying close attention to what the other had to say. But when Freud looked at the human psyche, he saw thorns, not roses, and he led us down a thorny path. His theory is deterministic and pathology-oriented. Biology was destiny. Freud looked beneath the surface and found sex and aggression. He made some interesting assumptions—that sex is our most powerful drive, that most of personality is formed by age five and that families are competitive, lusting and devouring. He reframed all good behavior, including art, love and work, as mechanisms for coping with evil impulses. In this quest for sexual and aggressive motives, he did the world no favors.

Freud didn't ask how culture affected the mental health of its members. He believed that pathology came from trauma within the family. In explaining human behavior, he ignored history, culture, economics and politics. For example, hysteria, a common problem among Victorian women, was attributed to childhood fantasies rather than to role expectations for women in Victorian culture. In "The Yellow Wallpaper," Charlotte Perkins Gilman writes of an intelligent, adventurous young woman who goes mad from lack of intellectual stimulation and opportunities to do real work. Her story explains more about women and hysteria in the Victorian era than does Freud's theory. But Freud influenced everyone—historians, philosophers, artists, politicians and even ministers. Humans in the Western world define themselves with concepts that Freud invented.

Following Freud's lead, many disciplines looked for mental pathology. Psychiatry, psychoanalysis and psychology became the study of human pathology. Therapists were trained to look for mental illness and dysfunctional patterns across generations. Families were invaded, analyzed and second-guessed. Most families withered under the microscopes. At one point family therapist Jay Haley asked his colleagues to identify a healthy family for research purposes. His colleagues, who were experts at finding pathology, couldn't find one. Haley concluded that we were so vigilant and skilled in our search for pathology that no family could look healthy for long.

Freud emphasized thinking and feeling. In fact, he was more interested in fantasies than reality and had almost no interest in what people actually did. That area was left to behaviorists, who invented a mechanistic "science" of human behavior. In their efforts to be scientific, the first behaviorists reduced the rich stew of life to a thin broth. Human action was described as stimulus/response chains. Behavior was seen as determined by outside forces, and will was accounted for by conditioning. Early behaviorists ignored everything important about humans—their inventiveness, curiosity, motivation and ability to love. They set aside all the truly interesting questions as too complicated to study. The meaning of life couldn't be examined in laboratories.

By the middle of this century, academic psychology was increasingly removed from clinical practice. Research studies, often of little relevance to clinicians, were written up in the dead language of the social sciences. Psychiatry was hopelessly ensnarled in outrageous treatments—lobotomies, electroshock and mind-numbing medications. Psychoanalysis had a language increasingly inaccessible to ordinary people. Psychoanalytic writing was for a well-educated elite. It was disconnected from the hurly-burly of real life. By the 1960s, the debates of analysts were like the medieval debates of bishops in Rome. While people dropped dead from the plague in their courtyards, the bishops argued about how many angels could dance on the head of a pin.

Meanwhile, social and demographic changes increased the need for therapists. As communities fell apart and organized religion lost its hold, the influence of therapy grew. People left their small towns and moved to cities and suburbs. They stopped working for their families and worked instead for big businesses. Young families formed far from their traditional family resources. As people became more isolated and stressed, they needed advice and comfort. The world changed so rapidly that old ideas about how to proceed did not work. People looked to therapists for guidance. Many people who believed that God was dead developed an inordinate respect for Freud.

In the late 1950s and 1960s, humanistic therapy blossomed. The humanists worked primarily with educated adults who lived in the era of Eisenhower politics and postwar prosperity. As children, many of these adults had experienced too much parental and community control. They tended to be perfectionistic, guilty and prone to self-criticism. Often their creativity and initiative were sapped by overconforming. After working with these depressed adults, therapists concluded that many parents stifled and hurt their children.

Carl Rogers said that people needed "unconditional positive regard" and wrote about the trauma to children who didn't receive that kind of love. Adults, especially educated adults, felt they had been traumatized by their conditional parents and were afraid that they would damage their children with conditional love. They tried to be more accepting and tolerant than their parents had been. But real parents can't give children unconditional love. First, they are human and don't always feel loving. Second, parents are responsible for socialization, which involves a certain amount of squelching.

I recall a case from the 1970s of parents who valiantly tried to deliver unconditional love to their four children. Their children lived in a totally accepting environment where they were not toilet-trained or weaned until they asked to be. The four-year-old was still wetting his pants and nursing. All the children screamed "I hate you" when they were frustrated, and the parents said they were glad the kids expressed their true feelings. Those children could have benefited from more conditional love.

The world has changed enormously and yet our theories haven't been upgraded to the new reality. I think of parents who are hopelessly confused by advice that might have worked well in the 1950s but is worse than useless today. One mother whose three-year-old was biting and screaming at day care said, "I don't want to impose my standards on him." A father said of his fifteen-year-old who was using cocaine, "That's her life, her decision. No one can really influence another person."

Therapists have many ways to approach human problems. There are family therapists, existentialists, feminist therapists and solution-focused therapists. There are also New Age therapies, such as past-lives or age-regression therapy, often with relatively unschooled practitioners. Some of these therapists are little more than charlatans who give our field a bad name.

Some therapists are loyal to a particular theory, while others integrate several theories in their own way. Over the years, therapists have developed many helpful ways to approach human problems—cognitive-behavioral therapy, skill-building and problem-solving therapies, relaxation and anxiety management training and therapy that helps people recover from trauma. There are many well-educated and socially conscious therapists who are working to protect rather than pathologize families.

Still therapy is dogged with long-term paradoxes. We work best with those clients who need the least help. YAVIS—young, attractive, verbal, intelligent and sophisticated—clients are our best customers. Oftentimes our clients are the family members who are sensitive, open and eager to learn, while other family members do not want therapy. Many disturbed clients won't come in voluntarily, and when they are forced in, they are not all that amenable to our advice. And sadly, we do not know what to do with psychopaths, who have no consciences and who inflict the most harm on others.

In addition to academically based therapies, we have a popular psychology industry that is easy to criticize. Much of popular psychology doesn't even come from psychology, but rather from business, public relations, chemical dependency and the personnel management field. It also comes from talk-show philosophers and various gurus who fly by the seat of their charisma. Popular psychology often borrows a few ideas from well-developed theories and turns these ideas into simple buzzwords and glib proscriptions. Whatever integrity and usefulness the original theory had is lost in the translation.

At its best popular psychology teaches communication skills, stress management and impulse control, but it has been oversold. Its hackneyed, imprecise language is part of all of our vocabularies. By now most Americans explain their situations in the language of pop psychology—"I'm from a dysfunctional family" or "My inner child is hurting."

Popular psychology uses generic language that reduces people to slogans and categories. A client says, "My wife is codependent" instead of saying, "Every time I play poker, my wife calls to say that our Chihuahua is throwing up. I have to go home and clean the carpets and take care of Pixie. Pixie's the Chihuahua, my wife is Franzetta." Or a client says, "I'm a woman who loves too much" instead of saying, "The last two guys I picked up at bars were losers. One gambled away his paychecks at keno. The other was a bullshitter who drank from his pocket flask on his way to AA."

Sometimes therapy derived from popular psychology encourages self-doubt, self-pity and self-absorption. It can give people labels rather than direction, and excuses rather than motivation. Sometimes therapy is a Band-Aid that gives people just enough support to stay in miserable situations. At worst, therapy can be an elaborate stall technique. Clients can tell upset family members that they are in therapy and working on problems, when in fact they are only in therapy. They can tell teachers that their unruly children are in therapy and the teachers will back off. Judges will give criminals in therapy a break. Sometimes alcoholics can keep drinking as long as they are in analysis.

I don't want to demonize our field or suggest that we do not do good work. Therapy by well-educated professionals has saved the lives of thousands of people, helped broken people mend and allowed stuck families to solve problems and move on. In general, therapists have worked for tolerance, understanding and decency within our culture. We have advocated for tolerance of diversity and the protection of the weak and disenfranchised. Furthermore, I am a mainstream therapist who has made many of the mistakes that I document. The mistakes were made with good intentions, while respecting the professional theories of the times. My mistakes were the same as those of many of my colleagues. I was slow to notice the changing world and slow to understand the implications of these changes for my work with clients.

When I remember some of my mistakes, I wince. I believe, as Pogo said, that "we have met the enemy and it is us." Our tendency to focus on problems is a question of training, tradition and certain paradigms.

It's a question of time and place. Our professional training fosters a certain worldview and attitude toward families. We look for flaws, sickness and an enemy within. Few therapists are fiendish plotters. In fact, most of us come into this field with a genuine desire to help others, but we all think and act in ways we've been trained. At one time, Freud and other theorists might have been immensely useful, but now their work is outmoded by the changes in our times.

The next section will discuss the major mistakes that therapists have made. But I must add a caveat here. I have spent my adult life being a therapist. I love the work. I have tremendous respect for many therapists and for the process of therapy. At best, therapy can save lives and rebuild families. It helps people "grow their souls." I criticize my field because I care about it. Our field is in a great crisis, brought on by economic pressures and our rapidly changing world. Therapy is beset by internal and external problems and in danger of becoming both outmoded and corporatized. If we do not examine our work and make changes, we will not survive.

TEN MISTAKES THAT THERAPISTS MAKE

1. Family Is the Cause of All Problems.

Einstein said that our theories determine what we observe. Given our theoretical base, it's no wonder we see pathology everywhere we look. When children are troubled we ask, What have these parents done wrong? Our professional language traps us into blaming families. Our words for distance tend to be positive—autonomy and independence. Our words for closeness tend to be negative—enmeshed, overprotective and dependent. Parental efforts to teach prudence and restraint can be labeled controlling or codependent.

At its worst, therapy undercuts families with the creation of phrases such as "emotional incest" and "covert incest." This "incest" involves no touching but implies intrusive or controlling parental love. I suspect that the only parents who have never been intrusive or controlling are probably neglectful. These phrasemakers have succeeded in framing love as pathological. But I would relabel most parental efforts as LOVE. Almost all parents want their children to be happy, well-behaved, productive citizens.

We have overemphasized early development and given families of origin too much responsibility for the lives of their members. We have overlooked how much people can learn as adults—especially from their love and work. Personalities can be changed by adult experiences. Many of us have had an experience of a friend stepping in when we needed help, a mentor teaching us what we most needed to learn or a family member carrying us love that enabled us to go on in tough times. These adult experiences are largely unexplored by our field.

Many therapists look for the source of clients' unhappiness in dysfunctional families of origin. The goal of therapy may be to identify family patterns that have caused problems in adult life and sometimes this identification is valuable. But this approach can unwittingly erode our clients' faith in their families. Some therapists even suggest that to feel better, clients must uncover past traumas inflicted by their families. Adults are encouraged to explain failures by blaming their parents. This can happen in subtle ways, such as by working on genograms where family weaknesses are thoroughly documented but family strengths are ignored. Or it can be direct, such as when therapists encourage clients to "detach" from families in order to heal.

Occasionally this family bashing can be carried to ridiculous lengths. I know a woman who went to a therapist to cope with the stress of a cancer diagnosis. Much to her surprise the therapist suggested that perhaps she had been molested as a child. This therapist said that maybe repressed memories were causing the cancer and recommended hypnosis to see if she could uncover memories of abuse.

Recently I met Lara, a young woman who had seen two other therapists. I asked her what she had learned from her extensive therapy. She said that she had done inner-child work and was learning to love herself. She no longer allowed her mother to "manipulate" her into coming home for Thanksgiving or other family events. Later, she told me she hated her job, drank too much and had no friends. These problems had not abated when she stopped going home for holidays.

Some therapists blame parents for adolescent turmoil. Of course, their adolescent clients have quickly supported this blaming. In fact, many teens suffer more from culturally created problems than from poor parenting. We have underemphasized the lessons that children learn from the media and peers. When children are delinquent or sexualized, we generally look within the home for cause. Sometimes that's the right place to look, but it's not the only place. Movies, TV, ads and music can sexualize children. Peers can also hurt children's confidence and mental health. Many children who feel loved at home face peers who denigrate and belittle them. They come to therapy devastated by the hurtful remarks they have heard in the halls of their schools or on the streets.

We often hear only one story about the family, and that may be the story told by the most dissatisfied family member. Listening to only this person's story distorts our view. Therapists are human and may take sides in a conflict without hearing all points of view. It's harder to sympathize with, and easier to judge, those family members not in the room. By sympathizing with the person in the room, a therapist may weaken the family. The therapist may say things like "You come from a dysfunctional family" or "Your parents sound manipulative." Others are given no chance to explain. Our attempts to support our clients may cement their outrage or feed into their sense of victimization.

Therapy can validate angry or dissatisfied feelings and that isn't always in the client's best interest. If the clients had talked to a family member, their negative thinking might have been challenged. For example, one time my son complained to his aunt about a grounding he received from us. She said, "Your parents were right to punish you. I would have been even tougher. Lighten up on them." That helped our family out. Americans suffer from the myth of parental omnipotence. But by the time kids are adolescents, their parents are not that powerful. Individuals from healthy families have the power to self-destruct, and individuals from harmful families have the power to succeed. People in pain often blame their families, but in reality life makes most people unhappy. Meaningless jobs, isolation, addictions, poor health, failed relationships, crime and poverty bring great sorrow.

Families have the tough job of socializing. In a world where many people rarely get constructive feedback, most families give feedback. They teach responsibility and skills. Families work because they are about much more than being likable. My son once said to me, "You're the only person who gets mad at me." I thought, Of course, I know you don't always wear your seat belt. I know you don't eat vegetables and fresh fruit. And I'm the one who cares when you are watching TV instead of studying. I love you too much to be indifferent about your behavior.

With institutions decaying, workplace ethics eroding and the sense of community fading, families are what remains between people and chaos. Parents tend to be more caring than the world outside. I think of all those mothers in ghettos trying to keep their boys off drugs and alive. I think of the parents of a local girl who was raped. She was ostracized by her peers for reporting the football-player hero involved. Only her parents stood by her.

I remember a farmer and his wife. Their daughter had seen our town's most noxious therapist and had cut her parents out of her life. The farmer, felt hat in his lap, explained that they had the daughter over for Sunday dinner the previous July. The wife had fixed fried chicken and had baked a chocolate layer cake. The parents were nervous, but felt the dinner went well and they loved seeing their grandchildren. When the daughter's family left, the farmer picked them a bushel of sweet corn to take home. Later he heard that the daughter felt ill treated at this dinner. He said to me in amazement, "Why, I picked her the best sweet corn we had." This family had been irreparably damaged by a therapist who, it is safe to say, would never bake a chocolate layer cake for the grandchildren.

Families are really what stands between individuals and impersonal corporate and governmental structures. If we take away people's belief in their families, what do we replace it with? If we have a culture of people who mistrust their own families, who can they possibly trust?

It's a common American belief that to be free of one's family is to be mentally healthy. Many tribes from all over the world believe that to be without family is to be without identity, to be dead. They are not far from wrong. An absolutely free self is an empty self. Families with all their inadequacies generally care for their members. In a communist country, without a family, a person has nothing between him/her and the state. In America, without a family, a person has nothing between him/her and the corporate consumer culture.

2. Therapy Has Been Hard on Women.

Freud worked in an era when women were without incomes, jobs, education or votes. All the early therapists were men. Men conceptualized our field, and their theories were androcentric. A good example of that is Freud's concept of penis envy, which has since been analyzed as power envy. In fact, if women had ruled in the 1800s, we might have an elaborate theory of pregnancy envy, as Karen Horney postulated later, or even of menstruation envy.

Therapists have a long history of scapegoating women. Characteristics associated with men, such as independence and dominance, have been labeled as healthy, while characteristics associated with women, such as connectedness and sharing of power, have been labeled weak and neurotic.

If children were in trouble the mother was held responsible. She was either too close and suffocating or too distant and emasculating. Mothers of schizophrenic children were labeled "schizophrenogenic" and blamed for the situation. Therapists believed that mothers induced autism with their coldness, and they labeled the mothers of autistic kids as "refrigerator mothers." Our field inflicted enormous damage on women who had the misfortune to have an autistic child or one with Tourette's syndrome or obsessive-compulsive disorder.

In formulations of childhood pathology, both the culture and genetics were ignored and instead, women were blamed. Women were accused of double-binding their families. That is, they sent their children mixed messages that supposedly made the children crazy. Little attention was paid to the double binds mothers were in when they had difficult children or to the fact that we all send mixed messages sometimes. And there were no equivalent labels for fathers, siblings or extended family.

Women were held responsible for the well-being of everyone in the family. If the husband was an alcoholic, the wife had enabled his drinking. Women were accused of provoking violence and being manipulative and masochistic. Until recently, when feminist psychologists have worked to enlighten us, our field has failed to relate women's depression to their position in our culture or to such factors as poverty, single-parent homes or high rates of abuse and sexual assault.

What effect did this have on women? For the most part they accepted the responsibility and blame for family problems. Women internalized their therapists' ideas. They read, took their children to therapy and tried to change. They felt guilty and dealt with things as best they could. They trusted therapists even as the therapists diagnosed them. Most women will do anything, including becoming mental patients, to help their families.

3. Therapy Has Pathologized Ordinary Human Experience and Taught That Suffering Needs to Be Analyzed.

The intense emotions we all feel—anxiety, anger and despair—all have been labeled pathological and "treated" by therapists. The system in which we work traps us into doing this. In order to be doctors, we must have sick people to help. Some psychiatrists have called sadness endogenous depression and have medicated people who are grieving. Some therapists have labeled people who love their work "workaholics" and implied they have a serious disease. We have labeled ordinary anxiety as neurotic when in fact anxiety accompanies life. Especially in this decade, a person doesn't have to be neurotic to discover the world is a frightening place.

A client recently said to me, "I must be screwed up to be in this much pain." I said to her, "On the contrary, being in pain is part of being human." She looked surprised at what was surely not a brilliant observation, except in the context of psychotherapy.

This pathologizing of ordinary behavior makes it impossible for families to survive a therapist's scrutiny. Sometimes couples in therapy are told that their problems stem from the way their parents handled conflict in their marriages. Overt fighting is harmful, while covert fighting is passive/aggressive. Either the parents handled conflict out of the sight of their children so that the children had no models for handling conflict, or the parents fought in front of their children and traumatized them. Most parents were either too present or too absent, too distant or too intrusive, too controlling or too relaxed. Parents either didn't express feelings or expressed too many feelings. It's lose/lose for parents, and all children can feel victimized. The game was rigged so that there were no right answers.

Therapists call those adults who coped well with difficult situations in their childhoods "parental children." I've known many "parental children"; a great English teacher whose father was an inveterate gambler, a good-humored accountant who in spite of her psychotic mother is a fine parent. To label these people "parental children" is to miss the point. The term "parental child" pathologizes adaptive behavior and suggests that strength and resiliency are a mental health problem. Many strong, interesting adults had difficult childhoods. From having to cope with adversity, they learned extraordinary coping skills. They became complex, responsible and interesting people. When we describe their personalities as flawed, we wrest defeat from the jaws of victory.

It helps therapists to remember that our theories come from a stilted clinical perspective. When people come to see us, they are at their most intense. When I see my clients in the real world, I realize how distorted our office view can be. For example, one couple discussed divorce in my office and they seemed so rancorous and unhappy that I found myself supporting their decision. Later that day I saw them riding bikes with their children. They were enjoying each other and the children. I wondered again about divorce. Obviously there was something happening in this marriage that I had missed in the office.

Therapy's worst offense is to reframe love as something negative, such as codependency, controlling behavior, emotional incest or even an "addiction to people." We have confused people about the healthiness of loving their own families. For example, a woman friend has a husband with a heart disorder. She's asked him to eat properly. Over lunch she said to me, "I'm not sure I have a right to ask him to see a doctor. Am I being controlling or codependent?" The parents of a gifted eighth grader reported sadly that Sonja was failing all her classes. The father asked me, "Is it wrong for us to care about our daughter's school performance?" When love is labeled in negative ways, we hurt people who are trying to help each other. We punish the people in the family who "give a damn."

Of course, some behavior can be judged as overinvolved and overprotective. Some people get their sense of self entirely from caring for others. Therapists can help people sort out when they are doing too much for others. We can teach people who need to learn how to take better care of themselves. But unfortunately, we haven't always encouraged those who do too little for others to do more. We have even left people unsure if doing for others is a sign of pathology.

I recently saw a book written for "adults hurt as children." This title sends the odd message that there are adults who were not hurt as children. In fact, all humans are fallible and all parents err. When we suggest that suffering can be avoided, we foster unreasonable expectations. We are sending the same message that advertisers send. Advertisers imply that suffering is unnatural, shouldn't be tolerated and can be avoided with the right products. Psychologists sometimes imply that stress-free living is possible if only we have the right tools. But in fact, all our stories have sad endings. We all die in the last act.

A woman carrying her dead child approached the Buddha and begged him to bring her child back to life. Buddha said, "Go to each house in the village and bring me a mustard seed from the one who has not known suffering. Then I will bring your child back to life." The woman carried her baby from house to house. She knocked on every door and asked the family if they had been spared suffering. Of course the woman couldn't find a house like the one Buddha described. Instead at each home she heard a sad story. She couldn't bring Buddha a mustard seed, but she did learn that life is suffering. This helped her accept her own fate as part of the human condition.

The human condition is about struggle and loss as well as beauty and joy. To call sadness depression is to trivialize it. As the Buddha story suggests, suffering is everywhere. At its worst, therapy has adults doing what I have heard described as "the great white whine." It disempowers people and gives them illnesses rather than direction, excuses rather than motivation.

4. We Have Focused on Weakness Rather Than Resilience.

T. H. White wrote: "The best thing for being sad is to learn something." Sadness that is inevitable need not be considered scarring. But for the most part, therapists have been more interested in damage than recovery. We have missed the stories about people who did surprisingly well under terrible circumstances. Why do certain people flourish in Hell's Kitchens? How do families survive and help others in dangerous ghettos? How does a person heal after a partner is killed? How does a criminal become a loving parent?

The focus on weakness is widespread in our culture. Victims and victimizers attract attention. Their stories are the ones we hear. We study those who fail—the Dahmers, Starkweathers and other "natural born killers." The heroes with daily courage tend to receive less attention than violent villains. Therapists follow in both a cultural and a professional tradition when we focus on pathology. There are exceptions, writers who have explored survival. Viktor Frankl's writing about the Holocaust is a fine example. Michael White and David Epston write today about solution-focused therapy. But therapists have generated much more writing on mental illness and victimization than on mental health and strength.

We have overestimated the benefits of stress-free lives and oversold the positive effects of smooth, nonchallenging childhoods. Too much pampering leaves children without incentive to grow. Painful experiences, if dealt with properly, can sometimes be good lessons. It's not the stress people experience, it's what they do with stress that matters. Some people give up, others work harder.

The optimal range of stress gives people sufficient challenges so that they are energized to grow and develop, but not so much stress that they cannot succeed. Constant defeat leads to bitterness, despair and apathy, but some defeat can lead to growth in motivation, compassion and understanding. Yearning can be a great motivator. Good copers experience their world as tough but manageable. With effort, they can be successful and this success brings self-regard.

The strongest, most resilient kids emerge from painful experiences with depth, energy and problem-solving abilities. I know a woman whose mother was schizophrenic and whose brother was a murderer. She sang in her crib and became a famous singer. As she put it, "I couldn't not sing." This woman is strong like tempered steel. Easy environments can produce hothouse flowers. As one friend of mine put it about a rather spoiled boy, "Sometimes a child's most basic need is not to have his needs met."

Lois Murphy, who studied resilience, found that one third of all kids don't regress with stress but put forth even greater efforts to solve problems. She found that the difference between normal and disturbed kids wasn't in a lack of problems, but rather in the ways problems were handled. Murphy felt that children too carefully raised were bland by adolescence. She concluded that while it was probably good to have basic necessities, it was important for kids to have some kind of "hunger." An object or goal just out of reach stimulated kids to maximal effort. She recommended that parents help kids find moderate challenges and suggested an optimal balance between gratification and frustration. Murphy quoted a mother of a strong child who said to her son, "This is a hard life and you'd better get used to it." The mother of a handicapped child told her son, "Everyone has a handicap. Yours just shows."

I think of the California condor, whose babies must peck their way out of tough, thick shells. Many chicks cannot do it and die in the process. One time some scientists tried to help the birds by opening the shells slightly. The birds easily pecked out of the shell, but they died anyway. They didn't develop the muscles they needed to survive. Those muscles came from the tough job of pecking out of the shell. Children are like that. Struggle toughens them for the future. The trick is to decide which stresses strengthen children and which weaken them. The important question is what does this child need to grow and develop? Some need more help, some need less.

5. Some of Our Treatments Have Created New Problems.

Iatrogenic illnesses are those illnesses caused by treatment. Often iatrogenic illnesses come from "not seeing the forest for the trees," or from not considering the effects of interventions on clients' lives. In the movie *My Dinner with Andre*, Andre tells of visiting his mother in the hospital. She's almost dead from starvation, pain and chronic health problems. But a surgeon has just operated on her arm and he tells Andre how great this arm looks. Andre realizes that when the surgeon looks at his mother he doesn't notice she is dying. He sees an arm.

I read a letter from a mother who called herself a TAP, a toss-away parent. She wrote that her daughter cast her out of her life after visiting a mental health center. She called what happened "family cleansing" and told a woeful story of her daughter being age-regressed, hypnotized and advised to get out of the family. This daughter had refused to speak to her family for several years. The woman was sad and bitter. I cannot help but think that both she and her daughter are now suffering from iatrogenic illnesses.

When I worked on a psychiatric ward, one of my first patients was a woman who was addicted to injections for pain medications. When the nurses wouldn't give her drugs, she would plead for shots of sugar water. She had been given so many shots over the years that she had learned to take comfort from injections. This addiction was an iatrogenic illness.

For the most part, we therapists are well-meaning people with honorable intentions. But we work with theories developed for a different world. Experts with good intentions can do harm. We need to be as scrupulous about the effects as about the intentions of our behavior. We do well to remember the Law of 26, which postulates that for every action one takes or fails to take, there will be a minimum of twenty-six repercussions. Furthermore, these twenty-six repercussions can be the opposite of the effects one hoped to cause. We need to be humble about our potential to do harm as well as to do good.

Generally, removing labels isn't the same thing as removing problems. But as Thomas Szasz discussed in *The Politics of Psychotherapy*, labels often create pathology. People are reduced to the sum of their symptoms. Labels can take away autonomy and responsibility and give clients the sense that they are not accountable. "Don't blame me for my Discover card bill. I'm manic-depressive." "I beat my wife because I am a victim of post–traumatic stress disorder." They can lead to self-fulfilling prophecies and undermine belief in the possibility of change.

People think labels are explanations. A client might say, "I lay in bed all day because I'm dysthymic." Or "I keep losing jobs because I'm a borderline." In fact, labels do not explain anything. They describe and they don't even do that very well. As Michael White points out, this labeling "steals the uniqueness from a person." No one is as simple as a label implies. A good share of the time experts do not agree about the proper diagnosis.

Unfortunately, the labeling process often takes the place of solving the problem. And labels can make people feel worse about themselves. Unfortunately for clients in therapy, to be covered by insurance they need to be labeled. Often these labels go into computers, where confidentiality may be a problem. So financial considerations foster simplifying, pathologizing and the dissemination of labels.

6. We Have Encouraged Narcissism and Checked Basic Morality at the Doors of Our Offices.

Therapy's non-blaming language has its uses, but it has also produced a sort of moral mush. Yet talking about morality is strong stuff for those of us trained in the 1970s. Speaking in terms of duty was called "musturbation," and the worst word in the English language was "should." Historically our field has shied away from moral judgments. Words like "duty," "responsibility" and "commitment" make us uneasy. Not only that but we have trained clients to expect that therapists will be people who agree with them and care only about how they feel. When we try to define ourselves differently, we crash into this old expectation.

We are trained to focus on the client and ignore the people in the client's life. This can contribute to an "I am the center of the universe" mentality. At its most superficial level, therapy teaches that feeling good is being good, and that duty and obligation are onerous chains, better off broken. Perls said, "To say I feel obligated is to say I resent." But duty is not necessarily a bad thing. Duty is social cement that enables a culture to survive. Without standards of conduct we are all simply pursuing our own hedonistic agenda.

Therapy can be a kind of lay confession. "I'll tell you my screwups if you'll absolve me of guilt and let me keep on doing what I want." Therapy can be used to silence others. A person under pressure from his family may respond, "My therapist said I'm doing the best I can." Or "I need to quit my job." Or "I don't have the energy to parent." Or "My affair is a statement about my marriage." Therapy can be used as an excuse for immoral or unethical behavior. A person might say, "My therapist told me I need out of this marriage." Or "My therapist says I can't stand the stress of visiting Mom in the old folks' home."

While it can be valuable for a person to have a calm, quiet place to talk honestly about problems, too much "massage therapy" can be harmful. At worst it can teach clients to "take care of themselves," without exploring the effects on those not in the room. Therapy can suggest glib answers to moral algebra problems. When is self-care selfish? What are one's duties to others? These are complicated questions.

I remember Bonnie, who had been in therapy with many other therapists. When we met she said proudly, "I learned from my last therapist that I shouldn't help people. I don't anymore." I remember Hannah, who was having an affair with a married man who had four kids and a wife with breast cancer. Hannah came to therapy because she did not want to feel guilty about breaking up this marriage. I think of a corporate head of a local company who came into therapy for the stress of having to fire longtime employees. He wanted help dealing with his guilt and quieting his conscience.

Therapy was invented in the Victorian Age, when most people probably felt too overburdened by their consciences. Freud considered the superego harsh and tyrannical, and in the context of large extended families in stable, religious communities, it probably was. But the world is different today. There's little evidence that Americans in the 1990s have rigidly overlearned conventional morality from which they desperately need liberation. Rather, all around us is chaos and confusion.

While there are still overcontrolled perfectionists today, they are in increasingly short supply. Our theory was designed primarily for neurotics who needed to be relieved of guilt. But the common clients of today are not guilt-ridden neurotics, but rather people looking for guidance and meaning. They often want help formulating rules about moral behavior.

Guilt is inner discomfort at not having met certain standards. Guilt doesn't necessarily lead to good behavior. It can translate into self-loathing, inaction or pious platitudes. Generally, love is a more powerful incentive to action. But the absence of guilt can certainly lead to bad behavior, and guilty consciences have inspired important acts of atonement. Many of our finest public buildings were built by guilty millionaires. Some therapists have suggested that all guilt is bad, but people with no guilt are psychopaths. Whether they roam our city streets, corporate boardrooms or the halls of Congress, they do us great harm.

Of course, not all therapists endorse a feel-good philosophy or abdication of moral responsibility. Albert Bandura's notions of self-efficacy and Aaron Beck's theories of depression both suggest that people feel better when they are helping others. Long ago, Hobart Mowrer pointed out that guilt is not an entirely useless emotion. He believed that some people, such as psychopaths, need to feel more guilt, not less. Michael Lerner encourages therapists to help their clients develop good values. Frank Pittman's goal in therapy is to increase and strengthen clients' characters. His goal of creating character is similar to my grandmother's belief— i.e., the purpose of influence is to create moral people. There are many good therapists who help people think clearly and make well-reasoned and ethical choices. They believe that therapy should be in the service of a good and ethical life.

William Doherty writes about these ideas in *Soul Searching*. He believes that therapists should enter into moral discourse with their clients. He argues that, at the very least, we shouldn't try to talk our clients out of their moral senses. He isn't recommending that therapists impose their beliefs on others. Rather he believes that good therapy increases moral sensitivity and builds character. Toward the end of therapy he asks his clients, "How can you use what you have learned in therapy to contribute to your work or community?"

7. We Have Focused on Individual Salvation Rather Than Collective Well-being.

Therapy has contributed to the cultural shift from collective political action to individual mental health. We've encouraged self-analysis at the expense of social change. I am reminded of a cartoon in which a person upset about famine in Ethiopia was told to take some Valium. At worst therapists have, to quote Ellen Goodman, "engaged in moral lobotomies." We have treated morality as a personal and pragmatic matter, not a community concern. We have abdicated our responsibility to speak to the moral and social issues of our times.

Our focus has been too narrow. We need to know how clients' lives affect other lives and the world at large. When therapists don't connect individual dilemmas to the broader world, clients often believe that their needs are the most important ones. That focus on self is not in clients' best interests. Narcissism leads to social isolation, shallowness, cynicism and ultimately to poorer mental health. People are their best and society is the strongest when we follow the Golden Rule, which emphasizes caring for the self and caring for others. Lives are meaningful and satisfying when they involve commitment, justice, truthfulness and community. When everyone is encouraged to look out for number one, our social climate is poisoned and we all suffer.

Some therapists have even accused altruistic people of avoiding their own internal issues. One striking example of this comes from the wife of a social activist in Latin America. Daily her husband risked his life helping victims of an oppressive regime. Her therapist suggested that her husband helped political prisoners because he was fleeing from intimacy with her. A few therapists have implied that altruism is unhealthy and premature in all except the self-actualizing. One author states: "You can't work on the social order unless you've healed the wound of your inner child." Would Martin Luther King, Jr., or John Kennedy have gone to work if they'd believed this?

Doherty points out that psychotherapy, as a cultural institution, has been stunningly successful. As other older institutions have eroded, psychotherapy has filled in the gaps. One-third of Americans have seen a therapist and all have been influenced by the language and concepts of therapy.

Doherty says, "The culture we helped shape for 100 years is in crisis, partly because people believed what we told them about the good life." He argues that currently our field is in deep trouble. There are many reasons for this but the two most important ones are our lack of relevance in a crumbling culture and the advent of managed care, which has created a "crisis in integrity." Therapists can do right either by our clients or by the health maintenance companies that pay us. A widespread reevaluation of psychology is under way. Therapists are asking how we can respect our long-held ideals of personal freedom and also acknowledge our culture's desperate need for family loyalty and community values.

In his book *We've Had a Hundred Years of Psychotherapy—and the World's Getting Worse*, James Hillman noted that one of the reasons our culture is falling apart is that intelligent people are going into therapy instead of becoming social activists. They're paying therapists for time to complain about work instead of organizing workers. Hillman wrote that therapy further erodes the planet by emphasizing inner, not outer, problems. He said that there is no evidence that people do more community work after they've had therapy, and in fact he suspects they do less.

There is actually some evidence from academic psychology that people who feel good are more likely to do good, and also that people who have been belittled are more likely to be racist and to belittle others. But there is little evidence that, as a group, people who have been in therapy are more likely to do community work. In fact, many clients choose to work on themselves in lieu of working on their communities.

Hillman had a wonderful definition of self—the interiorization of community. I like it because it connects us to our communities and suggests that if we live in lousy communities our lives will be in trouble. Therapists need a new point of view, one that encourages social action, not self-, or family, flagellation. We need to examine how the culture contributes to the mental health of its members.

A related problem is our focus on treatment rather than prevention. We have treated the casualties of lethal cultural policies one family at a time. We can help the mental health of families by speaking out on the issues of our times. We can support good day care and schools, gun control, national and state parks, social and medical services for the poor, a guaranteed minimum wage and programs that promote tolerance for diversity. We can support programs that protect children and enable more families to enter the middle class.

8. We Have Confused Ethical and Mental Health Issues, Empathy and Accountability.

A recent trend in America is to turn ethical problems into mental health issues. If people can define themselves as victims, temporarily insane, traumatized or under stress, they have no ethical responsibilities. No one is responsible for good or evil. We see it in our show trials. The

Menendez brothers, who killed their parents, claimed earlier abuse. We've had the "Twinkie" defense, the "I was drunk and didn't know what I was doing" defense and the "abused as a child" defense. If we can define ourselves as victims, any behavior can be justified. We've all become not guilty by reason of insanity. This confusion of ethics and morality leads us to moral impoverishment.

Popular psychology has contributed to the current general confusion about ethics. We worked to medicalize problems, such as alcohol addiction, that had formerly been defined as character defects or problems of willpower. This opened the door for non-blaming treatment, which is good, but it has left us a strange legacy. A man who gets drunk and kills his wife can plead not guilty by reason of temporary insanity. Even stranger, in the court of public opinion, his wife might be held accountable for enabling his drinking and abusive behavior.

A father in therapy discusses the beating of his daughter by her ex-boyfriend. He talks with wonder about the abuser's defense, i.e., that he was temporarily insane from jealousy. The father says to me, "Nothing is wrong anymore. Everyone can come up with an excuse for whatever they do."

I know a man who had a lengthy affair with a co-worker. When Blair tried to break up with her, she blackmailed him. He eventually was so trapped by her blackmail that he tried to hang himself. His wife found him and called 911. Blair was hospitalized and diagnosed depressed. He was told he had a genetic disorder and was put on medication. Now his wife is confused about how to respond to the affair. Should she be angry about his betrayal or glad that his affective disorder has been diagnosed? He's relieved to have an excuse for his behavior, but wonders why he never realized before that he was depressed.

Therapists quite rightly teach empathy. We encourage analyses of the causes of behavior. But this empathy and understanding should not eliminate accountability. Healthy parents say to their children, "We love you, but we have expectations." Good therapists want to understand their clients and foster moral behavior. Good psychotherapy promotes both empathy and accountability. Therapy should be part of a complex process to decide what is the right thing to do and how the client may find strength to do it.

We are a polarized society. The "right" focuses on accountability while the "left" focuses on empathy. Both sides are right. A society without accountability is a dangerous place. A society without empathy is fascist. A healthy society must say to its members, "We empathize with your troubles, but you must behave properly." A decent society teaches both empathy and accountability. On both counts we are all in this together.

9. Some Therapists Abuse Their Power.

Some therapists allow their clients to become too dependent emotionally. They take too much power and tell clients how to live their lives. They tell their clients to divorce, quit jobs or distance from family. I know of a young woman far from home who hated her job and missed her family. But she was in therapy with a therapist who told her, "Do not move back to Colorado. You need to work with me." The therapist also warned her that "she had issues with her family, and living near home might be harmful." Another therapist advises many of his clients to break with their families. He also encourages his clients to propose marriage in his office so that if they are rejected, he'll be there to help them.

It's dangerous when therapists imply that they will care for their clients. In fact, therapists who take away family have little to offer as a substitute. Therapists will not be there for clients when they cannot come up with rent or car payment, or when they are sick or need someplace to go for Thanksgiving dinner.

I remember Corina, who made a career of being a mental health patient. I was her tenth therapist. She'd been hospitalized a dozen times and been in counseling for more than twenty years. She wasn't schizophrenic or seriously mentally ill. She'd just learned to get all her nurturing from professionals. But on her birthday, her previous therapists weren't sending her cards or balloons.

10. We've Suggested That Therapy Is More Important Than Real Life.

Therapists have a tremendous amount of power. Even when we are careful, we can influence clients more then we intend. We often "colonize" our clients, and they end up adopting our worldview. For example, researchers found that the main way that clients who saw Carl Rogers changed was that they became more like Rogers. Even at our best we can inadvertently "inflict help" on others. Being helpful can render others helpless. Our solutions can become part of the problem.

Sometimes therapists have one set of theories for themselves and another for their clients. We don't want to be diagnosed but we will diagnose others. We don't want to be manipulated but we will manipulate others for their own good. Sometimes we fail to respect clients as people who can care for themselves. Or, we have led people to believe that only trained professionals can offer support and guidance. That's not true. Much of the best guidance comes from spouses, family, friends and co-workers.

Therapists are fallible beings. Our field has a great deal of ambiguity and dozens of models from which to work. Human behavior is infinitely complex. Almost nothing is certain. In fact, one of my favorite teachers believed that the most important characteristic in a therapist was a tolerance for ambiguity.

Therapists have their own styles and points of view. Two therapists involved in one case can be worse than none at all. Clients will get such different advice that they really won't know what to do. Therapists are not interchangeable. There are competent and incompetent therapists. My own experience suggests that, like plumbers, doctors or school-teachers, roughly a third of us are excellent, a third fine and a third substandard.

A good rule of thumb is that life is more important than therapy. Friends, family work, school, vacations and ball games are all more important than therapy, It's a mistake to take children from healthy, normal activity for therapy, because the goal of good therapy is to get them into healthy, normal activity.

Life is first. Clients may learn to trust in their relationships with therapists. But therapists should be transition relationships for them. After us they can trust other people and make some friends or reconnect with family. At best, a therapist is a consultant who helps people process life thoroughly. In terms of priorities for loyalty and attachment, therapists should come after family, friends and co-workers. We care about clients, but we are hired help.

STORIES

People seek explanations for their pain. In America right now there are several powerful stories. People hear that they are in pain because they don't have the right consumer goods, they are from a dysfunctional family or they have a chemical imbalance. Stories are theories, ways of explaining the universe to people. Psychologists, like all people, have stories to tell. Right now in America our stories have tremendous power. Clients come to us with what psychologist Michael White calls problem-saturated stories. They come seeking to understand their anger, sadness and anxiety, and they ask, "Why? What is the meaning of my behavior?" People who are miserable naturally look for something or someone to blame. We can help them find a scapegoat or we can help them place their complaints in a broader, more meaningful perspective.

There are endless possible stories. By now some are laughably outdated. Otto Rank's birth-trauma theory looks silly in the era of drive-by shootings and corporate takeovers. As "story doctors" we can tell clients that their problems are biochemical or that they are in an oppressed minority, are the baby of the family, have maladaptive behavior patterns or do not have enough fun or meaning in their lives. We can say, "You are the way you are because you are an Adult Child of an Alcoholic." Or we can say, "You are miserable because you gave up a child for adoption twenty years ago." Or we can refer to the Myers Briggs Personality Inventory and say, "You do this because you're an INTJ."

The explanations we give clients about their pain are enormously important to them. Our ideas help clients make sense of the universe. They can become self-fulfilling prophecies. Because our stories are so powerful in the lives of others, it behooves us to be cautious about what we say. I want to talk briefly about two stories that are popular right now.

One story is that people are in pain because their parents traumatized them. One author writes: "No matter how abuse is defined or what people think, you are the ultimate judge If you think you were abused you were. If you are not sure, you probably were." His book echoes the message of the recovery movement, which is—You are in pain because you come from a dysfunctional family, and if you want to recover, you must work through the grief your family caused and learn to nurture your inner child.

This movement also says that parental motivation doesn't matter, that even if no malice was involved, you could have been abused as a child. And sometimes it says that even if you don't remember it, you were probably abused and have repressed the memories. In this story, almost everything is blamed on the family of origin. Not wanting a child, wanting a child, depression, anger at one's children, addictions and sexual problems are because of inadequate parenting. This idea erodes families from within.

Another popular story is the codependency story, which pathologizes caring and leaves people hopelessly confused about the right thing to do. People become paralyzed between their impulse to help and their fear that helping is unhealthy. Especially mothers are confused. Women who care too much are labeled codependents and mothers who care too little are labeled cold and distant. It's hard to know the right place to be. But everyone else is confused too. Jesus, Mother Teresa and Abe Lincoln would all be considered codependents. They were not particularly good at taking care of themselves.

Wherever there is power, there is abuse of power. We therapists have not always critically examined our stories. Some of our stories have weakened families and disempowered individuals. We have undercut parental confidence and eroded family trust. Therapists who should have clarified and healed have muddied thinking and created rifts.

Whatever stories therapists tell, once they are in place they have great power. With great power comes great responsibility. We need to ask, What will be the effect of this story over time? How will it affect the client's relationship to others? With each story we need to ask, will this story make the client stronger or weaker? Will it heal family wounds or open them? Will it connect or disconnect this person from his/her community? Will it make our society a better place for all of its members?

All stories are not created equal. When our cultural heroes are scoundrels and takers we produce scoundrels and takers. When we idolize victims, we produce them. In a healthy society, the main stories are about exemplars. Our culture is filled with such people, but their stories are rarely told. I know so many people who are coping with extraordinary difficulties with extraordinary grace. I think of a woman who cares for her husband with Alzheimer's. I think of a young woman in a wheelchair at the Manor who manages to fill the other residents' days with joy. I remember how well some of my friends have faced their deaths. I think of teachers who work in demoralizing and dangerous conditions because they care about children. We need more stories of sacrifice, loyalty, kindness and strength through adversity. We become what we tell ourselves that we are.

Therapists hear many stories. We are in the unique position of hearing family stories. In Nebraska I hear stories of the loss of family farms, of young people dying from drugs and alcohol and of women with eating disorders. Recently there have been more stories of corporate takeovers with stressed workers and ethically compromised executives. Therapists have the chance to see how the broader culture affects the lives of many families. Themes become clear. We see what Hillman describes—that the self is the interiorization of the community. The pathology in the culture becomes part of the soul.

Therapists can see the tragedy, but we also see the courageous struggles and heroic solutions. We have the power to share these stories to give other families hope. We can teach empathy, flexible thinking, honesty and communication—all skills our culture needs if it is to survive. We can promote tolerance and respect for diversity. We can help families define themselves, protect themselves and connect with others.

Chapter Seven

How Therapy Can Help—
The Shelter of Each Other

When I wonder about the usefulness of my work, I think of Eileen, who came to therapy in the metal-toed boots and brown uniform of the cement company where she's employed. Eileen is physically plain, socially awkward and chronically apologetic. At our first meeting, she scanned my face for rejection, and her most common response to questions was "Why do you want to know that?"

Eileen was born to a father who disliked all people, including his own children. When he came home at night he yelled to his wife, "Get the dammed kids out of here." Eileen's mother did not want children, and especially not girls. She had trouble at Eileen's delivery and she referred to Eileen as "the one who almost killed me." Eileen was viewed essentially as household help. When I asked Eileen if she had ever felt special, she remembered that once her grandmother had made ham loaf because she knew Eileen liked it. Eileen choked up and said, "That meant a lot to me."

After a crummy childhood, Eileen moved into a crummy adulthood. She was too quiet and insecure to make any women friends. After several punishing sexual relationships, she decided she could do without men and without sex, which she never experienced as being connected to affection.

Eileen worked with guys who had pinups in their lockers and drove trucks with images of strippers on the mud flaps. She occasionally went to the bars after work and listened to her co-workers curse the boss and brag about their dates and beer drinking. But she was not connecting with them or anyone else. When no one sent her a card on her birthday, she decided to try therapy.

Eileen had never been valued and she didn't know how to value herself. She had been encouraged to be docile rather than authentic and quiet rather than creative. She had never experienced a relationship that felt good or was helpful. Eileen had few illusions about how kind the world is. In fact, her illusions were all in the opposite direction. She saw the world as unbelievably harsh.

At first, Eileen was jumpy and suspicious, ready to bolt out the door whenever I asked a question. But over time she trusted me. She told me how she felt, and sighed with relief that I accepted those feelings. Eventually Eileen's words tumbled out. In her eagerness to speak, she was unstoppable. She was eager to schedule two sessions a week as far into the future as my calendar would go. Her enthusiasm was understandable—this was the first place in her life where her opinions mattered.

I was touched and humbled by her enthusiasm. I worked to develop a warm, honest relationship. If she could have that with me, perhaps later she'd trust others as well. I encouraged her to explore who she was and what she thought. I wanted to give Eileen the conditions she needed to grow and to help her understand herself and her world.

I saw Eileen for almost two years. Gradually she set goals for herself and made important life choices. She invited her parents to come to her therapy, but they refused. Eventually she decided that her parents would never like her and quit worrying about their opinions. On the other hand, we searched her extended family for someone whom she could love and we found her aunt Shirley, her father's sister. She began writing Shirley and sending her little gifts. By the time Eileen quit therapy, she was going to Shirley's for Sunday dinners.

Eileen was proud of being able to do the hard physical labor that her job required. The job had good benefits and the wages were better than for other jobs she could qualify for with a high school degree. Eileen felt that even though the men on the job were pretty sexist, they treated her squarely. Over time she became friends with Ricky and met his wife and kids. After that, Ricky would quiet the other guys down when they got too obnoxious. He'd say, "Hey. There's a lady present."

Eileen learned skills for making friends—ask questions and listen carefully, be open and honest and be positive and low-key. She discovered needlepoint and knitting and joined a craft guild. The one she joined happened to be filled with kindhearted older women who took her under their wings and mothered her, something other young women might have resented but that felt great to Eileen.

Eileen valued the therapy, which she described as teaching her to take care of herself. As she talked, she learned what she thought about her own life. She learned she was interesting. She experienced what people should experience over the course of therapy, that human relationships can be deeply satisfying. And the work began with a simple connection between the two of us.

When I wonder if therapy can help, I think of the Green family. Melinda and Jeff began therapy by agreeing that their five-year-old son, Jason, was spoiled rotten and out of control. When he didn't get his way, Jason kicked and screamed, "I hate you." In public he insulted adults, hit children, threw his food and begged for every toy imaginable. He was afraid of everything—monsters, ghosts, shadows, thunderstorms and robbers. He wouldn't sleep alone and had terrible nightmares. The parents looked tired and guilty as they talked. They wondered if Jason's problems were biochemical or from poor parenting, the sugar Jason consumed, too much attention or not enough attention.

Both parents worked and Jason attended a big and not very good day care center. He watched about five hours of television a day, including the ten o'clock news. After her day job, Melinda worked nights as a Tupperware salesperson. Jeff spent time with Jason, but it was time in front of the TV.

I asked questions about the problems and also about what was working well in the family. I tried to convey respect for these parents' efforts to understand their situation. I suggested experiments. Perhaps Jason would sleep better if he didn't watch the late night news. Maybe if Jeff took Jason for a walk after dinner, he would be less restless and destructive. I could have made other suggestions, but I stopped. Melinda and Jeff agreed to try them. They seemed relieved that neither they nor their son had been labeled as crazy. They were grateful for a consultant. We agreed to meet weekly and figure out what would help their son be less frightened and spoiled.

Over time, we did a variety of things. I met with Jason, who was indeed a handful, and I tried to assess what he most needed to help him develop into a well-adjusted boy. I helped the parents enroll in a parenting-skills class. We talked about appropriate expectations for Jason's developmental level. I tried to offer the parents support, encouragement and some sense of focus. The therapy allowed everyone to calm down and approach problems in a systematic manner. By the end we were even laughing at some of the problems instead of seeing them as grim indicators that the Greens were failing.

In my work with both Eileen and the Greens what was right between us was quite simple—warmth, empathy, respect and uninterrupted time. I asked questions and suggested experiments. I complimented the clients when I could. Most of the time, therapy is this simple. One person agrees to listen and ask good questions while another person or persons explores his/her situation. The listener stays alert, curious and accepting. The talker or talkers try to be precise and honest. Therapists don't usually need fancy theories or elegant interventions. What's most important is common sense, experience helping people solve problems and basic human decency.

Good therapists do not give much advice. They stay out of the way when clients are succeeding. If it works they don't fix it. Good therapists help people sort out what they can and can't control. They can help people think clearly about goals and move toward them. Therapists can teach that all feelings are acceptable, but all behavior isn't. They can encourage people to express feelings honestly, but to behave properly. By emphasizing both honesty and good behavior, they integrate the wisdom of different eras. In the 1920s the emphasis was on proper behavior, and people rarely shared feelings. In the 1990s the expression of honest feelings is often valued, while behavior is overlooked. But feelings and moral behavior must be connected if families are to survive.

The fact that people have more choices today makes relationships more complex. We all require more skills to make relationships work. Unfortunately many people are not learning those skills in the real world. Therapists can teach relationship skills—conflict mediation, empathic listening, clear communicating, strategic praising and simple good manners.

We can attribute some of the difficulties people experience with their families to the fact that love intensifies problems. For example, I often say to teens who complain about their mothers, "Well, naturally she is worried, she loves you." We can remind people that all love causes pain and we can recommend talking, touching and laughing. I am advocating that we can reframe much of what has been called codependency as love.

It's important that the conditions be right for therapy. Generally families need time to sort out their situations and to find solutions to dilemmas. In fact, good therapy is really about protecting time. The language of healing and self-understanding doesn't unfold in sound bites. Truth isn't revealed in billable units. The human heart doesn't heal according to clock time. Faster is not always better. The problems that most Americans have today can't be fixed quickly. People need natural, biological time, not bookkeeper's time, to allow their stories to unfold.

Families come into therapy confused and angry about how they must spend their time. Many children spend their days in crowded classrooms. Many adults spend most of their time doing work they hate. Couples rarely have time for conversations, sex or dates. Children grow up in day-care centers, car seats and TV rooms. Therapists often need to "treat people's schedules," to use James Hillman's phrase.

Therapy is often the only time families are all in a room together talking about their situation. This time together talking is often all that needs to happen for things to improve. Talking and listening are healing. This is ancient wisdom. The Native Americans of the Southwest have talking circles in which everyone explains his/her point of view about situations or events. Everyone else listens carefully and tries to understand.

While I think therapy should be affordable and accessible to everyone, I worry about brief therapies and managed-care models. Therapists can't make instant rapport, like we make instant pudding. Hurried people shouldn't be hurried to solve problems. What is often most healing to clients is the knowledge that another person understands their reality. To claim to understand another person's life too quickly is both a lie and an insult. No one is simple and no one is like anyone else. I am not suggesting that therapy needs to involve three sessions a week for several years like traditional psychoanalysis did, but good work usually takes a while.

Therapists can help people clarify their values and set priorities. We can encourage people to use their time in accordance with these values and priorities. We can help people become wiser, more tolerant, flexible and aware. We can help them be less fearful, angry and lonely. We can teach sensible things—Examine your life and make conscious choices; don't just let events happen to you. Relationships matter and they must be tended to survive. Don't expect others to read your mind; communicate clearly. Don't hurt the kids. Don't attack others when you are in pain. Herman Melville was asked what helped people with grief and he said salt. "The salt of sweat, tears and the open sea." We can help people find their salt.

Good therapy is a meaning-building activity. It's about seeking the truth with all its ambiguity. In this era of infotainment and docudramas, we need places where the truth counts. We can teach lessons. Don't have affairs. Don't spend more money than you make. Don't lie or have secrets. Don't work seventy-hour weeks to buy jewelry and Valium. Love isn't always enough. Humor helps. Calmness helps. Addictions screw things up royally. It's good to do work that matters. When therapy succeeds, it is a miracle. It is the result of the caring, respectful connection of people working together to solve problems. It's a fine human endeavor, as worthy of respect as a good poem, symphony or field goal.

GOALS OF FAMILY THERAPY

1. We need to protect.

Therapists give families a place to build family identity and power. We can teach them how to protect themselves with their values, use of time and places, celebrations, stories and metaphors. This is simple, but it's not easy. Building family takes commitment and hard choices about priorities. I think of a blues singer who moved to our town from Chicago so that her son could grow up safely. Chicago was a better town for a career of singing the blues, but she didn't feel it was a better town for her son.

Building family means driving all night to a cousin's funeral or telling co-workers that you can't work Saturdays. It means avoiding the need to work overtime by going without a new car, or turning down a promotion that involves moving teenagers to a faraway city. It means missing *Seinfeld* to attend a grandmother's Eastern Star installation. It involves putting family first, something that is rarely convenient and not always even pleasant.

2. We need to connect families to others.

We can work to connect people with their histories and their extended families. Even the most difficult families usually have some potentially redeemable members. In the past, we have too often recommended distancing and cutoffs. While these actions are sometimes necessary, they are last-resort strategies. Once broken, fences are hard to mend. We can do families much damage when we separate members, even when those members are not getting along all that well. It's better for us to help in the healing. We can sober up people who are "intoxicated by their own rightness" and help families invent "mechanisms of forgiveness." As Peter Ustinov said, "Love is an act of endless forgiveness, a tender look which becomes a habit."

We can help families build support systems. As part of our assessments we can draw sociograms of resources in their neighborhoods—the older couple who loves children, the next-door neighbor who has offered to help or the owner of the corner store who knows the family. We can connect families to each other and encourage them to work for their common good. Churches are often islands of support. Recently there has been scoffing at the idea of Midnight Basketball leagues for kids, but it's a good idea. Community centers with supervised athletic and social events for young people can make a tremendous difference in the health of individuals and communities. Glenn Hilke said, "The most radical thing you can do is to introduce people to each other."

3. Be purveyors of hope.

The phrase comes from Don Meichenbaum, a cognitive-behavioral therapist who believes inspiring hope is the therapist's first duty and major contribution. If people feel worse about themselves and their situations after they come in, therapy isn't working. We can focus on learning, creativity, fun and good work. To paraphrase Robert Frost, therapists can encourage people to look backward with pride and forward with hope.

Hope isn't about facts that can be disputed, it's an existential choice about how to face adversity. As G.K. Chesterton said, "Courage is the power of being cheerful in circumstances we know to be desperate." That's a good definition of hope as well. As such, hope gives clients energy and focus. There is no such thing as false hope. The phrase is an oxymoron, like jumbo shrimp.

4. Be purveyors of respect.

Good therapists emphasize respect as much as caring. Therapists do care, but they also know that respect is a much more powerful motivator. Respect is connected to thinking as well as emotion and it's easier to link respect with specific behaviors. "I respect that you have stopped smoking pot because you want to be a good role model for your children" or "I respect that you will not join a gang."

Respect means that clients speak for themselves and are responsible for their own actions. Those family members not in the room also deserve respect. Therapists can support coping and reinforce resilience by asking—What did you learn from this experience? I think of Duke Ellington, who wrote, "I merely took the energy it takes to pout and wrote some blues."

Respect also implies no us/them dichotomies. Our theories must fit us. Psychiatric labels should be used judiciously, if at all. As Michael White said, "No one is as sick as their case history or diagnosis."

5. We can clarify thinking.

We help people differentiate between thinking and feeling and between truth and fantasy. Rather than handing out pardons, we can help people deal with reality. We can help families find pleasure in the right things. For example, last summer I stood on a beach at Cape Cod. I had always wanted to take my family to the beach and somehow we had never had the time or money. Now my children are grown and I watched other people's children dig in the sand and hunt for mussels. I heard the laughter and saw the parents' pleasure in their sandy, sunburned kids. I ached with sadness. I thought, On my deathbed I will not congratulate myself on the money and time I saved not bringing my children to the sea.

6. We can help families develop a strategy to make good decisions.

Most people are trying to do the right thing, but many people do not know what the right thing is and family members often disagree on this. We can help people learn a process for discussing choices in a way that includes everyone and leads to a fair, reasoned decision. I think of a poor family, deeply in debt, who came in to discuss whether the father should work at a dangerous job or the family should face homelessness. Or I think of two lesbians who came in for help with their adopted daughter's questions about their sexual preferences. They were unsure what to tell her and when and they cared desperately that they make a good decision about this. These are complex issues and families can use consultants about what strategy to use in making these decisions.

While poor families struggle to stay afloat and have neither time nor money, many middle-class families want both time and money. They don't realize that they cannot have both. Therapists can teach that the greatest gifts to family members aren't consumer items but gifts of time. We can help families formulate new definitions of riches. For example, Emerson defined wealth as "the number of things one could do without." Some of my favorite definitions of wealth include the number of sunsets the family sees each year or the number of times a week Dad is home after school with the children or the number of times a year the extended family enjoys itself at a get-together.

7. We can teach empathy.

Simone Weil said, "The only real question to be asked of another is what are you experiencing?" We can encourage people to turn off their machines, stop their rushing around and ask this of each other. We can encourage clients to call or write their relatives, to visit with the children on their streets and to invite a troubled neighbor to go for a walk. We can encourage people of different backgrounds to spend time together sharing their experiences. We can encourage rich people to share with the poor and people of different ethnic backgrounds to invite each other for a meal.

We can teach that people love only in the ways they can love. To make this point, a therapist I know reads families *The Gift of the Magi* by O. Henry. Too often people spend their lives searching for one kind of love, when all around them there is love if only they would see it. We can teach people to identify different kinds of loving—the husband who changes the oil in the car early Saturday morning, the child who watches his father's face for signs of respect, the neighbor who offers roses from her garden or the boy next door who stops so we can pet his kitten.

8. We can promote authenticity and creativity.

We can encourage people to tell the truth and be themselves. We can help people define themselves from within, rather than allowing the larger culture to define them. We can encourage people to "follow their bliss," as Joseph Campbell said. We can encourage them to write, play music, paint, cook, make quilts or cabinets, garden or tell stories to children, whatever they enjoy.

9. We can fight secrets, promote openness and encourage facing pain directly.

We can encourage families to tell the truth about family suicides, criminals, addictions, unplanned pregnancies, adoptions and abuse. Whatever the family is ashamed of must be discussed. As Adrienne Rich wrote, "That which is unspoken becomes unspeakable."

We are diminished by living with problems we try not to see. Secrets keep families from dealing with reality. They create alliances and estrangements. They keep things from changing and make people feel ashamed. Secrets teach people the destructive lesson that certain events cannot be handled. For families or individuals to be healthy, they must be able to integrate all of their experiences into their lives. Unprocessed experiences block growth and keep people from thinking clearly and realistically. We can encourage people to work through problems rather than avoid them. We can teach that almost all the craziness in the world comes from running from pain.

10. We can help families diffuse anxiety and cope with stress.

Families need ways to deal with things that are embarrassing, frightening, sad or upsetting. If families do not have good ways to cope with stress, they will have bad ways. We can teach families anxiety management and help people process their pain. We can encourage talking and listening, what trauma workers call "being and staying" with each other's pain. Therapists can teach wellness and healthy lifestyles. We can encourage families to eat properly and exercise regularly. We can encourage relationships with the natural world.

11. We can help families to control consumption, violence and addictions.

We can help family members assess their use of chemicals. If drugs, cigarettes or alcohol are creating problems in their lives, we can help them stop using them. We can teach impulse control, delay of gratification and frustration tolerance. Most of the unhappiness in the world is caused by people who are 90 percent happy, going for that last 10 percent. We can help families define for themselves the word "enough."

We can facilitate conversations between angry and hurt people. We can help families say violence is wrong. We can teach anger control. There are many good cognitive-behavioral models for this. We can teach family members that nobody deserves to be physically hurt or verbally intimidated. If the violence doesn't stop, we can help members leave dangerous situations.

12. We can help family members find the balance between individuation and connection.

We can help families settle boundary disputes. I think of a couple who was concerned about the wife's diabetic mother. They did not want her in a rest home, yet they were uneasy about her living alone or in their home. The couple was struggling with issues of duty, values and mental health. Were they taking care of themselves or being selfish if they decided to put the relative in a rest home?

I think of a young single mother who lived with her baby and her parents. She was in therapy to figure out how much help to take from her parents. Sometimes she felt they interfered with her parenting. They made suggestions about when to put the baby to bed and how to dress him. She was grateful for their help, but wanted more autonomy.

Some families are too enmeshed. Some parents do too much for their children. Siblings can interfere in each other's marriages. There are people who don't have a life or an identity and who borrow an identity from others. But therapists have tended to focus more on the dangers of this enmeshment than on the dangers of isolation. It's time for a corrective rebalancing. We help people the most when we acknowledge their needs for both connection and autonomy.

13. We can promote moderation and balance.

We can encourage work and play, altruism and self-love. We can, to quote an old minister, "comfort the afflicted and afflict the comfortable." We can help overly rigid people relax and casual people become better organized. We can help self-involved people think of others and people who are totally self-sacrificing to think of themselves. We can encourage people to do good deeds and find something to enjoy in every day.

14. We can foster humor.

As Jeanne Moreau said, "Life is tough enough without being unhappy on top of everything else." Humor was a survival tool of families in the 1930s. Often in the midst of sadness and stress, joking made life bearable. One psychologist I know often gives family members the assignment to tell a joke every night at dinner.

15. We can help people build good character.

Einstein said that the purpose of life is to become more fully human. We can help families allow their members to grow into all they can be. We must help families be both empathic and accountable. The culture is confused about these issues, and families echo the confusion. Families need both high expectations for their members and tolerance and tenderness.

———

I use assignments to help families clarify their positions, discover new things about themselves and stay motivated to work toward long-term goals. Assignments are experiments that let a family see what happens if they do things differently. They should be approached pragmatically— Does this make things better for our family? A family needn't be in therapy to follow assignments. Families can have weekly meetings on their own and invent assignments for themselves.

I ask families to record their victories. Family members keep track of successes and report on them when they come in. Victories can be defined as anything the family wants to do more of. For example, victories can be meals together, time spent having fun or honest conversations about conflict. Victories can be the number of nights that Dad and Mom have a quiet conversation or the number of times a single parent has the energy to read her child a story. I remind families that they needn't wait for a Nobel prize or a straight-A report card to record victories. Most victories in life are small ones. Small victories are significant when they involve overcoming personal weaknesses, helping others and making the self or the family stronger.

I encourage families to orchestrate "corrective emotional experiences." These are experiences designed to mitigate the pain of an earlier event. For example, some friends went to Denver when the wife had a brain tumor and needed emergency surgery. Two years later, after she had recovered, the family returned to Denver to enjoy the city. On a less serious level, a couple who fought at their favorite restaurant can return and have another dinner, only this time one in which they show great tenderness toward each other.

With adolescents corrective emotional experiences work better than punishments. Relationship-oriented reparations are often the most effective. A therapist I know suggests that when a teenager ruins a family dinner with a tantrum, he/she can be asked to cook and serve a candlelight dinner to the family on another night. Another therapist recommends that teenagers who are rude to relatives spend an evening putting photos in a family album. Reparations have the teenager working with an adult on useful projects that teach skills. A good reparation could include helping a parent paint the house, do the taxes or learn to use the computer. A good reparation could be helping with the gardening, the recycling or the care of an elderly relative.

After families have experienced trauma, I help them design healing ceremonies. A family whose daughter was murdered planned a memorial ceremony at her college campus and gave money for better campus security. This was an important event in the recovery of the family.

I recommend ceremonies of acknowledgment and forgiveness after an extramarital affair. Many marriages can be saved, but the couple must deal with what happened, express their painful feelings and resolve to move on. After betrayals, violence and losses, ceremonies can help with healing.

All families have unfinished business from the ways in which they have hurt each other and have been hurt by the outside world. In almost all cases, healing is possible with the right words and the right ceremonies. The more a family puts into a ceremony the more it will receive. My bias is toward out-of-doors ceremonies. As Thoreau said, "In the wilderness there is life." All experiences with the sun, water, the sea, forests and mountains can be healing. Even people who live in cities can find some outdoor places—rooftops, parks and walks along rivers and lakeshores can help families heal. Cities have trees, the sky, flowers, rain, stars—all the things people need for healing ceremonies.

I encourage families to make conscious choices about media. I know a man who loves the ancient Greeks and who reads his children only books written before 1900. He allows no TV or radio in his home. His children love literature and are calmer and more relaxed than most children I know. Another family sold their TV and gave their children the money from its sale. The kids bought hiking boots and snowshoes and soon forgot that they ever had a TV.

Another family has their children count commercials for sugary products, for alcohol and for designer clothes. Then the parents discuss the numbers and messages with the children. They "deconstruct" advertising with the kids. One mother I worked with was so upset by the kinds of magazines available to teenage girls that she refused to allow them in her home. Then she discovered *New Moon*, a magazine that allows no advertising and is by and for girls.

I encourage families to examine their relationship to media and to make conscious choices about what they will and won't consume. This involves research, dialogue, experiments and oftentimes conflict resolution. But in the end the family has made decisions and not just let the outside world happen to them. It's a deeply satisfying experience.

People act more intelligently when they have good, accurate information. In the 1990s it's hard to know what's true. For example, we hear such contradictory things about crime rates, global warming and healthy diets. It's hard to feel we have accurate information on which to base decisions. I try to help families upgrade their information sources. For example, I encourage families to learn together to use the reference desk at the local library.

I do encourage clients to read some of the self-help literature. For example, I recommend David Burns's book *Feeling Good* and *The Guide to Personal Happiness*, by Albert Ellis and Irving Becker, for depression. I like Harriet Lerner's book *The Dance of Anger*. But before I recommend books, I read them and make sure that they offer good factual information and that they don't encourage clients to feel like victims of dysfunctional families.

Successful adults often report they were inspired as children by books about heroes. I recommend works about good people overcoming adversity. For example, I like books such as Eugenia Ginsburg's *Into the Whirlwind*, about her experiences in Stalin's camps, or Zitkala-Sa's stories about her Lakota Sioux girlhood in the early part of this century. I like biographies of people who have accomplished things—Albert Einstein, Georgia O'Keeffe or the astronauts. I lend out autobiographies—Margaret Mead's *Blackberry Winter*, Ben Franklin's diary and Mark Twain's autobiography.

Children like to read of heroic children. As a young teen I read *The Diary of Anne Frank* and also John Gunther's story of his son's cancer, *Death Be Not Proud*. Those books inspired me to do my best with my relatively easy situation. Modern books I like for teens include *It's Our World, Too! Young People Who Are Making a Difference*, by Phillip Hoose, and *Real Lives*, a book written by teens who designed their own educations. Librarians can help families find stories that are just right for their children.

I encourage the gifts of attention, lessons, encouragement and experiences. I know a family who walks on a nearby ridge every time the full moon rises at sunset. Another friend writes long letters to all her grandchildren every week and tapes them stories for their bedtimes. A client spent months making a quilt for her nephew, a quilt that let him know how much he meant to her. I know a grandmother with a very limited income who hand-copies all her favorite recipes for her grandchildren when they graduate from high school.

As I will discuss in Chapter Eleven, I encourage families to develop rituals. These can be for seasons, significant family events and rites of passage. When adults are surveyed about what they remember most fondly from their childhoods, most fondly recall time outdoors, holidays and vacations. So I encourage families to have time outdoors, vacations and holiday meals. Again these need not be elaborate or expensive. A vacation can be a weekend camping or visiting a relative. Time outdoors can mean sitting on a city stoop and identifying the constellations.

I encourage families to increase their expressions of affection. Families often need to be reminded to hug each other, to compliment each other and to say how they feel about each other. I encourage people to write notes, make short phone calls, do small favors and express affection in whatever ways it can be received. It's great to go visit graveyards where family members are buried, to see homesteads and hometowns. I advise families to buy the plane tickets, take the crosstown bus or drive the hundred miles out of the way to see the grand-aunts and visit cousins. I think of an elderly client who visited family members who had been lost to her since the Holocaust. This reunion was one of the most healing experiences of her life. Another client had been separated at birth from a twin brother who had serious deformities. She tracked him down in a care facility and began a relationship that has been healing for her and life-saving for the brother.

I recommend that parents schedule once-a-week breakfasts alone with their adolescents. It's a good time to talk about life. I encourage these breakfasts to be a free zone in which grades, chores, rule violations and money are not mentioned. Rather, parent and child can just visit. It's a connecting experience that helps hold the relationship in place during a difficult time.

I design experiments to help people sanctify time. These can be simple things, such as the custom of an old friend who takes his wife to the opening game of the Kansas City Royals every year. My co-worker Jan takes off the first school day of every year so that she can be home to hear about her children's day. They can be more elaborate things, like setting aside certain times as special. Many local families travel to central Nebraska every spring for the annual migration of the sand cranes. Other families in our state have long traditions of coming to our football games.

I encourage minivacations where the family makes a few moments special. Small rituals at dinner, such as saying grace, unplugging the phones, turning off the TV and lighting candles, can hallow family time.

I suggest writing. Here are examples—write essays on gifts you received from your family of origin, write what you learned from your father and your mother. I like letters—letters of intent, letters of reconciliation, thank-you letters, promissory notes and love letters. When I teach, I ask my students to interview an older relative and write long papers on that person's life. Many of my students feel that it's the best learning experience they have in college. Many touching stories have come from this assignment. One student, an angry drug user, was about ready to drop out of school. He interviewed his grandmother, to whom he had barely spoken in years. In the course of his ten hours of interviewing her, they became reacquainted. Now Corey goes to his grandmother's for lunch every day. He mows her lawn, she sews his tattered jackets. He is no longer thinking of dropping out of school and even his drug use is declining.

I encourage sons and fathers to write each other. I often encourage adult siblings to write each other long letters about their feelings. A colleague of mine asks siblings of his depressed clients to write to him. He solicits letters about the strengths and virtues of the depressed sibling and then reads them in the therapy sessions.

I encourage married partners to write each other yearly "state of the union" letters. These letters include what they look back on with pleasure, what they see in the present and what they hope for in the future. They also include promises by the writer about the ways in which he/she will work to be a better mate. These letters can be powerful, and over time they document the growth of the marriage.

When the nuclear family is struggling, it's good to bring in aunts and uncles, cousins and grandparents. Most people are touchingly eager to be useful. Sometimes the extended family is part of the problem and we can discuss this. Respecting people enough to ask their opinions about solutions can make miracles happen. Other times they are an important resource. An uncle can play basketball with a delinquent teenager. A grandfather can help watch the young children of an exhausted single parent.

Family reunions are important. It's great when children can go visit relatives for extended stays. In this culture we groan at the mention of long family visits, but they can be wonderful. Americans have been mass-marketed the benefits of privacy, but privacy can mean isolation. Children are gregarious and love family around them.

I always ask clients what they know about themselves—their births, their first words and their early habits. There is tremendous variation in how many good stories families have, how much detail the members know about their own lives. People are hungry for this. Families can provide the details. I encourage families to stay connected—via letters, telephone, videotapes, audiotapes and e-mail. Families tell each other the most powerful stories.

A friend of mine told me about her trip to Singapore. She talked to a local woman about the different living arrangements in the two countries. In Singapore several generations of family live together. My friend explained that here each nuclear family lives separately. The woman from Singapore asked in amazement, "Where do the children get their stories?"

Today, before we can analyze a family, we must build it. In the 1960s, only certain kinds of families needed to be "built"—that is, they needed rules, structure, hierarchy and values. Today most families need those things. Many of the ideas about therapy no longer fit the times in which we are living. We must update our conceptual thinking to match the new reality. Actually clients are ahead of many therapists. They know the culture is crazy. But oftentimes they are confused by all the different popular-psychology explanations of family malfunctioning. They doubt themselves in all the wrong ways.

Therapists must update our conceptual schemas of families. Even twenty years ago, a common task was to help young families form strong boundaries between themselves and their extended kin. This was a time when parents-in-law were likely to live nearby and to want Sunday dinners together every week, when grandparents gave grandchildren too much candy and interfered with parental discipline and when many families had "clothesline police" to check on when they were doing their laundry. Therapists helped these young families push back overinvolved relatives and make space and time for their new families. They helped couples set firm boundaries between themselves and their often intrusive parents. But while young families used to be overwhelmed by family, today young families often have no time with extended family. No one in the extended family knows their children or gives them anything. Young families often need to be connected, not distanced, from whatever family resources are available.

Of course, most families have difficult people. As I write this I am thinking of my friend's aunt Charlotte. At get-togethers, family members do their best not to get stuck with Charlotte. She's a chronic complainer and an incessant wet blanket. She is angry because no babies in the family have been named after her and because the hosts don't prepare her stewed prunes properly. Her favorite topics of conversation are how she is abused by the world at large and how she told off someone who tried to screw her. It's understandable that no one bonds with Aunt Charlotte. Almost all of us have an "Aunt Charlotte," a person in the family whom we do not enjoy. But almost all of us are lucky enough to have others whom we truly love and value.

Families need to be connected to role models, the natural world and community resources, as well as their kin. In the 1990s therapists' main job is to protect people from the toxins in our greater culture and to connect people with each other, with their extended families, friends and communities. We need to work to reconnect children and adults, rich and poor and young and old.

Therapists can fight those who give simple answers to the complex problems that families face. Too much that is written about families is simplistic and romantic. Glib homilies such as "All you have to do is love your kids" have damaged families. Most families are neither hotbeds of pathology nor founts of virtues. Most of us live in families that have elements of both the Waltons and *Mommie Dearest*. We think that our families are both uniquely interesting and uniquely crazy. And each of us believes that he/she is the sanest member of this crazy group. Unfortunately, many therapists have looked at the cup of family as half empty. I am suggesting we see it as half full.

We can politicize, not pathologize, families. We can help them see that their enemy is a culture that takes their time and money, overstimulates their children and leaves them with junk. We can help them see the extra burdens that women often carry and encourage them to work for social changes that make things fair. We can encourage wealthy families to share their resources with the poor and educated families to share their knowledge with those who need it desperately. We can encourage altruism and fight cynicism.

Therapists can take stands against racism, homophobia, sexism, violence and ignorance. We can support all kinds of people and families and encourage tolerance for diversity. We can be organizers as well as analyzers and give clients the hope they need to change their communities. At best we can be an antidote to too much technology, consumerism and loss of community. In a political climate of demagogues, we can model tolerance and respect for all points of view. We can remind people of what is truly important and help them find meaning in a confusing culture. We are a force in the culture that advocates for people in all their variety and complexity. Our interest is not Gross National Product, but the human spirit.

Again, therapists are among the great storytellers of this century. Because our stories are so influential, we must choose them carefully. I contend that we haven't been careful enough. Stories such as the codependent story, inner-child story or the dysfunctional family story increase human misery. They create strife in families and leave clients feeling weak and alone. They hopelessly confuse people about accountability and about proper behavior. They can lead to cutoffs and broken hearts. Good stories empower, create connections and heal. They leave clients feeling loved and loving, stronger and more capable of handling their own lives.

It's time for a major examination of our stories. Which of our stories should we keep? Which are person- and family-building stories? Psychologists have other important questions to address. What role should psychology play in the next century? How do we raise children who are loving, nonviolent and productive? How can we support all kinds of families in our culture? How do we create empathy for people different from ourselves? How do we foster a sense of community for 300 million people in this country and four billion people on the planet?

Part II

THE WEIGHT OF THIS
SAD TIME

WHAT MADE SENSE even thirty or forty years ago is counterintuitive today. For example, in the 1960s I admired the irreverence, rebelliousness and wildness of the beat poets. Kerouac and Corso, Ginsberg and Orlovsky were wonderful foils for sleepy suburban citizens. They were a counterbalance to all the certainty, uniformity and smugness of the Eisenhower era. But today, Americans are a lost and uncertain people. While some politicians may boast that they know the answers, in most families smugness is in short supply. When the culture is having a nervous breakdown, wildness and chaos are less appealing. In the 1950s, America may have needed iconoclasts. Today we need healers, people who try to make broken things work.

Similarly, for most of our history, therapists have worked in well-organized cultures with relatively monolithic value systems. Families were embedded in extended families and in communities. Values rarely needed to be reinforced by therapists—that happened everywhere else. Rather, therapy offered people a more accepting environment in which to explore personal issues. But as our old monolithic belief systems have crumbled, the problems today aren't throwing off stifling constraints. Rather, they are our lack of shared guidelines with which to organize lives.

In the next three chapters, I tell stories of families who are struggling with the issues of our times. Some of the stories will be about families who are overwhelmed and failing to make it. Other stories will be about families who have coped with resilience and dignity. The contrasts are not absolute. In all of the families I know, strengths and weaknesses are inextricably blended.

I organized these stories around three central themes—character, will and commitment. I don't claim any kind of inclusive treatment of all the issues that affect families. Rather, I wrote about the families that came to mind. I tried to select rich and poor families, families at different developmental stages and families from different ethnic backgrounds, but I am limited by where I live and whom I see in therapy. Mostly I see middle-class white people in Nebraska. Occasionally I have worked with African-Americans, Hispanics and Native Americans, and I consulted with the Refuge Center, where I met Asian families. But I do not claim to present stories that reflect the diversity that is America.

I have several other caveats. Of course I, like all therapists, have had cases where I failed totally. I haven't told any of those stories for two reasons. One, I don't think they are as instructive as cases in which families make some progress. Also, because I want this book to give families hope, I have focused on stories with at least some victories. But I want to be honest that my ideas do not work for every family.

Also, much of my work is the same as that of other therapists. I teach people to relax and manage their stress. I teach problem solving, negotiating and communication skills. I help clients learn to be assertive, to manage their depression with cognitive-behavioral techniques and to control their anger and impulses. I listen as clients talk about trauma. I try to help clients develop parenting skills and wellness programs and I try to help clients who have eating disorders and addictions overcome their compulsions. But for heuristic purposes, I write very little about this work. Instead, I focus on what I do that is perhaps different from other therapists. While this helps the reader understand my theories, there may be a cost. The reader may feel that I am more unique than I am.

With these caveats in mind, let me tell some stories. I tell them to give readers a sense of how other people's families are doing. I suspect that readers will discover that other families are struggling with many of the same issues that they are. Also, I want to give readers hope that there are solutions to many of the difficult situations that families face. There are things families can do to make their lives saner.

Chapter Eight

CHARACTER

I would define character as that within a person which governs moral choices. Character implies both thought and feeling, history and action. The moral education of children is about character—it is teaching the young to make wise and kind choices. Character grows over the lifetime and is influenced by everything. As William Least Heat Moon said, "A man becomes his attentions. His observations and curiosity, they make and remake him."

When we lost track of character and focused on self-esteem, therapists made a mistake. Character is a bread-and-butter concept, solid as a loaf of rye or sourdough. By contrast, self-esteem can be a cotton candy kind of concept. Originally self-esteem had a precise meaning and some real utility, but by now it's a word, like the words "communication" or "abuse," that has become meaningless. It's a tired word that functions mainly to keep graduate students cranking out publications and the self-help books selling.

Myriad master's theses and doctoral dissertations demonstrate the correlation between low self-esteem and virtually every problem. Some of the research is so obvious as to be trivial—slow learners, unwanted or sexually abused children and obese women are likely to have low self-esteem. But most of the research on self-esteem is simply misunderstood. It is correlational research that shows merely that two phenomena occur together.

Correlations say nothing about causality. Many people assume that people with high self-esteem will accomplish more, make better grades, sell more products or whatever. In fact, if there is a cause-and-effect relationship, I think it's likely to be in the opposite direction of what is popularly assumed. People who have skills and accomplishments feel good about themselves. Self-esteem is probably the result, not the cause, of good work.

Often insecure adults try to bolster their self-esteem with compliments. Many listen to self-affirmation tapes as they drive to work, or they ply themselves with programmed messages that they are good people. These self-affirmations have a place, but they have been oversold as a panacea for a difficult life. If a person's work is meaningless and his/her relationships are fragmented, self-validations will go only so far. Then the person needs to make real changes.

It is important for people to receive credit for good work, and criticism can indeed be damaging. But true self-esteem comes from the belief that one is making the world a better place. It's a by-product of a life lived wisely. In fact, self-esteem, like viewing Halley's comet, is best accomplished if not looked for directly. Self-esteem cannot be given to one person by another and it cannot be induced by self-hypnosis. I'm reminded of the biblical debate between faith and good works. Faith alone, in the absence of charity, leads to sophistry. When we focus on self-esteem instead of character and good works, we feed into narcissism. Self-esteem, if real, is self-regard and comes from ethical behavior.

The difference between narcissism and self-regard confuses clients and therapists. Narcissism is self-absorption. All one's energy is spent massaging the self. Narcissism implies a lack of interest in anything that isn't self-referential. In contrast, self-regard has to do with behaving in accordance with one's value system. It implies a moral stance on the universe and a centered sense of who one is. Because the self is defined and rooted, there is energy to look outward. People with self-regard can see others as real and interesting, not merely as vehicles to meet their needs. Self-regard implies self-knowledge, which is always hard-won. Narcissism implies self-preoccupation. Narcissism says, Look at me; self-regard says, I know who I am when I look at you.

In America we are encouraged to be narcissistic, to constantly examine ourselves for dissatisfaction and to evaluate everything in terms of what's in it for us. Ads tell us to think about our smallest needs and to put our whims first on our list of priorities. We've been trained that the important question is "Does it make me feel good?" I just read an article about an older woman who drove medical supplies to Nicaragua. When she returned, people asked her if she enjoyed herself. She said, "Enjoying myself wasn't really the point. I was delivering medicine. But most people cannot conceive of any other reason for doing something."

Many clients are more worried about their children's feelings than their behavior and they focus more on their self-esteem than their character. They want their children to be happy more than they want them to be good. It's understandable that parents feel this way, but it's misguided. Happiness ultimately comes from a sense that one is contributing to the well-being of the community. In reality, making wise moral choices is the most direct route to true happiness.

Clients often believe that somehow praising their children will improve their self-esteem. But aimless flattery is useless. It's worse than useless; it teaches children that they can slide by. When expectations are too low, children become slackers. One of the greatest gifts a parent can give a child is to teach him/her how to work.

Two teachers in Minnesota talked about their classroom experiences. Pam said, "Parents know the language of popular psychology. They describe things in psychological terms."

Joanne said, "Some parents send us a mixed message—build my child's self-respect but do not require anything of him. Make sure he feels good about himself, but do not make him uncomfortable. Parents act as if we can buy and package self-esteem. Like it's salve that we can rub on."

She stopped and sighed. "I know we can damage children by being too critical. It's important for us to be aware of the psychological effects of our remarks, but we shouldn't just manufacture praise."

"Parents seem mixed up about accountability," Joanne said. "They want us to teach their children responsibility, but they are angry at us if we hold them accountable."

"Some parents think it will hurt their child to be reprimanded, so they write notes pleading mercy for unfinished homework," Pam said. "They are missing a chance to teach their children responsibility. In the long run children suffer when they aren't taught to act properly. Hollow words of praise can't fix the deeper problems."

Many modern parents have the belief that low self-esteem is a concrete condition, like low blood sugar, that a doctor can fix. Parents have the mistaken idea that praise will make their children feel good about themselves. But false praise doesn't improve children's self-esteem. When children are working hard to do the right thing, little praise is necessary. Children know when they are being useful. This isn't to suggest that we shouldn't praise children for good work, but rather to say that the good work, not the praise, is what helps children feel good about themselves.

The stories that follow look at various aspects of character. In the first story, Victoria wanted me to fix her son's low self-esteem. Andrew had been loved but not challenged, and he was growing up passive and mildly depressed. The next story is about a young man of good character who was preparing to leave home. Shawn and his mother, Hannah, were sorting out how close was too close, an issue complicated by several factors. Hannah was a single parent and her older parents depended on Shawn for yard work and errands. Also Shawn was gay and worried about how he would fare in our intolerant culture. Yet he didn't want fear to have power over his life and overly determine his decisions. Ann's and Flossie's story is of a family struggling with addictions, divorce and too many therapists. The conflicts about limits and discipline between Ann and her former husband make it almost impossible for Flossie to feel protected by her parents. The last story is about Izella and Lloyd, who are older, poorer and less sophisticated than most families I see. Their youngest daughter had recently died of AIDS. Even though they are in poor health and raising their granddaughter, they both work full-time at a factory that requires physical labor.

ANDREW (16) AND VICTORIA

Victoria, dressed in a white sundress that showed off her tan, carried a copy of *Crazy Wisdom*. She wore ankle bracelets and had turquoise beads woven into her hair. Andrew was smaller and paler, with narrow shoulders, a nose ring and dyed yellow hair. He wore faded jeans, old boots and a T-shirt that said, "Eat shit, corporate America."

"I'm here for Andrew," Victoria said. "He has no friends. He has terminal low self-esteem. Maybe he needs some affirmations."

Andrew shrugged. "I'm not doing anything wrong."

"Andrew, honey," Victoria said. "You aren't doing anything. You need a life."

"Andrew is what I call severely gifted," she continued. "Last quarter, he made an F in study skills. That takes some doing in this era of grade inflation."

Andrew sighed. "I was sick."

"Andrew has asthma, lactose intolerance and irritable bowel syndrome," Victoria said. "Last semester he had chronic fatigue syndrome."

I asked about interests. Andrew shrugged.

"I've offered to pay for guitar lessons, but he's not interested." Victoria sighed.

I asked Victoria about chores, work, rules and consequences. "I don't like to be the heavy. I want Andrew to do what's right for him," Victoria said.

We talked some about the past. Victoria was the youngest daughter in the family of an Iowa banker. She had everything a child could want—family support, art and music lessons, expensive camps and travel. In the early 1970s, she attended college at a posh private school. She majored in art history, but soon was cutting classes to drop acid and smoke dope. Most of her education was outside the classroom. Her college career reminded me of the Bob Dylan line "You've gone to the finest schools, Miss Lonely, but you know you only used to get juiced in them."

In her sophomore year, Victoria got pregnant. She dropped out of school and moved back to her small Iowa town. At first her family was angry and rejecting. Her parents worried about their reputation. Her mother blamed herself; she felt that she must have raised Victoria wrong. All the siblings were upset that Victoria, with all her privileges, would choose to "ruin her life." But after Andrew was born, her parents cheered up and forgave her. They made sure that Victoria could afford to be home with her son. Victoria's older siblings were more judgmental, especially her brother Joe, who was, to quote Victoria, "a solid but smug citizen."

When Andrew was a toddler, Victoria lived in Boulder. Then during Andrew's elementary years they moved to Santa Fe, where Victoria studied Native American religions. For a brief time, while his mother was involved with a writer named Jake, Andrew had a "father figure." But Victoria eventually left Jake. As she put it, "He wanted to settle down into a traditional family and that scared the hell out of me."

After Santa Fe, they lived in India, where Victoria visited various holy places. Then, when Andrew was in eighth grade, they rented an apartment in the Village. Andrew went to a private school for gifted kids and Victoria joined a Sufi sect. But Andrew was arrested for selling pot in Washington Square Park and Victoria decided that they needed the "stability" of the Midwest. An aged aunt had died and they moved into her mansion. They still traveled, though, mainly to Europe, India and California.

As Victoria talked about their trips, Andrew casually illustrated all the moves that stewards make when they demonstrate safety features in planes. She stopped talking to watch, and he recited an entire airplane safety talk. We laughed and Victoria said, "Maybe he should be an air steward. He knows more about airports and flying than anyone else in the world."

As Victoria shared their history I noticed how different these two were. Victoria had a new lover, fitness and watercolor classes and a job at an art gallery. She belonged to the local Zen temple. She was the archetypal "trust fund hippie." She had enough money to support her spiritual growth, her travel and her cultural pursuits. But the life that energized and excited Victoria seemed to drain Andrew. All this diversity had worn him out. When I asked him what he thought of all the travels, he shrugged his thin shoulders and said, "Whatever."

Several problems had led Andrew to a state of total lassitude. Andrew needed more long-term relationships to give his life depth and perspective. Victoria had very few expectations of Andrew and rarely insisted on good behavior. All the money was a problem too. Having a job gives people a reason to get out of bed in the morning. Rich people often have trouble structuring their lives. There's more drift and ennui.

Victoria was so worried about stressing Andrew that she hadn't allowed him enough challenges to grow. Challenges, successfully met, produce resilience. Andrew had the resilience of a gardenia. Victoria had worried about Andrew's feelings, but she hadn't worried enough about his skills. He couldn't do much besides fiddle with his computer. I doubted he could change a tire, throw a softball or cook a meal.

Finally, there was Victoria's fear of truncating Andrew's growth by imposing a belief system on him. Victoria assumed that because Andrew was bright, he could develop a philosophy on his own. But Andrew had been given so many options that he seemed paralyzed.

Today Victoria's face reminded me of another line from the 1960s, the Electric Flag line "Behind your broken mirror you only see unhappy eyes." Victoria had grown up the center of attention, with every external need gratified. For someone so flighty, she'd had too many choices, too much sail and not enough centerboard. Her drug use hadn't helped her think clearly about her situation. Nor had all her therapy gurus. She was adrift and unsteady, but I liked her honesty and sense of humor. I found her simple admission that she had made mistakes disarming and I respected her genuine concern for her son. She loved, to quote her, "my yellow-haired good guy."

I was unsure where to begin with Andrew and Victoria. Usually I would start with chores, rules and expectations. But Victoria didn't believe in those things. I asked about his aunt and uncle, cousins and grandparents. Maybe Andrew could visit someone who could teach him to work. I wanted him to be involved in some activity where he was actually learning a skill—woodworking, guitar playing, gardening, anything. Andrew needed to see how most of the world lived. He was ready for a little "shock therapy."

Victoria said that an Iowa reunion was coming up, but she hadn't planned on going. She dreaded seeing her judgmental brother and prissy sisters. She said woefully, "I have nothing in common with those people." But I pushed her to reconsider, and to her surprise, Andrew agreed with me.

I suggested they prepare for this reunion carefully. Victoria could draw Andrew a family tree and tell him what she knew about people in the family. Andrew said he'd like to visit his great-grandparents' homestead and the graveyard where all the family members were buried. I suggested getting out any old pictures and talking over the family history. We scheduled a session for a week after their return from the reunion

Session Two

Victoria and Andrew arrived late and Victoria explained that they had stopped to buy Gas and Shop cappuccinos. Victoria carried a bag of purchases from Under the Rainbow Tarot and Mystical Equipment. Andrew had holes fashionably cut in the knees of his jeans, but his nose ring was missing. He explained that he took it off for Iowa and couldn't find it later. I asked about the reunion.

"It was better than I thought it would be," Victoria said. "Of course, I thought I'd be burned at the stake."

She laughed and sipped her cappuccino. "Seriously, after all these years, nobody seemed to care much that Andrew was born out of wedlock. My sisters and brother were just happy to see us."

Andrew said, "They were geeky, but I liked them." He pulled out a picture of Joe's son Reuben, his ten-year-old cousin, and said, "Reuben asked me where I had been all his life."

"I was angry at all of them. I let that keep us away. But things change. Even Joe has calmed down," Victoria said. "It felt good to be with people who had known me my whole life. We had some things in common— like our grandparents, our family vacations and old pets."

"We walked out on the homeplace," Andrew said. He pulled out a horseshoe and some nails that he'd found. "I didn't get sick the whole time I was there."

Victoria winked at me. "He sounds like someone out of *Heidi* or *Anne of Green Gables.*"

Andrew said, "We're going back at Thanksgiving."

Victoria said ruefully, "I don't think I want to spend a lot of time in Iowa. Once a year is plenty for me. But you can go there. Just don't become a Republican." She turned to me. "Dad offered to teach him to play golf. What do you think?"

I asked Andrew what he thought. "I'll look pretty weird on the course with all those guys in white pants and polyester shirts. But if Granddad will take me I'll go."

I congratulated them on re-finding their family. I predicted that many good things would come from these new connections. Then I asked if Andrew might consider looking for a job.

SHAWN (17) AND HANNAH

Early Monday morning, I met with Shawn and his mother, Hannah. Shawn wore black jeans and a black jacket with a button that said, "Closets are for clothes." When he came in, he handed me a flier for *Jesus Christ Superstar,* the senior play that he would be in the next week. Hannah was a feminist lobbyist whom I'd seen before on TV. Then she was relaxed and confident but today she was stressed. I asked what was going on.

"We need help making decisions about Shawn's future," Hannah said.

"We are both pretty emotional and an outside party might help us think clearly."

Four years earlier Hannah's husband had died of a heart attack. Since then Hannah and Shawn had leaned on each other. Like many single mothers, Hannah worried that they were too close and that she was being too controlling about the college decision. She said, "I couldn't bear Thanksgiving and Christmas without Shawn." She looked at me imploringly. "I want to be involved in Shawn's life. But I don't want to suffocate him."

"I want to be near Mom," Shawn said. "But I'd like to live where there are more gays."

"Shawn's been out since junior high," said Hannah. "Safety is an issue. He's been harassed."

"Insecure idiots feel compelled to prove their manhood by hassling me. Recently though, it's gotten worse." Shawn pulled out some notes and read one aloud. "Die, die, gay scum" and another, "Look behind you, queer boy."

I asked about suspects. "There are some kids at my school who would do this." Shawn pushed back his hair. "The cruelty of some people is unbelievable."

Hannah shuddered. "We don't think there's much more we can do. Shawn's locking his car doors and staying near friends at school. But we're not sleeping well."

"Especially you, Mom." Shawn hugged his mother. "You're the one having nightmares. I'm actually tougher than you think."

Shawn had red blotches on his neck , but he spoke calmly. "We've notified the police, but so what. It's hard to get fingerprints off paper."

"This will pass. We'll survive it, " Hannah said. "But it adds another dimension to our discussion of colleges."

She explained that they had lived in the same house since Shawn was born. Her parents lived in town. Shawn had friends from kindergarten days who were fiercely loyal. At school everyone knew him from plays. She said, "Shawn doesn't really want to move, but he wants to be accepted for who he is."

"I'd love to go to NYU or San Francisco State. But cities aren't exactly Meccas these days. Cities have gay bashing. I don't know where I'd be safer." Shawn gestured expansively and continued, "I'd miss everyone. My grandparents are getting old. When they need help, I want to be here for them."

Hannah added, "Shawn doesn't like to give thugs power over his life. He wants to live where he can get the best education. I agree with him intellectually, but emotionally I want him to protect himself."

"New York and San Francisco are exciting places, but I'm a low-key person," Shawn said. "I don't want to be on Broadway. I want to do children's theater and community playhouse."

Hannah said, "Shawn mows my folks' yard and helps them with the garden and home repairs. He goes there for lunch on school days. We don't want to split up our family, but we want Shawn to have every opportunity. We don't know how close we should be."

It was good they were here. We could discuss the issue of how close is too close, which in our culture is a particularly difficult issue for mothers and sons. I could help by assuring Hannah that her desire to stay connected with Shawn was not pathological, but healthy and understandable. I could label what she feared was codependency as love. In a culture that looks suspiciously at mother-son closeness, I could give Shawn permission to love his mother.

I hoped it would help them to talk about the harassment. Being chronically afraid wears people down. The decision about college was a difficult values clarification task. Shawn needed to sort out what was more important—family or educational opportunities, the anonymity of a more diverse but less interested world or the warmth, and sometimes intolerance, of the hometown.

I recommended that they visit schools in New York and San Francisco. I also stressed that no decision was irrevocable. The choice of a college was an experiment. Shawn could begin at our local university and see how he liked it. Or he could leave for a while and come back. The most important thing was the care and thoughtfulness of their decision-making process.

After they left, I thought of them. It made me angry that good families worried that closeness was pathological. Their closeness was what gave them hope and support. Shawn and Hannah were healthy people living in a society that was making their lives needlessly difficult. I hated that other boys had to prove their manhood by hurting Shawn. Like his mother, I was scared for him. Shawn was likable—funny, gentle and smart—a character at seventeen. Hannah was resilient and loyal. I hoped I could help them make a good decision. I made a note to buy myself a ticket to *Jesus Christ Superstar.*

ANN AND FLOSSIE (11)

Ann looked edgy and exhausted, ready to cry. She fumbled awkwardly with her purse and then clasped her hands together to stop their shaking. Flossie sat defiantly on the couch, a thin girl with a Tropical Splash Barbie. In spite of Flossie's angry posture, there was a dullness in her eyes that belied an underlying sadness. Ann said, "Flossie was released from the hospital yesterday and already we're in trouble."

The previous night Flossie had hit Ann after an argument about rules. Then Flossie had run to a nearby QuickMart and had returned only when Ann promised she wouldn't be punished. This morning Flossie wouldn't go to school. Ann was frantic—she had to go to work. It all was overwhelming.

The first time Flossie was hospitalized was after she beat up a classmate and ran away from school. The truant officer took her to a nearby hospital, where she was evaluated and admitted to the children's unit. She was diagnosed with attention deficit disorder and put on Ritalin. On the unit Flossie met children who were into drugs, alcohol and crime. She was encouraged to talk about her parents' divorce and her problems at home. Unfortunately, while Flossie was in the hospital Ann had been given no guidance, and the day before, when the insurance ran out, Flossie had been discharged. Ann felt as lost as ever, only now they had no insurance coverage to pay for further help.

After hearing Ann's story, I was surprised that she would trust another mental health professional. But I realized what brought them in wasn't so much trust as despair. As Ann talked, Flossie interrupted with remarks such as "You're so stupid" and "You're lying." Ann seemed resigned to this kind of rudeness but embarrassed that I was seeing it. Finally I asked Flossie to wait in the lobby.

Ann spoke more freely with her daughter out of the room. She felt Flossie was vulnerable and that it was her fault. She and Jack had married as teenagers. When she was pregnant, Ann had smoked marijuana. Flossie weighed only four pounds at birth and was a colicky, demanding baby. Jack was a heavy drinker who was unwilling to help much with

Flossie. "He was too young to be a dad. Babies made him nervous," Ann said.

Ann had trouble with breast-feeding and felt bad when the doctor recommended she switch to bottle-feeding. Six weeks after Flossie's birth, Ann returned to work as a bank teller. She hated leaving Flossie in the crowded day-care center with its overworked staff. With the pressures of working and caring for an infant and with the stresses of her marriage, Ann developed insomnia. She tossed and turned all night, then staggered to work in the morning. She visited her doctor, who prescribed sleeping pills. Ann said, "For a while I was hooked on them." She shook her head sadly. "Our family was a mess."

Jack was a hard-charging salesman. He depended on Ann for social life, household chores, cooking and sex, but except for money, he gave her little in return. He worked long hours and then came home plastered. He called Ann's discussions about their relationship "whining."

Over time Jack and Ann had less and less to say to each other. They tried therapy. Ann explained it to me. "The therapist would say to Jack that I meant this, and then to me that Jack meant that. It was like we were so complicated and emotionally constricted that we couldn't actually talk to each other. But therapy didn't help. Maybe if the therapist had moved in with us . . ."

When Flossie was nine, Ann came home early one day and found Jack in their bedroom with her friend. She wasn't actually surprised. In fact, it was almost a relief to have a good reason to call off the marriage. Ann divorced Jack and dropped her friend. But the affair was just one of many problems. She said, "I left Jack because I hated what I became in that marriage."

Ann and Jack had spoiled Flossie, but the divorce made things worse. Ann was overworked and depressed. Jack was self-absorbed and indulgent, a Disneyland dad who treated Flossie to candy, movies and shopping trips on the weekends.

Like many people who behave badly, Jack needed to monsterfy the person he had hurt. If Ann weren't a monster, how could he justify his lousy behavior toward her? So as time went by, Jack demonized Ann. He told Flossie that he felt sorry she had to live with someone so emotionally disturbed. He implied that it made sense that she would act up. Ann said, "Jack wouldn't have taken Flossie for all the money in the world. He just liked sabotaging me."

Flossie's behavior worsened. She saw monsters coming out of the walls and the closets and she begged to sleep with Ann. She hit other kids and refused to do her homework. She developed a manipulative and dishonest style of getting her way. When Ann wasn't right on top of her, Flossie ran wild. And as she became more difficult, Ann's parenting fell apart. She'd let things slide and then blow up. Ann didn't believe in physical punishment, but twice she lost her temper and slapped Flossie. Jack reported her for child abuse.

After a while, everyone was in counseling. Ann sighed. "At the time I felt that all the treatment in the world couldn't fix such a catastrophe. Jack and I had jumped off a cliff. Therapists could only ask us how we felt about falling."

Jack saw a therapist to help him cope with his impossible ex-wife who was abusing his daughter. Ann saw a therapist who helped her find her inner child. Flossie saw a play therapist who watched her bang mommie and daddy dolls together and yell "I hate you." In family counseling Jack explained that Flossie was in pain from the emotional abuse that Ann inflicted. Flossie said she loved her dad and hated her mother. Ann told me angrily, "Of course she preferred Jack. He bought her toys and ice-cream bars and let her do whatever she wanted."

The therapist encouraged Ann to use time-outs, but they didn't work. Ann explained, "Flossie loved her room. She watched television, played Nintendo or called her dad." In family therapy, Flossie was encouraged to talk about her anger toward her mother. Ann said bitterly that this approach was "less than helpful." Jack suggested that Flossie would be fine with him. Finally Ann refused to go back to the counseling. She said, "All the suggestions were about how I should change. I was holding down a fifty-hour-a-week job and broke from all the mental health care. I resented being labeled dysfunctional. I'd like to see how the therapist would have handled my life."

But today Ann admitted she maybe should have stayed in therapy. Flossie had gone downhill after they quit. She was labeled a conduct disorder and sent to a special room for kids who can't tolerate regular classrooms. Flossie was in the children of divorce group, but she was expelled after she called the teacher a bitch.

Ann was crying by now. She said, "I'm frustrated as hell. We've spent thousands of dollars. We've had Flossie to several therapists, all of whom told us different things. The school wants her on medication, but I didn't see any improvement when she was on it before. The hospital said she needed long-term treatment, but they charge fifteen thousand dollars a month. Mostly what she did there was watch television and play Ping-Pong."

I handed her Kleenex. She blew her nose and continued. "I know it would be giving up, but I'm ready to give her to Jack. I'd have to force him to take her. He enjoys second-guessing me much more than he'd enjoy raising her himself."

As I watched Ann cry, I thought that my profession hadn't helped her much with all our tests, labels, advice and bills. Too many therapists were worse than none at all. We offered conflicting advice and hopelessly confused her. By now Ann felt more inadequate and disempowered than when she first sought help. With so much conflicting information, she just couldn't seem to get her feet on the ground.

I suspected Jack had done his daughter a great deal of harm by undercutting Ann's authority and by interpreting Flossie's bad behavior as a reaction to inner pain. Perhaps he could tolerate Flossie during the times he had her, but apparently no one else could. I wondered if there were relatives nearby who could step in. Perhaps extended family could diffuse some of the tension between Jack and Ann. Maybe they could agree to a few simple rules for Flossie, such as a policy on swearing and hitting and an insistence that she go to school.

We talked about hospital programs. I said that some children need an assessment of their psychological and social situation and some need medication and treatment planning. When children are out of control in ways that could get them killed, hospitals are sometimes necessary. But in general using hospitals for children's problems is like using a Volkswagen for a paperweight. It's cumbersome, expensive and counterproductive.

I asked to talk with Flossie. Ann said, "You may want to chain me to your front door so I don't leave her with you." I smiled. Flossie reminded me of the boy in the O. Henry story *The Ransom of Red Chief*. That boy had been so dreadful that the kidnappers had paid the parents to take him back. Just to make sure Ann didn't leave me with Flossie, I suggested that she stay in the room.

Flossie plopped down on my couch with Barbie. With feigned indifference, she waited for my questions. On the surface, Flossie was a hurricane of outraged entitlement, but under the surface I detected confusion. Flossie was too powerful and that was scary for her.

She said, "I hate Mom. I can't live with her. I just can't."

"What makes it hard to live with your mother?"

"She's always yelling at me. She may act nice around you, but with me she acts crazy." She sniffed indignantly. "She won't let me get a gerbil."

I said rather sternly, "What have you done to be kind and helpful to your mother?"

Flossie swore under her breath and looked out my window.

Ann looked pathetically heartened by my remarks. I felt for her. Ann had minimal support, lots of people second-guessing her and resources that turned out to be Trojan horses. I recommended we meet with the school people and talk about how to reintegrate Flossie into the classroom. I suggested that Ann contact her parents, who lived nearby, and ask if they could come help her with Flossie. I assigned Ann the task of making a list of rules and consequences for Flossie. I gave a small lecture on respect, which was probably futile but seemed less harmful than my other options. I told Flossie that if she and her parents came to see me we would try to understand her situation. I said I had faith that at some point in the near future she could be a normal girl again and not a chronic mental health client.

I asked to see Jack in the next few days. I wanted his perspective and I wanted to make a plea for his cooperation and support of Ann. Also, he needed to be firmer with Flossie. Perhaps I could suggest that having a dad who set no limits caused children immense inner pain. I asked Flossie to write me a list of all the things she had to thank her mother for. She looked stunned by the assignment.

I hoped Ann could later form a parent support group in her neighborhood. Ann was busy and I knew organizing a group would be a hassle, but Ann was alone and isolated. Neighborhood parents could bond together and support each other. At least it was free.

In the not too distant future, I wanted Flossie out of the hands of mental health professionals. All the therapy hadn't helped Flossie calm down and grow up. Rather the therapy had simultaneously given her excuses for her bad behavior and made her feel different from other kids.

Flossie could be saved, but it would require work with the family and school. Ann especially would need support in her parenting role. Jack would need guidance in how to be a truly helpful father, not merely an indulgent one. Mainly I wished we could turn back the clock. I wished that Ann had been granted more time off at Flossie's birth, that Jack hadn't jumped into bed with his wife's friend and that Ann and Jack had come in for marital therapy before things were so unfixable. I wished Flossie had never been hospitalized. We made an appointment for the next week.

Session Twelve

I'd seen Flossie and Ann for three months now and things were slowly improving. I wished I could have taken more of the credit, but much of it went to Ann's parents. We had included them in some of our discussions and they had made a commitment to helping their daughter and their granddaughter through the crisis. They volunteered to watch Flossie every other weekend. This was a godsend. Ann got a needed break and yet Flossie was with people Ann trusted and who trusted and supported her.

Flossie's schoolteacher had also helped. She'd been strict with Flossie, but also supportive and positive. She praised her good behavior and sincere efforts and saw through her manipulations. Flossie had settled down under her care. The teacher had Flossie tutoring a younger girl in reading. Flossie was going out for track, which helped burn off some of her energy.

Ann was still pretty overwhelmed, but with my support and the weekends off, she was recovering a little energy and optimism. Her sleep was improving, and like most of us, she did better when she wasn't exhausted. Twice Jack had been in with her and they had agreed on some guidelines for Flossie. He was an active alcoholic and a real blamer, but the therapy held him accountable. He knew that if he trashed Ann, we would all discuss it in therapy. That slowed him down some.

Our last session had dealt with mother-daughter misunderstandings. There was a great deal of pain and anger on both sides. I asked each of them to tell the other about her life, about goals and sadnesses, about what happened during the day, about how she felt about herself and about what she saw as her major struggles and victories. While Flossie talked, Ann listened. Then Ann talked and Flossie listened. At the end of the session, Flossie said, "I didn't know you had problems too." As Ann put it, "We are much more alike than I realized."

Today's session was to discuss their healing ceremony. Ann had taken the day off from the bank and looked younger in jeans and a sweatshirt. Now that Flossie was off Ritalin, she was growing again and she looked an inch taller than a month ago. She had turned her Barbie into "Track Star Barbie." Both were excited to tell me about their ceremony.

"We couldn't think of anything for a while," Ann said. "But then Flossie got the idea of designing a shoe box for each year. We wrote everything good and bad that we could think of about every year and we threw it in the appropriate shoe box."

She smiled at Flossie. "I was surprised at how many good things we could both remember."

"In last year's box, Mom stuffed the hospital bills and police reports," Flossie said.

"And you put in your report card and your note about running away." Ann sighed. "Anyway, we had eleven boxes stuffed with junk, mostly bad but some good. We took it to Platte River State Park for an overnight campout. That's where we had our ceremony."

Flossie interrupted. "It was fun. We rented a tent, which took us forever to set up. We hiked the trails and walked over to watch the sunset on the river. Then we built a fire and roasted hot dogs."

"We unloaded all our boxes and used a flashlight to read what we had written. We started at year one and sorted the bad and the good. We burned the bad and put the good notes back in the boxes." She paused and looked at me. "I don't know if a psychologist would approve of that, but it felt right to us."

Flossie finished the story by explaining that afterward they roasted marshmallows. They fed each other perfect marshmallows and then looked at the stars and the fire until they were too sleepy to stay awake.

Ann said, "Flossie fell asleep in my arms. That hasn't happened since she was two years old."

I said I thought their ceremony was wonderful and asked their permission to share it with others.

IZELLA, LLOYD AND MINDY (4)
Izella and Lloyd were referred by the employee assistance person at the dog food factory where they worked. Izella's blood pressure was high and she had arthritis. The counselor was worried that, caring for a young child and working full-time, Izella might get sick. She also worried that Lloyd,

who had been a serious gambler, might start going to the dog tracks again.

The counselor told me a story to illustrate Izella's earthiness. Another woman had been complaining to Izella about her boredom and depression. The woman said that she didn't sleep well and was worried about whether to redecorate her dining room. Izella had listened politely, then said, "You think you've got problems, I just found out my granddaughter has head lice." The counselor laughed. "I want these people to have the support they need to raise Mindy."

On a windy April day, Izella limped into my office. Her hand shielded her lower back from its spasms. She was a heavy woman with thin gray hair and a plain face. She wore polyester slacks with hose underneath and a slick orange top. She moved awkwardly over to the couch, which she dropped into with a sigh. She reminded me of something my aunt said, about "needing porters to carry the bags under her eyes."

Lloyd followed her, clearly uneasy to be in a psychologist's office. He was wiry, black-haired and still rakishly handsome if you ignored the wrinkles and tattoos. He wore jeans, cowboy boots and a starched white dress shirt. When he smiled he revealed a gold front tooth.

Izella said, "We're here about our grandbaby, Mindy. We made big mistakes with our own kids and we don't want history to repeat itself."

Mindy had come to live with them after Izella's daughter died six months before. They had been devastated by her slow, painful death. Lana had been a sweet girl, the most loving of all the children, but she had problems with drugs and men. As Izella put it, Lana was "a bum magnet." Lana had found men who liked cocaine. Over the years any money she had "went up her nose." Her last partner, Mindy's father, had left her when he found out she was HIV positive. She was six months pregnant with Mindy at the time.

Izella wiped her eyes and said, "Watching Lana die of AIDS was the hardest thing we ever did."

Fortunately Mindy wasn't HIV positive, but she had been born prematurely and addicted to crack. She'd been a colicky baby and slow to develop. Her speech wasn't good and she had trouble sitting still. Her first years had been with a sick, drug-addicted mother. Izella and Lloyd had watched her some, but mostly she'd lived with Lana.

When Lana died, Mindy moved in. Mindy was small, awkward and developmentally delayed. Lloyd and Izella found caring for a young one difficult. They moved slowly and needed their sleep. Carrying Mindy hurt Izella's back. But Izella said, "Me and Lloyd want to do all we can for her. If you think she needs special help, tell us where to go."

This couple had survived a great deal. Izella prefaced her family history by saying, "You may not believe my family stories." She had many memories of poverty and shame. Her father had been the town drunk and her mother had been overwhelmed by bitterness. As a baby, Izella had been hospitalized for malnutrition. She said, "Maybe that's why I have my weight problems today. As a child, I couldn't get enough food."

Mostly they ate potatoes. She said, "In the South poor folks were either potato or bean families. We were a potato family. Us kids wouldn't eat beans no matter what." Her mother never gave compliments, especially to Izella, who was chubby and plain. Izella had happy memories of a grandmother who sometimes baked her molasses cookies. She still ate molasses cookies when she was sad.

Izella married her first husband when she was fifteen, "just to get away from home." As she recalled her years with Raymond, Izella shook her head. "He was mean as a snake. I don't know why I put up with him all those years. I guess I got pretty beaten down."

She had three children with Raymond, and actually she left him because of the children. She would put up with abuse herself, but wouldn't let Raymond inflict it on the kids. One night at dinner her son spilled juice and Raymond picked up the boy, threw him on the floor and kicked him. Izella fought him off, but her son had two broken ribs and a black eye. After Raymond left the house, she took her son to the doctor. Then she returned home and packed up the other kids. Raymond threatened to kill her if she didn't return. But she said, "Living with Raymond was worse than being dead."

She and the children were often hungry. She said, "Once Mom gave us a bushel of apples and that's all we had for a week. Another week we lived on Spaghettios sandwiches." But Izella found work as a waitress. She said, "I was bone tired all the time, but I paid my bills and kept the house clean. The kids got birthday and Christmas presents."

Lloyd also grew up poor in the South. His mother had a humped back from picking cotton. When Lloyd was eleven, his dad died in a farm accident and Lloyd supported his mother and younger sisters. He said, "By the time I was eighteen, I'd worked more than most people do in a lifetime." Lloyd worked in the oil fields all through his twenties and sent money home. He got married when he was thirty and fathered three kids. But the marriage lasted only seven years. He said, "I was the problem. I was as considerate as a wild boar." He'd sent his first wife child support for fifteen years and still kept in touch with his kids, who were grown and lived in Florida. He and Izella went down to fish with them every other year.

Izella met Lloyd when she was fishing at one of the muddy lakes around Lincoln. "He came over and helped me rig catfish lines."

Lloyd laughed. "I always knew I'd marry a woman who fished." They dated for several months and then flew to Las Vegas for their wedding. Izella loved the shows and had a good time, even though Lloyd lost all their honeymoon money playing blackjack.

Lloyd was good to her and her kids. He never let his bad habits interfere with work. He made good money, he just didn't hold on to it well. They lived in a trailer south of town. Izella gardened and raised chickens. Just the night before she had set out the tomato plants. Lloyd continued to take her and the kids fishing. Until the kids started having trouble, they were happy.

Izella's son was killed in a car accident when he was nineteen. He'd had alcohol problems like his dad and was driving drunk. Lana dropped out of school and drove them nuts with her choices of men. But their other daughter, Lora, was the success story. She was married to a man who managed a Burger King and she had a good job as an X-ray technician at a hospital. Lora and her husband had two young children and were buying their own home. Izella and Lloyd were tremendously proud of that. As Izella put it, "She's the first one in the family to be a property owner."

Lloyd and Izella's work got harder as they aged. Izella had her back and heart problems, but at least Lloyd had quit drinking. He said, "Izella couldn't handle all their problems and me drunk at the same time." But after years of heavy drinking, Lloyd's liver was "pretty much shot." He said, "A bottle of Southern Comfort would kill me."

They lived in the same trailer they'd had since they were married and, except for their Florida trips, bought nothing but the basics. For years, Lloyd had lost his paychecks at the tracks and he'd "borrowed" money from Izella's credit cards. He still gambled, but not as much. Izella managed their money. She gave Lloyd a little for Powerball and keno. He dreamed of buying a house and a Cadillac. As Izella said, "We'll never own a house unless he does win. Five bucks a week isn't much to keep a dream going."

Izella had none of the blessings and all of the curses of this stage of life. She had led a life of poverty, neglect and abuse. But she had kept her spirits up through difficult circumstances. She was a hero in the truest sense of the word, someone who could endure chronic adversity with dignity. Izella reminded me of Japanese shibui-style pots: dull sienna brown on the outside and inside, a glazed and sparkling blue, surprisingly beautiful.

Lloyd had his serious flaws, but he too was loyal and loving. He'd worked hard his whole life and had less than a thousand dollars to his name. He'd made many mistakes, but he'd learned some things along the way. With his beloved grandbaby he wanted to be more careful. Children had become more precious to him as he grew older. He would do whatever was necessary to help Mindy, including seeing a therapist.

Lloyd and Izella were tough around all the broken places. Like many people who have suffered a great deal, they'd learned to appreciate what they could in each day. Little things made them happy. Izella liked the polka mass at her church. Lloyd bragged he'd won a Thanksgiving turkey at bingo. They loved to buy Mindy a new toy or dress.

At one time they had consumed pretty much everything noxious that our culture sells—tobacco, gambling and booze. But as they got older they had sorted out their priorities and made reasonably good decisions about what they would consume. They were spending less time at the dog tracks and more at the lake, less time drinking and more with their grandchildren.

Izella pulled out pictures of the grandchildren to show me. She'd just taken all the grandkids to Kmart for professional photographs. Lora's girls were blond and serious. Mindy had red hair and dimples and smiled rakishly like her grandfather. We talked about a parenting education group and Head Start for Mindy. I recommended that they read stories to her and take her to the library for books. I supported their efforts to have her outdoors—gardening and fishing with them. I encouraged them to spend as much time as they could with Lora and her family. The other children would be good for Mindy, and Lora sounded good for Lloyd and Izella.

At the end of the hour I congratulated them on their courage and self-sacrifice. I asked them if they wanted to reschedule. Izella said, "I believe it might do us some good." Lloyd was more restrained. "It wasn't as bad as I thought it would be. I liked your advice about going fishing."

Chapter Nine

WILL

I define will as the ability to act on the basis of one's values. Often will is a problem for adults who came of age post-Vietnam, post-Watergate, post-Chernobyl and post-Exxon-Valdez. Since birth the current generation of young adults has been fed a steady diet of junk food and junk values. The information they have received is unsorted and unconnected. It makes the world one giant word salad. Their values come from ads, talk shows, popular psychology, music, comics and movies.

Plato said, "Education is teaching children to find pleasure in the right things." This generation has been educated via the media to find pleasure in many wrong things—alcohol, casual sex, violence and consumption. Cynicism is king. Ideas are trivialized and the sacred becomes profane. In the popular culture, everything is a joke—murder, dismemberment, cruelty, politics and religion. There is so much information and so little sense.

While many of our young adults are moving gracefully into responsible adulthood, many are in trouble. This generation is sophisticated, cynical and tired. There's a morass of angst. Some young adults are dissatisfied with corporate consumer values. They drop out of mainstream culture and go trekking in Tibet or work minimum-wage jobs and write poetry. Some reject the emptiness of our modern times, others struggle to join the middle class. Some become religious to cope with the moral chaos around them.

This generation doesn't read much. Many young people know more about soap operas than Shakespeare, more about gangster rap than government. The decision to have sex can be as casual as the decision to see a movie, and as meaningful. Many young adults have had dozens of sexual partners and no real relationships. There is lots of "shacking," "boning" and "getting play" and not much sexual joy.

This generation is the "I want" generation. They have been educated to entitlement and programmed for discontent. Ads have encouraged this generation to have material expectations they can't fulfill. Money confers moral superiority and poverty is considered a moral crime, a sign of personal failure. Poverty means that you can't have what you have been programmed to want. Poverty means danger—high-crime neighborhoods, cars that break down on dark streets and jobs in places that are at high risk to be robbed.

Many young adults feel passive and disempowered. The world is harsh and conscience is perceived as a luxury. Most young adults are good-hearted but have little faith in social change. They see activists as naive and they limit their acts of goodness to friends and family. Work is not seen as an opportunity to create good on the planet, but as a way to make money. Young adults sense that things are terrible in the broader culture and so they try to care for themselves.

This generation has been sold down the river and they know it. Their cynicism and anger are understandable but tragic. Cynicism is not an energizing emotional state. It is harder, but much healthier, to care, to try to make the world better. However, caring sets them up for mockery and possible failure. It's safer not to care.

The stories in this chapter are about young people searching for guidance. Gabe and Vicky Lou are ill prepared for the parenting responsibilities they now face. Their junk-value system just doesn't serve them very well. Aubrey hates high school and makes a bold decision to educate herself. The last stories are of two families with young children. Edwardo and Sabrina are exhausted and demoralized from their lack of time and money. As things get tough, they blame each other. But they rush to do what's best for their family as soon as they can see it. The last story is of Grace, who models how to survive as a single parent. Grace's moral capital is greater than the wealth of many of her peers.

GABE, VICKY LOU AND HAROLD (2)

An emergency room doctor referred Gabe, Vicky Lou and Harold to me. The night before, Gabe had yanked on baby Harold's arm and accidentally broken it. As Harold moaned in pain, they'd driven to the hospital. The doctors treated Harold's arm and his shock and reported the parents for child abuse.

Harold was thin and grubby, with a sparkling white cast on his arm. His blond hair was dirty and uncombed, his face tear streaked. He wore only a T-shirt and a heavily loaded diaper. I wondered why the nurses hadn't washed him up while they had had a chance. He snuggled in beside Vicky Lou, with a plastic bottle that looked like it contained Kool-Aid and stared at me with wide blue eyes. I smiled at him and he burrowed deeper into his mother's side.

Vicky Lou was chubby, with heavy makeup and perfume. She'd been a runaway from abusive parents. When she got pregnant, she was making her living as an exotic dancer. When she mentioned the dancing, she gestured toward her stomach and said, "I wasn't such a fat cow back then."

Gabe was nervous and unshaven, already wrinkled from weather and tobacco. When there was work, he built levees on the Missouri. Other times he did construction work or collected unemployment. He was a man of few words who depended on Vicky Lou to explain things. But when she talked he smiled scornfully, as if he were above such mundane events as conversations. As Gabe sat awkwardly in my office, he reminded me of Tennessee Williams's line about "the terrible stiff-necked pride of the defeated."

Vicky Lou explained that they had met at her club and had been going out only a few weeks when she got pregnant. When she told the news to Gabe, he was upset. He was already paying child support for two children by mothers in Alabama and Oklahoma. Gabe let Vicky Lou move in, but he was waiting to "see how things worked out before getting hitched." When he said this, Vicky Lou looked yearningly at him. He folded his arms and stared with great interest at the wall calendar.

Gabe and Vicky Lou had no family nearby. Gabe had a few drinking buddies. Vicky Lou liked the woman who ran the convenience store down the street, but she talked to her only when she went in to buy snacks or disposable diapers. During the day Vicky Lou watched the talk shows and soaps. At night she and Gabe bought a pizza and a twelve-pack and rented a video. He liked Jackie Chan martial arts movies. Her favorite movies were *Dirty Dancing* and *Pretty Woman*.

I asked about Harold's injury. Vicky Lou said, "He was running around like a chicken with his head cut off. I gave him way too much candy.

Gabe yanked his arm, just to slow him down, and he must have pulled it funny because it broke."

Gabe reluctantly explained that the day before he and his co-workers had been laid off "temporarily." After getting their pink slips they bought some Jim Beam and drove to a lake. Gabe got home late and wanted Vicky Lou to fry him some eggs while he watched the ten o'-clock news. Gabe denied being drunk when he pulled Harold's arm, but he admitted that alcohol didn't improve his disposition any. He said, "Vicky Lou should have put him in bed hours ago."

Vicky Lou nodded in agreement. She lived in an environment that reeked of failure, a world of heavy drinkers and adults who hit their kids. Except when she was dancing, she'd never received much attention. Gabe had belted her a few times. She didn't like it, but it seemed normal. Sometimes she felt she deserved it. Mainly she was worried about my report. She didn't want any "do-gooders" taking Harold away from her and Gabe.

The layoff came at a bad time. Gabe and Vicky Lou were overdrawn at the bank and buried under credit card debts. Every day Vicky Lou got harassing calls from companies that had been eager to extend credit but were brutal when payments weren't made on time. They were two months behind on their car payments and expected it to be repossessed at any time. Finally Gabe concluded, "I owe a guy for two tickets to the Ted Nugent concert."

One night when Gabe was out drinking, Vicky Lou had ordered jewelry from the shopping channel. Next month the payment would start on the couch they had bought a year ago on the "buy now pay later" plan. Already Harold and their dog had ruined the couch. Gabe had some gambling debts that he didn't want to discuss. As we talked, he rubbed his chin nervously. Finally he said, "I ought to just shoot myself and be done with it."

Gabe had quit school in the ninth grade and he was easy pickings for anyone with something to sell, be it alcohol, nicotine, TV sets or pickle cards. His family had no health insurance or savings. When he got anxious about his situation, he got drunk or hit somebody. Vicky Lou seemed so young and unformed that she reminded me of a John Prine song about "the oldest baby in the world." She faced problems that would overwhelm a good coper—money crises, parenting problems and an alcohol-dependent, abusive mate. She had no diploma, job skills or family support and her career as an exotic dancer clearly was over. Her options were limited—she could stay with Gabe or be on the streets. She felt guilty about her weight, her spending and her nagging and she blamed herself for Harold's broken arm.

I asked Gabe and Vicky Lou what they needed. Gabe said, "We don't need nothing. Nobody gives a damn about us anyway."

"We could use a thousand dollars," Vicky Lou said. She looked meaningfully at Gabe. "And a wedding."

Both Gabe and Vicky Lou needed more parenting themselves. Vicky Lou needed a mother to help with her son and her budget and to encourage her to stand up for herself. Harold needed a father who didn't drink or hit his wife. They hadn't been well parented, and in any era they would have needed help from the broader culture. Unfortunately, in our current culture there were many people eager to capitalize on their ignorance.

Gabe and Vicky Lou had learned all the wrong lessons. They were hooked on the worst junk our culture peddles. They spent money they didn't have on things they didn't need. Meanwhile, their real needs, for health care, decent wages, parenting assistance and community support, had not been met.

I felt overwhelmed as I pondered where to begin. They could use relationship and financial counseling, parenting classes, day-care relief and nurses' visits to check on Harold. Harold could use Head Start and a visit to the dentist. Vicky Lou could use assertiveness training and a tutor to help her pass the GED. Gabe needed job skills and alcohol treatment. I thought of how expensive these services were and how unlikely it was that they could all be arranged. I felt angry that as a culture we make it so easy for families like this to fail.

Over the long haul I wanted to help them with their relationship to chemicals and consumption. This couple needed help sorting out their relationship to the broader culture. Instead of just letting things happen to them, they needed to screen what they would take in and what they wouldn't. For the short term I recommended that Vicky Lou take Harold outside, to a park or a swimming pool. I suggested they watch a sunset or look at the stars and think about what was really important to them. This advice confused them, but they humored me and nodded okay. I doubted they would do it. I referred Gabe to an anger control group. His jaw set and lips tightened. I wondered if he would go.

In fact, Vicky Lou was right. They did need a thousand dollars. Gabe would get unemployment for eight weeks and then they'd be hungry. Our town had some minimum-wage work available, but a family can't survive on that money. I brushed away my thoughts about their future.

Harold was dozing by now and Gabe picked him up carefully. The boy hung on trustingly to his father's bony shoulders. Vicky Lou picked up the bottle and padded out after them. After they left, I watched through the window as the family piled into their soon-to-be-repossessed car. Harold was off to a tough start.

AUBREY (16)

Late one October afternoon I met Aubrey and her parents. Aubrey had purple hair and a septum pierce and wore an unusual combination of clothes—hiking boots, tights and a flannel shirt over a silky pink undershirt. She plopped into a chair and looked defiantly around the room. Her parents looked much less lively. Gene, dressed in a rumpled suit, explained he had a meeting with his elementary-school staff in an hour. Muriel looked frazzled as she announced she had too many students in her fifth-grade class. I asked why the family was in my office.

Muriel said, "Aubrey's been out of school since October tenth. If she isn't there tomorrow, she'll be kicked out."

"Be still my heart," Aubrey said sarcastically.

"Aubrey says that she can't stand the boredom of school, but I wonder if that's a bunch of hooey, an excuse for laziness," said Gene.

Aubrey spoke again. "From the great gene pool that is my being, I am grateful that I didn't inherit the tendency to use the word 'hooey.' "

"Aubrey has a smart mouth," said Gene wearily.

"What happened on October tenth?"

"I had my sixteenth birthday and I wasn't legally required to go anymore. I was sitting in government class when I realized that I didn't give a flying fuck about federalism or anything else I was hearing that day." She yawned elaborately. "I've hated school since junior high. I'm going to be a musician."

Aubrey had a litany of familiar complaints about her junior-high days—lots of name-calling and teasing, girls hurting each other, boys being too sexual and aggressive, a rape in the school bathroom and guns in the parking lot. And she had complaints that were her own. She hated "titty twister days" and flip-up days when boys flipped up girls' skirts. Two boys who were failing English destroyed her creative writing project. Someone drew a swastika on her friend Emma's locker. Aubrey hated the pain that racism caused her friend. She and Emma talked about dropping out together.

"School was fucking awful," she said. "I acted the way my parents taught me to act, no one would speak to me."

She laughed. "When I dressed wild and took up smoking, I dazzled my peers. Within weeks, I was invited to all the parties. You wouldn't believe the parties—kids getting drunk and sick and getting laid in bathrooms. Fuck."

She leaned forward and waved her arms dramatically as she spoke. "I hoped high school would be better but it was worse. Our school had gangs. My classes sucked canal water. Some of the teachers were okay, but they spent all their time controlling the troublemakers. Kids were assholes to each other."

We talked about drugs. Aubrey asked, "Did you ever hear that saying 'Reality is for people who can't handle drugs'? That's what high school is like. All the cool kids used. Emma and I dropped acid and went to shows."

"We always thought Aubrey needed the socialization of school," Muriel said. "But we aren't sure now that we want her socialized."

Gene turned to me. "We suspected that Aubrey was using, but we couldn't control her. We both work. It was impossible to hire a sitter for a teenager. The drugs scared us."

"Let's not go there," Aubrey interrupted. She waved away her father's concerns. "I hardly use drugs at all. I'm more worried about my friends." She told us about Molly, who was in a relationship with a drug dealer and had tried crack; about Heather, who grew marijuana in her window box, and about Candice, who was stockpiling pills for a suicide attempt. Even Emma smoked pot before school. Aubrey worried about busts. As she put it, "Everybody learns that it's cool to do drugs, but if they are caught they're locked up forever."

As I listened to Aubrey talk, I thought, No wonder she hates school. The halls were emotional mine fields. Who could concentrate or relax with all this going on? I asked if her friends could talk to school counselors. Aubrey shook her head. "The counselors don't have time to talk."

"We've suggested other friends," Gene said. "But Aubrey claims that all groups have their problems."

Aubrey interrupted. "I've outgrown school."

When I asked her what she wanted instead, she knew. "Travel, playing in a band full-time, editing a zine, visiting San Francisco."

"Aubrey is a plan-hatching organism. She constantly cooks up ideas for herself. Her plans aren't very practical and that creates tension between us." Muriel looked at Aubrey and continued. "She says things to me I would never have said to my mother. Sometimes I'm too shocked to respond."

"It's hard to watch Aubrey screw up her life," said Gene. "The hardest thing about parenting is that you can't protect your kids from themselves."

"Especially when we don't want protection," said Aubrey.

"Right on," said Gene sadly.

Gene and Muriel wanted Aubrey to explore the world and be safe, to get on with her peers and yet not be self-destructive. Muriel said, "Aubrey had to make decisions in junior high that I didn't make until college." Gene said, "Kids don't respect adults like they used to."

Aubrey said, "Most adults don't have a clue what life is like for teenagers."

I returned to the immediate crisis. "What will happen tomorrow with the school?"

Aubrey said, "I won't go back. You can't force me."

"No one wants to force you," said Muriel.

I agreed with Aubrey that, especially in our big schools, kids were tough on each other. The teachers and counselors were generally good, but they had too many students and too little control to make things work. On the other hand, not all teenagers are capable of structuring their time and learning without schools. I asked the family if they thought Aubrey could learn on her own.

Gene said, "She's not learning much now."

"Give me the chance," said Aubrey. "Let me prove what I can do if I'm not being told to do it."

Muriel suggested that Aubrey stay out of school for the rest of this semester and experiment with her time. Meanwhile she could see me in therapy. Then we could all meet in January and make a decision about second semester. Gene agreed without much enthusiasm but because he felt he had no choice. He was mostly worried about whether Aubrey could get into a good college. Aubrey said, "I'll never go to college."

I recommended books about teenagers who structured their own learning. I also suggested that Aubrey do at least five hours of volunteer work a week with older people. I wanted her to be around people who were older and wiser than her peers and who had different value systems than the ones she encountered in school. Aubrey and I scheduled a session for the next week.

After that first session, Aubrey reported being much happier. She volunteered at a nearby rest home and she liked it. The first day she befriended an old man who was so disfigured by facial warts that most of the volunteers avoided him. Over time she became devoted to Oscar and insisted that others were missing an opportunity to know a truly great person. Oscar liked her immensely and told her stories of his life on a South Dakota farm. He had been a musician in a little polka band and he fondly recalled his travels. He even found her some faded old brochures that the band had used. Soon she was dropping by the home every day to check on Oscar. She made him tapes of Brave Combo, a band that combined polkas and rock and roll. He played them as he fell asleep at night.

For the first few weeks she lay around watching talk shows, but soon she was bored. She read zines from around the country and practiced her drums. She formed a band with some young women she met at a show and they rehearsed regularly.

Aubrey struggled to be a good person in a chaotic universe. She had an amusing style. When she liked what I said she responded, "Go, girl." She used colorful words such as "de-stressify" or "bunk," a synonym for awful. Often she began our sessions with a dramatic comment such as "I may look happy and well adjusted, but I am not." Or "I dwell in irresponsibility." Then she'd bring up an important question. One time it was "Is it wrong that I love my mother so much?" Another time it was "Should I try to change the world or just work on myself?"

In our tenth session, Aubrey plopped onto my couch and announced, "I am so sick of sex that I want to find a desert island." Lately Aubrey had hidden her beauty as best she could by wearing extra-large overalls and flannel shirts. But even with old clothes, purple hair and a nose ring, her delicate features and alabaster skin shouted "beautiful."

That day her complaints reminded me of a Russian song. A beautiful girl harassed by drunken men sings, "What shall I do with my beauty? What shall I do with my love?"

Aubrey sighed as she told me about lewd remarks, unwelcome touches and pregnant friends. Aubrey had friends with herpes and genital warts. She said, "Most kids know everything bad about sex, but they still do it. It's not just guys. I know girls who jump guys' bones whenever they can. They get drunk so they can block out their fears." She confided that a guy she thought was cute had asked her out, but she was afraid to accept. She said, "He probably just wants to get laid."

Aubrey explained that since she hit seventh grade, guys had pursued her. When she dated, guys wanted her as a trophy or they wanted to control her. A guy she liked in eighth grade bragged about their sexual activities to his friends. Aubrey settled into the couch. "I screwed around a lot in junior high. I didn't really have boyfriends, just guys I'd get high with or meet at concerts. I thought they liked me. I was fucking naive. By the time I finished eighth grade, I'd had it with sex."

"Have you had any serious relationships?"

Aubrey inhaled sharply.

I waited. "What happened?"

"At the beginning of ninth grade I met Alex. He was a musician. I was flattered that he liked me. We met in the mosh pit at the Dead Milkmen. We slept together that night."

Aubrey looked out at the darkening late-afternoon sky. "I got a lot of attention dating Alex. But from the start, things weren't good. He was self-centered and sexist. Plus he was always loaded. It was fun to walk into parties with him, but in private it wasn't much fun."

She looked sober and sad. "I think he was some kind of sex addict or something. He wanted to do it all the time. He overwhelmed the fuck out of me."

I asked if she tried to break it off.

"At first I thought—I'm with Alex, I must be having fun. It took me a while to realize how miserable I was."

She shrugged. "We broke up and he threatened to kill himself."

She looked at me with eyes wide. "I was relieved when I heard he was moving to North Carolina. I thought, I'll never have to do it with him again." Aubrey began to cry. "I wish I were a lesbian. I really don't want to deal with men any longer."

Aubrey was not currently sexually active, but everyone assumed that since she had been she would be again soon. Even her doctor wouldn't put her on Acutane, an acne medication that can cause birth defects, unless she was on the pill. Aubrey asked, "Why is he so sure I will have sex?"

Aubrey was only sixteen, but she'd had more experiences in her lifetime than most women my age have had in theirs. I handed her some tissues, and when she stopped crying we talked about the kinds of sex education girls get in America. One is from loving adults who say wait until you are mature, responsible and in a committed relationship. The other is from the popular media, which says sex is cool, go for it and don't worry about the consequences. Aubrey said, "In a way I want to have sex. I have hormones, you know. I get turned on. But it's hard to know what I really want versus what I've been programmed to want."

We talked some about sexual decision making, about setting criteria for relationships. I asked her to think about what needed to happen before she'd feel comfortable having a sexual relationship. She laughed. "You mean like actually talking first?"

Aubrey could be serious for only so long. She smiled and asked, "Would you like some cheese with my whine?" We talked about the present. She'd been listening to lots of new music and recommended I check out Edward II, a Celtic reggae band, Slow Down Virginia and Commander Venus. She loved Liz Phair and Bikini Kill. She said that her all-girl rock-and-roll band finally had a name, Hemlock. She was practicing her drumming six hours a day and writing original tunes. Hemlock had its first gig at a local coffee house the next month. She was a founding member of the local chapter of Riot Grrrl, which was a rock-and-roll club inspired by feminist punk musicians. Aubrey was editing the local Riot Grrrl's zine.

Aubrey rubbed her brow. "I saw *Little Women* three times last week. I envied Jo so much. I wish I could have lived then. People were so civilized and wholesome. I hate to live when everything is so hard."

I thought about myself and my friends at Aubrey's age. We were reading Cather and the Brontës, baking cookies for bake sales and building floats for homecoming parades. We felt wild and bold when we listened to Elvis or Roy Orbison. Our big issues were grades, who would be first chair in band or who would make it into select chorus.

I was pleased by Aubrey's progress in just ten sessions. She had mellowed a great deal on the topic of her parents. She was losing some of her anger and adolescent narcissism. In high school, her self-absorption was reinforced by her self-absorbed peers. It helped to be around Oscar. Aubrey had some freedom to define herself in nonsexual ways. She was under less pressure to be a beautiful object. Also, Aubrey had made some decisions about drugs and alcohol. For a while she struggled with the question "If I don't experiment now, will I feel later I missed an important experience?" But she saw the damage drugs were doing to Emma and her other friends and she decided for now to cool it.

We had talked about the importance of having a moral center, an internal compass to make decisions about right and wrong. It was easy to lose this center in the world of high school. There are so many different messages about right and wrong that it's hard to know what is truly best.

I encouraged Aubrey to write an essay entitled "Truth," which defined what she believed in. She made her own personal ten commandments and told me, "My religion is kindness." After these discussions I encouraged her to define victories as times when she acted in accordance with her deepest values. She wrote her victories down and brought them in to share with me.

Aubrey seemed much happier than when we first met. She was working hard at things that genuinely interested her. She had an important relationship with Oscar, who was teaching her things she needed to know. She was off chemicals and involved with friends who shared her creative interests. She wasn't as angry at her parents or the world. She asked if I would see her friend Emma in therapy. Aubrey mentioned studying for the GED and taking some music-theory and creative-writing classes at the university. The following week the whole family would be in for our evaluation session. I wondered if Gene and Muriel would want her to return to school.

SABRINA AND EDWARDO, ERNESTO AND JORGE (TWINS, 3)
Sabrina had shiny black eyes and healthy olive skin, but she looked exhausted. Edwardo, dressed in a gray factory uniform, looked tired as well. He told me he worked a rotating shift—a week on days, followed by a

week on evenings and then a week on the graveyard shift. He was twenty-five, but he looked younger, like he should be playing high school basketball, not working a sixty-hour-a-week job.

Edwardo said, "We are here to make our marriage better. We don't believe in divorce."

"Besides," Sabrina added, "we've cared about each other since the day we met."

Edwardo smiled. "We met at a high school track meet. I was attracted to Sabrina's hurdle jumping."

Sabrina laughed. "You were attracted to my body, admit it."

They dated for a year and married young. The twins were an expensive surprise. Since the boys' birth, life had been tough. Edwardo and Sabrina cared for each other, but they had definitely fallen out of love. Edwardo said, "I know my problems at work aren't Sabrina's fault, but sometimes I take my anger out on her." Sabrina said, "We almost never see each other, and when we do we argue about who is going to take down the trash or bathe the twins."

"If you could stay up past nine, we might have more of a relationship," Edwardo said. Sabrina nodded miserably and explained that she was always tired. At Kmart she supervised twenty-six checkers. She was on her feet all day, dealing with disgruntled customers, spills, returns and broken scanners. Some days she had time to wolf down a corn dog or taco, other days she worked through the lunch hour. At five, she managed to get out of there and into rush-hour traffic. She picked up the boys, who were fussy and tired. Lately the day-care operator complained that Jorge might be hyperactive. He hit other kids and drove the caregivers crazy. Sabrina was worried that the woman would kick the twins out. The Jolly Tots wasn't great, but they could afford it. Sabrina knew the boys were physically safe, if not terribly well entertained or cared for, and there weren't other options.

Sabrina's day didn't slow down after work. At home, she turned on *Sesame Street*, changed clothes, looked at the mail and called her mother, who had breast cancer. Sabrina explained that her mother wasn't a complainer but she was demoralized and in pain. When they talked on the phone, Sabrina ached because she wanted to hug her mother so badly. Instead she would talk to her until the kids needed something and then hang up with tears in her eyes. Later she fixed dinner—on a good night she made burritos or hamburgers, on a bad night she microwaved pot-pies.

Sabrina did the second-shift work—the shopping, errands, bill paying and cleaning. When Edwardo was on late shifts, she was essentially a single parent. When he worked days, Edwardo sometimes made it home by seven. Other nights he called to say he was working a double and wouldn't be home till after 11. Those nights she ate with the boys, gave them baths and read them a story. Then she fell asleep lonely.

Twice lately Edwardo had fallen asleep driving home from work. His bosses saved money by having fewer employees and working them constantly. Overtime was cheaper than paying more employees, who wanted benefits. Besides, they had a dozen ways to avoid paying overtime. Edwardo liked his co-workers but not his bosses. He explained that new managers had been brought in from out of state. As he put it, "The local guys couldn't stomach the work these guys do. These new guys don't know us or our wives. It's all numbers to them."

The worst thing was no family time. He missed Jorge and Ernesto's holiday play at day care. He missed the mariachi masses that he and Sabrina had once enjoyed together. He had worked the last Thanksgiving and also the night that Sabrina had arranged a sitter to celebrate her birthday. He said, "I feel trapped; I have to support my family, but in order to do that I have to be gone all the time. I hardly know the boys."

Both Sabrina and Edwardo had been required to take stress management classes at their jobs. Sabrina said, "I don't need stress management, I need time with *mi familia.*" She continued, "Last Tuesday Jorge had a temperature of a hundred and two degrees. I was more worried about missing work than his illness. Edwardo and I fought about who should take him to the doctor."

Sabrina loved to jog but had given that up. She said, "For a while I put the boys in a double stroller and jogged along the highway near our home. It was impossible." Edwardo loved to play the drums, but he said, "Since the boys were born, the closest I've come to drums is the car radio."

This couple rarely had a date. Edwardo complained they almost never had sex. Sabrina said, "It's hard to feel sexy if our conversation for the day has been whether Ernesto's diarrhea is serious and who is responsible to change the air filters in the heating system."

Edwardo and Sabrina rarely saw anyone except their co-workers and each other. Edwardo worked most Saturdays, so Sundays were errand and catch-up days. For him, a good Sunday meant he got the yard mowed, Sabrina fixed a real meal and he got to watch sports on television. For Sabrina, a good Sunday meant she caught up on housework and had time to play with the boys.

In spite of the couple's hard work, they had money trouble. Day care was expensive, their house payment was high and they had two car payments to make every month. They paid for cable so the boys could have the Disney channel and they tried to keep them in toys and nice clothes. The boys liked all the expensive stuff advertised on TV. Even though they couldn't afford it, Sabrina and Edwardo felt so guilty about their absences that they often caved in and bought them what they wanted.

Sabrina felt bad about her time away from the boys. She said, "I returned to work when they were eight weeks old. I feel like someone else is raising my kids. Their day-care people saw their first steps and heard their first words. For a while Jorge cried when I picked them up from day care. He felt more at home with the staff there than he did with me."

Edwardo said, "I'm not sure a therapist can help us. What we really need is a seventy-six-hour day."

This couple's schedule needed treatment. The pathology was external to the family. I recommended that Sunday evening be family time and that Sabrina and Edwardo show each other some affection every day, not necessarily sex but kissing, back rubs or simply words of appreciation. With great difficulty we scheduled another session.

Session Three

This session the topic was Sabrina's mother's health. The chemotherapy was making her mother nauseated and dispirited. Sabrina wanted to spend more time with her, but there was no way to manage that. She moaned, "I feel guilty when I am with my mother and guilty when I am not." Sabrina's mother was in a health maintenance organization in which she saw a different doctor every time. Sometimes she had long waits in crowded offices. Sabrina wished she could go with her mother to these doctors. She was more assertive than her mother and would ask questions. She wondered if her mother should spend her meager savings on a private doctor. Her money would do her no good if she was dead. On the other hand, if her mother lived, she needed every penny she had.

Edwardo told Sabrina, "I want you to be with your mother whenever you need to be. We'll manage." But he was swamped at work and hated to have his sons in day care all the time. The boys missed their mother; Jorge's behavior was getting worse. Edwardo said sadly, "I don't see how we can keep this up much longer."

He shook his head and wondered aloud, "Back home most families had six kids or more. How did our parents do it?"

On the bright side, the family was spending more time together. Edwardo told his boss he wouldn't work Saturdays and so far he hadn't been fired. Sunday nights, they were going on outings or playing children's games, which Ernesto and Jorge both loved. Sabrina and Edwardo had a regular sitter for Friday nights and were going out on dates. They were managing to say "I love you" and had even given each other back rubs a couple of times.

I congratulated them on their progress and encouraged them to keep track of victories, which we defined as spending their time in accordance with their deepest values.

Session Fifteen (six months later)

Today we reviewed the changes that Edwardo and Sabrina had made. They had many victories to report—evenings in the park with their boys, time holding hands and family dinners with Sabrina's mother. The twins would be four years old next week and Sabrina was planning a big family party for them. Her mother was watching them today while Sabrina shopped for balloons and party favors. She said she was buying them a few practical gifts.

Sabrina looked happier than the first day we met. Her face was younger and some of the tension was gone from around her eyes. She'd quit her job and was home full-time with the boys. She and Edwardo had invited her mother to live with them. At least for now her cancer was in remission and they were all appreciating this "good time." They'd pooled their financial resources and everyone was better off. They had less money than when Sabrina was working, but they had enough. Sabrina's mother had her daughter's help and time with her beloved grandsons. Jorge and Ernesto had a live-in storyteller. The boys had thrived under their mother's and grandmother's care.

Sabrina finally had a schedule that a human being could manage. She took her mother to the doctor and the cancer support group. She was taping some of her mother's stories and encouraging her mother to label old pictures. Sabrina had many projects going. On Fridays she met her best friend for lunch. She planted a garden and was building a sandbox for the boys. The twins were helping. She jogged during the boys' nap time and felt good that she was physically fit again. She said, "I don't know how I ever worked. "

Edwardo still hated his job and he missed time with the family. He wanted to find a different job, one with benefits and a decent salary, but also a set of demands that he could meet and still be a good family man. He said ruefully, "There's not a lot out there for guys with a high school education and ten years' factory work."

But at least his time at home was better. He came home to a relaxed wife and a real meal. The boys were calmer and he was proud of what they were learning. He loved to hear that Sabrina and her mother had taken them to the zoo or even on a leisurely trip to buy jackets. Now that they weren't always in a hurry, outings were fun. Sabrina, not the sitter, told him about his sons.

The family had made some hard choices. They had realized that they could have more time or more money but not both. They had chosen time. Edwardo now carpooled to work so Sabrina could haul the boys and her mother around town. They gave up shopping, except for essentials, and they didn't eat out.

The marriage was stronger. As Edwardo put it, "We're falling in love again." As the stress level of the family had dropped, they were bickering much less. Sabrina was grateful that Edwardo worked so that she could stay home. Edwardo was grateful that she took good care of him and the boys. Sabrina even reported that she had a glimmer of interest in sex. Edwardo said wryly, "After three years, it's about time."

We talked about what they had learned in therapy. Sabrina said, "I learned the toll that work was taking on my life. I thought the problem was Edwardo, but it wasn't. We were fighting each other, but the problem wasn't us, it was the pressures on us. I learned I could get off the merry-go-round."

Edwardo said, "I got warned at work about letting my mother-in-law live with us. But it's been great. I love to hear her tell stories to the boys and they love their *abuela*. I've learned that when Sabrina and I are un-

happy we need to look at the choices, we need to attack our problems
and not each other."

GRACE (21), EVETTE (4) AND NATASHA (3)

Grace came to therapy because of insomnia and anxiety. She said, "I can't
relax. I worry about work. I worry about money. I've had some bad things
happen that come back to me at night." Her family doctor had offered
her sleeping pills but she said, "I knew that was wrong for me. I wanted
to solve my problems, not drug myself up."

Grace was an African-American who grew up in the poorest section
of our town. At an age when most young women are in college or working at their first jobs, Grace was on her fourth job and supporting two
daughters. She made a little more than $700 a month, out of which came
child care, rent, groceries and car insurance. Fortunately she had health
insurance that paid for therapy. She said, "Let's just say money doesn't
grow on trees or anywhere else that I know of. We never have enough."

She had long hard days. Grace said, "When the alarm goes off at five
forty-five, I shower and read the paper. Then I wake up the girls. Evette's
a morning person and she hops right up, but Natasha has to be coaxed."
She smiled. "I usually tickle her feet or give her a back rub."

"I fix them cereal and we pack their backpacks. We get dressed in my
room. I show them how to do things, fix their hair or tie bows. Right now
Evette puts her socks on so that the heel is on top." She laughed a rich,
throaty laugh. "We're working on that."

Grace continued. "I drop them off at their day care and work till five.
My happiest time of day is when I pick them up. They smile and run toward me like they haven't seen me in a week."

Grace pushed a stray hair back into her ponytail. "We run errands and
head on home. The girls take turns helping me cook. I'm always doing
more than one thing at a time. I'll be making salad while I talk to Natasha
about how to deal with a bully. I'll give Evette alphabet letters to print
while I pay the bills."

Grace continued, "After dinner we cool it. We're too tired to do much
else. I let the girls watch a little television, after I make sure the shows
don't have sex or violence. They know they aren't to watch those kind
of shows, and when they come on they'll prompt each other to turn them
off."

She paused. "I rented *Hook* this weekend. I thought it was a movie for kids, but there was swearing and violence. We had to stop watching it."

I asked about music, especially rap music, and Grace said, "I don't listen to music that I don't want the girls to hear. I want to set a good example for them. They think that what I do is right, so I want to be right."

I told her I was impressed by her energy level and commitment to parenting. Grace said, "There are just two things that are important to me: my girls and my work."

I asked about Earl. Grace said, "I should have come to see you years ago, when I first met him. But I didn't even know how to get help at the time. I was young and dumb."

Grace's face became serious. "Mom warned me not to mess with Earl. He was bad news. But I didn't listen to anybody at that time. I was seventeen when Evette was born. Three months after Evette's birth I was pregnant with Natasha."

"How did you feel about having a baby at seventeen?"

"I thought my life was over. And right after Evette was born, Earl forced himself on me and I was pregnant again."

Her voice became dull and hard. "That year was a bad dream. My parents wouldn't let me live at home, so I lived with Earl. One time he beat me so badly I was unconscious. He called my folks to say that maybe he'd killed me." She shook her head. "After that, they let me move home."

"While I was pregnant with Natasha, Evette and I had a tiny room in their attic. Dad said I could stay there as long as I was in high school. He was harsh but right. I needed that diploma."

"I wanted to abort Natasha. I drove to the center and watched their stupid films. Then the doctor examined me and said it was too late. That was the hardest afternoon in my life." She sighed. "I worried that any baby conceived the way Natasha was would have problems. I felt nothing for Natasha when she was in the womb. Her delivery took forever. At first I thought she was ugly. She was skinny, pale and bald. I kept her in bonnets."

She sipped some tea and looked out the window at the gray sky. "I wasn't a good mother to her. I cuddled Evette, but I left Natasha in her crib. I did the basics, but no more. I didn't get into being her mother until she was about eighteen months old. Then one day she called me Mommie and that softened me up."

She smiled. "But Natasha is great. We joke about the abortion attempt. I tell her she was a fighter. Even back then she knew what I was up to and stopped it."

I asked how she survived that first year. She answered, "I moved into a little apartment with no furniture. There was a guy that shot up heroin in the basement. For several months we lived on the floor. Then the land-lord took pity on me and brought in a few scraps of junk. But I took my girls to the day care at the high school and I graduated in the spring. I qualified for food stamps and WICS.

"Those first years, when both girls were in diapers and on bottles, are a blur. I remember one winter day when it was about five below and I had to get the girls to day care. I had one baby under each arm and a giant diaper bag as I slid toward the car. I put them in and scraped ice off the windows. Then the car wouldn't start. I was trying hard to make my life work, but I was eighteen and broke."

She sighed. "Earl kept turning up. I realized that eventually he was going to kill me. The last time he broke into my place, I called the po-lice. My neighbors agreed to testify. Earl hassled me about pressing charges. He said I was setting him up to be punished by white people. But this wasn't about color, it was about my safety."

She paused. "He's been in jail for about a year now. That is the best thing that ever happened to me. I feel slightly in control of my life."

She sighed. "Running from Earl took so much energy. Since he's gone I've grown a lot. I like my job, although the funding may be cut. I have a foothold on life." Grace paused and looked earnestly at me. "But I still get anxious. I'm not sure I'm over all the stuff with Earl. Sometimes I think of him at night. I don't sleep well and then I'm tired with the girls."

I asked her about resources, friends or family who might help her with the girls. Grace saw her family regularly but said her mother "doesn't do child care." Grace said, "Mom's attitude is you made a choice. You be re-sponsible for that choice."

I respected Grace's mother's point of view, but it was clear that Grace could use help. I asked her to think about extended family, neighbors and friends, anyone whom she might talk to about her situation. Grace mentioned her older sister Tina, who was also a single parent, with one little boy. Tina had offered to help and Grace had been too proud to ac-cept. I suggested she might rethink that decision.

I talked to Grace about being an exhaustible resource. For her girls' sake she must take care of herself. She'd be no good to them if she got sick or seriously depressed. I recommended she exercise over her lunch hour and that she find a few predictable ways to be good to herself. As Grace left she flashed me a smile. "This helped," she said. "I'll see you next week."

Session Two

Grace looked better today. She told me that she was exercising some and she had called Tina. They had agreed to clean their houses together on Saturdays and to let the kids play together while they took turns running errands. She said, "Tina is one funny lady. We need each other."

Today Grace had her two daughters with her. She was worried that all their early stress might have damaged them somehow. This session was to be a mental health checkup. The girls didn't look like sisters—Evette was dimpled, with black curly hair and flashing eyes. Natasha was small and pale, with light brown hair. Evette was talkative and bold. She loved being the center of attention and would interrupt her mother with comments or kisses. Twice she crawled up on Grace's lap and once she came over and hugged me. Natasha sat beside her mother with her hands in her lap. She observed everything, especially her mother, with soulful eyes.

Grace looked with pride at her girls, touched them frequently and laughed often at what they said or did. Both girls knew their ABC's and Grace said, "That's because we read stories every night. I want my girls to do well at school."

Grace settled into the couch and said, "Their behavior has to be good. I can't be with them all the time. If I couldn't trust them to act right, I couldn't leave them at day care."

Natasha said, "We tell the troof." Grace patted her shoulder. "I know you do, baby."

I asked about various developmental milestones. The girls were on time or ahead of schedule with all of them. I asked about sleep and nightmares. Grace said, "Natasha still has nightmares. She comes in to sleep with me about once a week."

"What do you dream about?"

Natasha looked me square in the eyes. "Mama getting killed."

"Are you worried your mother will be hurt?"

Evette nodded.

Grace said, "The girls don't like to talk about Earl. I don't know if that's good or bad."

I asked the girls to draw some pictures. Natasha scribbled but Evette drew spring scenes—tulips, trees and birds' nests. I asked them what they would wish for if they had a wish. Evette said she wanted $50,000 and a trip to Disneyland. Natasha said, "I love now."

"Thank you, baby," Grace said. She looked at me anxiously. "Do you think the girls are okay? They've seen Earl hit me. He never hurt them, thank God, but he scared them."

I said, "We'll have to see. What happened to your girls could leave scars, but it doesn't always. What happens later is important too."

I recommended that Grace create some healing rituals. Some could involve the girls. They could tell their bad memories and then tell their dreams for the future. They could talk about the bad things Earl did and then talk about the good things that other adult men had done for them.

Grace needed to heal herself before she could move on. Her individual rituals might need to be more complex. She needed to acknowledge, understand and forgive the damage that Earl caused before she could even think of dating another man. After I explained, Grace asked, "Do you mean I should burn some of Earl's stuff?"

I said that could be part of it. She could also write about her experiences with Earl and burn the letter. She could forgive herself for her youthful mistakes. She could design a ceremony of hope. Grace was silent as I talked about rituals that might help her move on. She held her girls tightly and blinked her eyes to keep from crying.

At the end of the session I encouraged Grace to seek out kind, good men for her daughters to know. I said, "A good uncle or neighbor can be an antivenom to an earlier poisonous experience."

She hugged the girls. "Their grandpa is good to them."

We rescheduled for another week. Grace would think about healing rituals. I said as they left, "The girls seem to be doing great now. They are smart, well behaved and well loved. They have a wonderful mother, a real survivor."

Chapter Ten

COMMITMENT

Recently on public radio I listened as a quadriplegic was interviewed about his life. He'd had polio as a boy and lived with his parents well into his twenties. He spoke lovingly of his folks and was clearly aware of their sacrifices and grateful for their care. For some reason, the interviewer couldn't accept his positive attitude. He kept suggesting that somehow the man's parents had failed him. He kept asking if the man resented his parents. He asked, "Don't you feel they should have made an effort to have children over to play?" The polio victim explained that there were no support groups to offer parents advice on such things. Besides, he argued, his parents were protective of him and kids were cruel. But the interviewer remained determined that his parents could have done more. I thought how easy it was for the interviewer to second-guess parents who had cared for a quadriplegic child for two decades. I wondered if the quadriplegic man felt differently about his mother and father after this show.

I first thought about attitudes toward parents when I was a college student at UC Berkeley in the late 1960s. Friends told me how controlling, neurotic or cruel their parents were and what an enormous battle it was to free themselves from their evil domination. I formed images of fathers similar to Big Daddy in *Cat on a Hot Tin Roof* and of mothers out of Philip Wylie's *Generation of Vipers*. Then the parents showed up. They were soft-spoken couples from Iowa or Illinois who took us out to spaghetti dinners and asked about our classes. I realized that being sophisticated and adult in America required a certain belittling of one's parents.

America's belief in independence leads us to value rebellion in our children. Our culture is extreme in its message that to grow up people must reject their parents. In *The Wild One*, Brando was asked, "What are you rebelling against?" He replied in his surly Brando way, "What have you got?" That's a very American question.

We are a culture that portrays parents as baggage, impossible to ignore but generally a pain in the neck. Teenagers hear that families are a hindrance to individual growth and development, and sadly, teens who love their parents are made to feel odd. This sets up teenagers for trouble. Just when adolescents desperately need their parents' guidance and support, they are culturally conditioned to break away. They must tackle difficult questions about sex, drugs, peers and chemicals on their own. Rebels do not ask for advice and help.

One afternoon I visited a friend whose eight-year-old daughter was helping her with some cooking. They worked calmly and with obvious pleasure. I congratulated the daughter on being a good helper. She said shyly, "Mom is making me help." I laughed and said with mock disbelief, "Oh really, you didn't want to spend your afternoon working with your mom?" But later I was angry at myself. This girl and her mother so clearly enjoyed each other. The girl's words were an apology for that pleasure and my remark suggested that, indeed, it wasn't normal to want to work with one's mother. I had so automatically validated the child's effort to distance from her mother. Next time I would say instead, "You and you mother work so well together. It looks fun."

Our American love of rebellion makes the whole idea of commitment confusing. We are unclear whether loyalty is healthy or unhealthy, good or bad. But commitment is about being there when it's not convenient or easy. It's about steadfastness in the face of change and crisis. The stories that follow all explore some aspect of commitment. Billy is a boy to whom no one is committed. There are millions like him all over America. The Lu family, who have Vietnamese values about commitment and loyalty, crash into American culture with its very different values. The Rainwater family illustrates how helpful extended family can be in times of emergency. An extended family can survive situations that would take a nuclear family down. And finally, the Cohns are committed to family theoretically, but the parents work long hours and their extended family is a thousand miles away.

BILLY (11)

After Billy broke into his school and smashed all the trophy cases, he was sent to a holding facility. A judge had asked me to evaluate Billy and today I flipped through the stack of reports by caseworkers. The thick file told a sad story. When Billy was one, a neighbor reported his mother, Isabella, for leaving him while she went drinking. There were abuse reports—Billy had a broken collarbone, two dislocated shoulders and he'd been scalded "accidentally." Isabella had been ordered into therapy and parent education classes. Her boyfriend had been jailed for child abuse. Certain events were described over and over—"Mother not home when I visited at our agreed-upon time," "Mother won't return calls," "School nurse is concerned about Billy's safety," "Mother appears unmotivated, may be drinking." Other events leapt from the page—"Billy was found in the cab of a pickup outside the Skylane Bar. He was hungry, cold and soiled." "After she slapped Billy in a Safeway parking lot, Isabella was picked up for drunk and disorderly conduct." Even before I met Billy, I felt defeated. He was both trouble and in trouble and there was no place I could recommend that was likely to heal him.

Billy was waiting at a battered table in a pea-green room with bars on its windows and a year-old calendar on the wall. The room was hot and smelled of tobacco, and the first chair I sat on was broken. Billy wore camouflage clothing and a leather thong necklace with a skull charm. On his left arm was a homemade tattoo of the peace sign. He was small for his age, with red hair and ice blue eyes. As I entered the room, he looked up from his efforts to deface the table with a ballpoint pen and grinned at me. A stack of unfurled paper clips was scattered around him.

I asked how he was doing. He shrugged and said, "Okay. There's a pool table and free popcorn." Then his voice broke and he asked, "When do I get out of here? Dad was gonna take me to the state fair."

I couldn't answer him. Until Isabella was murdered by her live-in boyfriend, Billy had lived with his mother. After that he lived with a grandmother until she went into a rest home. Billy had met his biological father only once. The year Billy was five, his dad showed up at Christmas with a bike. He promised to keep in touch and to take him to Worlds of Fun. But he never returned. Billy had been in six foster home place-ments in the last three years. I asked Billy which dad was planning the state fair trip.

"Max," he said indignantly. "The dad I live with. Who do you think?"

"Have the Jensens been to see you?"

"Mom brought me peanut butter cookies." He dug into his pocket and pulled out a picture. "Here they are."

Mom was a large woman whose face was blurred in the picture. She held a toddler in her arms and had three other children around her knees. A big black dog lay at her feet. Dad, who leaned against the clapboard house smoking a cigarette, was skinny and none too healthy. Billy proudly identified each family member, including the dog. "That's Coalie. The best hunting dog in Thayer County. That's our house out on High-way Ten." As he talked, I realized that he hadn't been told that this fam-ily didn't want him back.

I asked, "Tell me about the other families you lived with."

Billy had a good memory. Family number one lived on a farm. He learned to milk cows and kill chickens. They made him work hard, but he liked it there. When the mother had twins, she didn't have time for him anymore. The second family was religious. He grimaced as he told me, "They prayed all the time and didn't do anything fun. They made us go to bed at eight at night. Yuck." He'd lasted there ten days. The third family kicked him out when, among other things, he called their daugh-ter a motherfucker. He shook his head. "She was the spoiledest little princess you can imagine."

Billy asked to be removed from the fourth family because the father was abusive. Twice he'd lost his temper and slapped Billy. As Billy told it, "The first time I deserved it, but the second time I wasn't guilty. I know my rights." In the fifth family the mother had cancer and was unable to care for him after her chemotherapy. Billy said, "I liked her a lot. Could you find out if she's dead?"

Finally there were the Jensens, whom he'd been with for seven months. Max was a janitor, Lulu ran a day care. He said, "The other kids get on my nerves. I want to be an only child." He liked Lulu and said, "She made a quilt with my name on it. I am going to keep it forever and then give it to my children." But he conceded, "She has her bad days when if you're smart, you stay out of her way."

And he liked Max, who had taken him hunting twice and fishing once. When he talked about those trips, he lit up. I heard about the four doves they bagged, the pheasant that Max shot but Coalie couldn't find and the squirrel Billy killed, cleaned and ate for breakfast the next day. He talked about the bluegill and perch he and Max caught in a lake near their town. With his grubby hands and bitten-down nails, he showed me their size.

As I listened I felt my own anger rising. Someone needed to tell this boy what was happening. Not me, but someone who had a relationship with him, his caseworker maybe. But Billy couldn't remember who his caseworker was. There was so much turnover at the social service agency. I asked about his grandmother and his face darkened. He said, "I don't like to talk about her."

I asked if he remembered his mother and he looked angry. "Why are you bringing this stuff up anyway?"

"Okay," I said, "we don't have to talk about that. But we do have to talk about why you vandalized the school."

Billy picked up the pen and began poking it hard into the table. In a few seconds it was broken. "I've told a hundred people about that already." He sighed elaborately to reinforce his point.

"Please tell me."

His voice grew harsher. "I don't know why. I hate the principal and the boys pick on me. I was just gonna paint the lockers with shoe polish, but when I got inside I went crazy."

Billy looked his youngest and saddest when I asked about school activities. "Sports suck. They're pussy," he said. "And I don't want to read."

Even before this recent event, Billy had had a police record. He'd stolen a bicycle when he lived with his grandmother. Twice he vandalized buildings. He shoplifted, mostly action heroes and Power Rangers. His favorite was Lord Zedd. Amazingly, he'd never hurt anyone.

Billy had always been the new kid somewhere. Teachers and kids would just start to know him and he'd move on. His math was way below grade level and he couldn't read. Worst of all, he'd never been in Little League or played soccer or basketball. At recess he was the last boy chosen for teams. He pretended he hated sports, but I didn't think it was an accident that he'd chosen to smash trophy cases.

I asked him to draw a picture of himself. He drew a boy whose chest was crossed with bullets, Pancho Villa style. He had guns strapped to his waist and a knife in each hand. The face in the drawing was very different from the freckled face I saw before me. That Billy had big pointed teeth and angry eyes. In the background were rockets, swords and machine guns. In case I missed the point of the picture, he had written "Kill, Kill" across the top. For a while I just looked at it, then I said, "The boy in this picture is really mad."

He said, "He's a paid assassin. He works for the CIA. He only kills bad guys."

He liked *Rambo* and *Terminator* movies and the *Halloween* series. He took pride in how much gore and suspense he could tolerate. Billy launched into a description of heads being blown off in the last movie he saw, but I cut him off. It was obvious that he could have narrated violent scenes for a long time.

Billy was a heartbreaking combination of angry and vulnerable. With his life, I didn't think the vulnerable part of him would last too many more years. I looked at his serious face. Something in the thrust of his jaw showed how fiercely he was fighting for his dignity. His body posture signaled "Respect me." I wondered what I could ask that would allow him to speak of his life with some pride. I asked what he wished for in the future. He wanted a motorcycle, a million dollars and a big-screen television. And yes, he wanted a family.

Billy and I picked up all the ruined paper clips and threw them away. Billy asked about my family. Did I have kids? What were their names? Had I ever taken them to Worlds of Fun? He walked me to the locked door of his unit. He would have kept talking forever.

When I left, I had to resist the urge to tousle his hair. He needed to be touched so badly. But it wasn't fair to promise him more connection than I would be providing. Instead I shook hands. I made a note to make sure he had a good caseworker who could stick with him. I would ask the caseworker to find out about his fifth foster mother's cancer and let him know. I'd urge the caseworker to talk to his current family about taking him back.

It is unlikely they will. Most foster kids get dumped when they get in this much trouble. And in fairness to this family, Billy was a handful— angry, energetic, undisciplined and dishonest. The mom already had four kids and the dad had obviously been kind. Those hunting and fishing trips were the best things that had ever happened to Billy. In fairness to the family, I wouldn't want to take Billy on and I suspect that I had more time and resources than Lulu and Max had.

Perhaps the state would pay for family counseling. But I knew that was unlikely because of recent budget cuts. Maybe the caseworker could appeal to the mom's big heart. She had brought him cookies, after all. I didn't even want to think beyond the Jensen family. Surely a seventh foster home wouldn't turn things around and I hated institutions for boys. Often they took in kids like Billy and turned out hard-core delinquents.

The really frustrating thing was I knew that Billy could be saved. He liked adult attention and family. He yearned for mothering and he could elicit it. Within three minutes of our meeting, he had me feeling maternal. He had strong feelings, but if he had help sorting them out they would be manageable. There were things to hook him into—animals and fishing. If he could learn to read and play basketball, he might even have a chance at school. These small favors didn't seem too much to ask to save this boy's life.

As I drove back to my office I kept picturing Billy's face and small, nail-bitten hands. He was right on the edge—a budding psychopath or a savable child. He still hungered for warmth and closeness. His dreams still had people in them.

I would make some calls, write a report pleading for more support for the Jensens or his next family. If he had a next family, I wanted him to be an only child or maybe have older brothers who might protect him at school. He could benefit from being the baby in a family. But even as I thought of what Billy needed, I was reasonably certain that I couldn't get it for him. The reality was I was just one more person in the stream of bureaucrats who had flowed through Billy's life, observing the damage that was taking place, caring but ineffectual.

I stopped my car and gathered up files to take to my office. The late morning air felt clean and cool. I allowed myself a minute-long fantasy about Billy's life. In my version he was in the Jensens' home getting ready to go camping. Coalie was beside him. Lulu was in the kitchen fixing sandwiches and Max was pulling out the fishing poles. The other children were on the couch looking at picture books. A country music station was playing on the radio. The sun was shining.

THE LU FAMILY—VU, TRINH, LILY (18) AND GIANG (16)
The Lu family came on the recommendation of the school counselor. Giang was in trouble for smoking on school grounds, truancy and poor grades. The previous week he'd been involved in a fight with some Cam-

bodian students and the counselor had said that unless he calmed down, Giang would be expelled.

The parents were dressed in clothes from a Goodwill basket. Vu had on tan slacks, a blue suit coat and a T-shirt advertising Budweiser. Trinh wore a purple pants suit covered by a bulky olive-green sweater and shiny red shoes. The children looked like they belonged to different parents. Lily was dressed in expensive slacks and a silky blouse. Her short hair was fashionably cut, her makeup was model quality. Giang wore jeans, a black shirt and a black leather jacket. His brand-new motorcycle boots shouted expensive.

The dignified parents sat side by side with their hands in their laps. Trinh spoke some English and seemed to understand most of what was said, but Vu was totally dependent on translation. Both parents seemed ill at ease and unsure what a therapist was. In such a strange place, Lily took charge and introduced everyone. Vu smiled, revealing a mouthful of gold teeth. Giang shook my hand. He spoke good English, and occasionally interjected something as Lily translated for her parents.

Lily said, "Our family is here to cure Giang. Until this year he has been a good son and brother, but now he acts like a gangster. In our country we would take him to an herbal doctor, but in America the teachers said we should come to a psychologist."

I asked about the family's history. In a matter-of-fact manner, Lily explained that they had come to this country five years earlier, when Giang was eleven. Before that they'd been in a camp in the Philippines and before that in Vietnam. After the war, Vu and Trinh were sent to reeducation camps. The children stayed with Vu's parents and almost starved during the time their parents were away. Lily said, "There were many days when we had only sweet-potato broth to drink."

Trinh described her camp and Lily translated. It was a rice planting camp where the guards worked the prisoners eighteen hours a day. They punished the workers mercilessly when they didn't make their quotas. Once the guards broke an old lady's hips to teach her a lesson. Another family was forced to watch their oldest son's execution. They were told they'd be shot if they showed any remorse while he was beheaded. Even children were forced to kill other children. Trinh said, "Many times I was so sad that I wanted to die, but I stayed alive for my children."

Vu talked rapidly and loudly about his situation in Vietnam. I had the feeling he rarely talked about this. After long days in the rice fields, the workers were kept awake with lectures on Marxism. Once when Vu fell asleep, his punishment was to be buried alive and left to die. As he waited for his death the second night, an old farmer dug him up. The farmer gave him a chicken and said, "Forget my face so that I will not be killed for my actions." Vu crawled through snake-infested jungles in the dark. He said, "My only goal was to be reunited with my family. If I hadn't believed in that, I would have died."

Vu managed to reach the Philippines after several months and eventually was able to arrange his family's escape. For Trinh and the children, the boat trip was horrible. The boat was overcrowded and dangerously leaky. There wasn't enough food or fresh water and the people were terrified of pirates, who often robbed the immigrants of everything. Also the pirates kidnapped and raped young women. Lily was prepared to jump overboard if pirates overtook their boat.

Fortunately they made it to the camp where Vu was. They built a cardboard shack and studied English while they waited for visas and an American sponsor. They lived for a long time in the camp, but eventually were able to come to Lincoln. They had other relatives they were hoping to bring over and they sent money to Vu's parents and Trinh's sisters.

The family lived in a small apartment. They had trouble with the language and customs and they missed their families. Even though Vu had been a lawyer in Vietnam, in America he worked in a water-bed factory. Trinh had a job as an aide in a rest home.

The United States was very different from Vietnam. The values of our culture of consumption were not Asian values. The parents held on to the old values as best they could, but the children were trapped between the two worlds. To be successful Americans, the children would have to do things differently than their parents. Here men and women married because of love and divorced if the relationship wasn't happy. In Vietnam marriages were arranged and eternal. In Vietnam children were respectful and obedient. In the United States children talked back to their parents. Lily explained that her parents didn't know how to deal with Giang because problems like his seldom arose in Vietnam. Vu and Trinh had never seen a son insult his parents or disobey their orders.

Lily said that in Vietnam men were the masters, but here men lacked authority. Everyone in the family spoke more English than Vu, so he was always dependent on someone to translate. Giang could lie to him and he wouldn't know the difference. For example, Giang had told him that there was no school on Mondays and Vu believed that. Once he told his father that all boys at the school had to wear black leather jackets. Lily shook her head in reprimand as she told me these events.

Lily explained that in Vietnam only her father had driven, but here he couldn't get his driver's license. Only Lily could drive. She'd learned at school. The family had bought a used auto and she chauffeured everyone around.

Lily explained that the men had the most trouble in the new culture. The children learned English faster than their parents did. The wives could keep their familiar roles of cooking, caretaking and housekeeping. But many men were without work and succumbed to alcohol. Some beat their wives and children as they lost control of their families. She sighed. "Father hasn't begun to drink, but he is angry and sad."

I asked Lily to explain how the family felt about America. She said that the family liked the freedom and the safety. They were grateful to have food and a home, but they didn't like the lack of respect. They were from a society that respected elders. Here the children did whatever they wanted. Lily paused and said, "I act the Vietnamese way but Giang acts like an American."

The parents didn't like some American customs. It struck them as very insulting to pat children on the head. In Vietnam only animals were patted in this manner. They disliked the drinking and sexual activity of most American teenagers. They felt it was wrong for children to move away from home when they graduated from high school. As Lily put it, "Who will help the children with their problems if they are far from home? And what if the parents need help?"

Giang said that he hated school. He and Lily took ESL classes and stuck with the other Vietnamese students. Some American kids called them dog eaters and accused them of not paying taxes and of stealing jobs from Americans. Other kids told them to go back where they belonged. When Lily reminded him that some of the students and teachers were kind, he angrily brushed her comments away with his arms.

Lily said that going to high school had caused some problems at home. She explained that in Vietnam students were praised for conforming, but here students were expected to think for themselves and even argue with their teachers. At school she was rewarded for being creative and thinking for herself, while at home she was praised for being obedient. "I have to change the way I am many times every day," she said wistfully. "It is hard to be an American and a good daughter at the same time."

I asked Giang about his troubles. He scowled, but at his parents' urging, he tried to explain. "I want to hitchhike to Los Angeles, where there are more Vietnamese. I don't hate my family, but they don't understand anything about my life." He gestured toward his parents. "They have never been to a movie in their lives. They don't know who the Rolling Stones are. They cannot help me figure out what to do."

Vu interrupted and Lily translated. "He says that he and Mother would sacrifice anything for us, but they expect us to obey. Giang has been influenced by bad children.

"I do what my parents say, but it is difficult," Lily said. "I don't argue or interrupt. I do not date yet because in our culture girls don't date until they are in their twenties. I ask my parents' permission to go out with friends." Her mother patted her hand and Lily smiled at her. She continued, "I want to study law and buy my parents a nice house. I want to bring honor to our family."

"I want to make money," said Giang. "Here you are nothing unless you have money." He gestured toward Lily's nice clothes. "I bought her those. She was teased when she wore old clothes. Now she is respected." Lily sighed. "It is hard to make enough money in America."

I felt humble dealing with this family. I knew so little about their world and I sensed that modern psychotherapy meshed poorly with Vietnamese traditions. I smiled when I thought of applying our Western models to their problems. What would they think if I used phrases like "inner child," "superego" or "dysfunctional family"? In Vietnam suffering was expected to be endured. There was no tradition of talking about feelings. Family loyalty was valued in Vietnam. Now I was asking people to talk about problems within the family.

Still I think it was good they were in therapy. I suspected that the family needed help working through the trauma of the past. After all, Vu had been buried alive and they had all almost starved. We would do post-traumatic stress therapy. Also, the Lu family had lost their extended family, which was their major support system. Perhaps I could help them find new support systems.

I tried to explain what therapy was. "It's a place the family can talk about the past and learn new ways of solving problems." Everyone looked polite but baffled. Vu asked about medicine and I said I had no medicine. Lily asked, "How can you cure Giang with no medicine?"

Trying to sound more confident than I was, I said, "Therapists help people communicate and negotiate disagreements."

They nodded politely and I continued. "The ways you solved problems worked in Vietnam. You had many traditions to hold things in place. Family was around to support you. But here your family is more alone. There are many new ideas to discuss. Sometimes people in the family disagree. As a family you need to talk your problems over."

The family talked in their own language about whether to return. While they talked I thought about their situation. Before they came to America, this family had been separated a great deal. They had yearned for each other and risked their lives to be together. They had suffered external pressures, but internally they were strong. In America, they were less sure of what their enemies were. They both liked and disliked broader American culture. They had many more disagreements within the family.

The children especially faced a serious dilemma. To fit into American culture they had to become less Vietnamese. In some ways the values of the cultures were diametrically opposed. Vietnamese society is authoritarian and adult-dominated. Respect and obedience to parents are supreme values. American teenage society couldn't be more different. To succeed is to be independent and autonomous. The children were caught between two worlds. I hoped that their Buddhist beliefs might hold their lives in place and give them a healthy perspective on the junk culture of the 1990s.

If this family returned, my goals would be to help them heal from trauma and to cushion their crash into American culture. It is hard to make a commitment to both consumer culture and the traditional family. I wanted to help them integrate two very different value systems in a way that worked for their family. They would have to make many choices about what to accept and reject from our culture. They would have to work hard to hold on to what was good from Vietnam and find what was good here.

The family talked in an animated way for several minutes. Finally Lily turned to me. "We will come back. We have faith in American doctors. They helped our family last year when my mother had pneumonia. We ask you to help us now." I hoped I could merit their faith.

THE RAINWATER FAMILY—BETTY, LILLIAN AND RANDY (14)
Lillian and her mother came to my office to talk about Lillian's son, Randy. Lillian was a librarian with a quiet, serious demeanor. Betty, her mother, had snapping eyes and a laugh that was suffused with humor and energy.

Lillian said, " I should begin this story about two years ago. Randy and I lived in Kansas City with my husband. Grant was a good husband and father. Wherever he was, people had fun. But he had problems with money." She paused and swallowed. "He shot himself."

Lillian swallowed hard and continued. "At first Randy and I were in shock. Later I was angry at Grant for doing such a stupid and selfish thing. But at the same time I wondered if I could have saved him."

"After Grant died, they lost their house," Betty explained. "Grant had made good money. But Lillian only worked part-time."

Lillian continued. "It was hard. We moved to an apartment in a bad part of town. Randy worried if I would die. He started acting up and I didn't have the energy to control him."

Betty said, "I worried that my grandson would get into trouble. I heard there were drugs and guns in the schools. I invited them to come live with me."

Lillian and Randy left Kansas City and moved in with Betty. The family was Lakota Sioux and there was a long tradition of generations living together. The family had more money together than they did when they were apart. Randy got on a ball team. Lillian had someone to talk to about her pain. A tiospaye formed around Randy and Lillian and helped them through their darkest days.

Lillian said, "It was a good decision. It saved us." She explained that for a while she didn't work. Their first summer in Nebraska, she and Randy visited all the places that Grant had loved. They visited the Sand Hills and the Black Hills, went to the Rosebud and Pine Ridge. Their old relatives told Randy stories about his father. They gave him presents and magic charms. Randy's uncles took him hunting. The relatives didn't say it directly but they conveyed to Randy that they would teach him what he needed to know to be a man.

After summer ended Lillian returned to her mother's house. Betty and Lillian sometimes disagreed, but they worked things out. As Betty said, "We tell each other the truth even when we're angry." Lillian got a job at the library. Betty worked part-time at Quick Stop. But Betty had time to watch Randy and fix the meals. Both women went to his ball games. Lillian smiled as she explained that every night they had dinner together. Everyone reported on their days. After dinner Lillian helped Randy with his homework. When he went to bed, Lillian talked to her mother about Grant. Many nights she cried herself to sleep. But she tried to spare Randy the brunt of her grief.

This new family had many tough times. In spite of Betty and Lillian's best efforts, Randy got into trouble at school. He wasn't turning in his papers and he was hanging out with the troublemakers. He wouldn't discuss his father and he had times when he wouldn't talk about anything. He had nightmares. When he was home he wanted his mother or Betty nearby at all times. He seemed fearful that they might be hurt.

Lillian said, "That's why we're here. We don't think that Randy is recovering the way he should be. We wanted a consultant to help us help him."

"Do you think he should be in therapy?" Betty asked.

While it's dangerous to say no to a question like that, I suspected that Randy wouldn't do well in therapy. Boys his age are not generally articulate about their feelings and they don't like talking to middle-aged strangers with Ph.D.s. Therapy can make them feel weird. Often they are better off talking to family and dealing with their pain by actions.

I also suspected that Betty and Lillian had the resources within their tiospaye to help Randy. We talked about Randy's uncles. One of them lived nearby. He was a good hunter and could teach Randy his skills. Betty believed that the combination of family and the outdoors would help Randy heal. She wanted them to attend powwows and learn the traditions. She thought that perhaps hanging a dream catcher above Randy's bed would help with the nightmares.

I recommended a few things. Perhaps Betty or Lillian could visit the school and talk to the teachers about Randy's situation. Randy needed a tutor, perhaps an older boy who would help him catch up on his studies. Lillian could find him some books on the death of parents that would help him understand his situation.

The ball team was a good idea. I encouraged Lillian to help him find some new hobbies—a part-time job, drawing, music—whatever would give him pride in himself. He was at the age where he was forming an identity. I wanted him to form it around positives. But I also suggested that Randy needed to talk more about his father's death. The women had tried to protect him by crying when he was asleep. Perhaps that was a mistake. Randy needed to see their grief in order to express his own. He needed to know that people wept for his father. I recommended that they discuss Grant in front of him, maybe even pull out some pictures and letters and gently encourage Randy to talk and cry.

I also suggested some healing ceremonies to help Randy accept his father's death. I said, "I probably don't need to advise you on designing these." Betty smiled. "We can do that with our own people."

I congratulated the Rainwater women on their closeness, thoughtfulness and hard work on Randy's behalf. I asked them to come back in a few weeks and let me know how Randy was doing. Lillian said, "Perhaps we will invite you to a special ceremony for him." I said that I would be honored to attend.

THE COHN FAMILY—JONATHAN (50), NANCY (45) AND RACHEL (7)
When I spoke in Chicago I stayed with the Cohn family. They were originally from New Jersey but now live in a suburb filled with Tudor-style houses, BMWs and backyard swimming pools. We talked in their living room. Jonathan, who worked on his computer at home, emerged from his study around eight, "after California closed down." He microwaved burritos made with tortillas that a co-worker of Nancy's had FedExed from Albuquerque. As we talked, Nancy knitted and Rachel drew me pictures. After about half an hour, we took a break so that Nancy could read Rachel a story and Jonathan could show me his computer. Later Rachel gave me a drawing of butterflies in a prairie field.

Jonathan was a hard-charging man who worked for an international organization. He spent up to ten hours a day in front of a computer screen. Most of that time was work-related, but some was for pleasure. His friendships were "on the net." Jonathan described himself as a "guy who needs lots of stimulation and lots of options." He was very bright and his skills were portable—he had job offers in Stockholm and New Delhi to consider.

Nancy had just started a new job as the designer of Home Pages for a national ad agency. She was an art history major who taught herself computer skills to be more "salable." She had a prestigious job that paid well, but she said a bit ruefully, "This wasn't exactly what I planned to do with my life."

Rachel was a confident and precocious seven-year-old. Until Rachel was five she'd been at home with nannies, but now she went to a special and expensive school. Her parents glowed as they described Maple Tree School. Jonathan took her there every morning, even though it added an hour to his day. The school was a working farm, with horses, sheep and rabbits, hay fields, a garden, an orchard and an aviary. The children all had jobs. Right now Rachel gathered eggs and helped weed the beans. Jonathan said that Rachel was outside most of her nine-hour day, getting lots of sunshine and exercise. Nancy liked the teamwork. Together the kids and teachers made cheese, candled eggs and fed hay to the animals. At the end of her day, Nancy drove to the farm and inspected Rachel's work. I was struck that this New Age child with wealthy, intelligent parents was having the same experiences that my mother had had as a girl in eastern Colorado.

———

Nancy said, "We don't watch TV while Rachel is awake. Jonathan thinks it is evil. Mostly we read to her or play games. We know parents who have full-time help on weekends and who never see their kids. But besides being with Rachel, we don't do much. We go to temple. Jonathan's on the symphony board. Otherwise, we're at home."

"We're older parents, which means we're tired parents. We sowed our wild oats years ago. We've done the social thing and we're ready to forgo it," Jonathan said.

I asked about extended family. Nancy had grown up in New York City. Her parents were both dead and she rarely saw her two brothers. Her family had not been a happy one. She quoted her mother as saying, "We're too poor to get a divorce." Still she had aunts, uncles and cousins in the city and memories of big family dinners. But she no longer kept in contact with most of her relatives. She said, "I'd like to, theoretically, but I'm always bushed."

Jonathan's father was dead and his mother lived in Brooklyn. He had one brother in Alaska, whom he described as his best friend. He hadn't actually seen him in three years but hoped to visit him next summer. Neither Jonathan nor Nancy seemed to miss their families for themselves, but they did feel bad for Rachel. Nancy said, "When I grew up I had my brothers and cousins to play with. Rachel is much more alone." Jonathan said, "She's an only child and that won't change. I regret that she won't have a lifetime best friend like I have in my brother."

Rachel piped in, "When is Grandma coming to see us?"

Jonathan answered that she would come next month. Then he proudly told me that he had bought his mother a computer and taught her to use e-mail. Before she had been lonely, but now she "chatted" with people all over the world. She was working on a family tree. Rachel and his mother e-mailed each other every day. He said that before e-mail, he dutifully called his mother once a week, but now he met her daily on the Internet. Thanks to computers, they were much closer now than they'd ever been. Their correspondence was cheaper, too. Nancy said a bit sharply, "That's if you don't count the cost of computers."

We talked some about money. Jonathan said, "We're not big consumers, but we like to be able to afford experiences."

"The more we make, the more we spend," Nancy said. "I worry about Rachel. We know families that spend twenty-five thousand dollars on Bas Mitzvahs. She wants Reboks that cost eighty-five dollars and she wants designer jeans." She sighed. "She doesn't get that from us."

I asked about kids in the neighborhood. Nancy sighed. "This is kind of a bedroom community. We don't really know our neighbors. We never see any children. Of course, if there are kids, they're in their fenced-in backyards."

"We don't let Rachel go outside alone," said Jonathan. "Last spring a girl was kidnapped in our area. Other children have been frightened by strangers."

Nancy said, "There really isn't much to do outside."

Rachel looked up from her drawing and said, "I like Blackie."

Her parents laughed and explained that Blackie was a cat who visited their house for scraps. Nancy said, "We all look forward to Blackie's visits."

It was Rachel's bedtime and she gave me her drawing and kissed her dad good night. Jonathan offered to surf the net with me. His study had several computers, all turned on. We sat down in front of one. We looked at France Net, Pubhiker's Guide, beautiful pictures of a Catalina sailing yacht and a discussion group for older parents. Jonathan couldn't help proselytizing—he talked about the incredible amount of information available, the ease with which he could chat with colleagues all over the world and the opportunities to find people of similar interests.

"Computers make the world smaller," he said. Jonathan showed me Home Pages and explained how small companies could advertise cheaply to targeted markets. We looked at jewelry from the Southwest and at restaurant ads from Boston. But he said that he never bought anything over the net because he didn't want to give out his credit card number.

He spoke of the computer as a source of family togetherness and talked of his genealogy research over the Internet. He and his brother were creating a family tree with pictures. He said, "I wouldn't even know my nieces if we didn't have chats." He said that he was keeping a record of Rachel's experiences and quoted a computer guru as saying, "If you want to immortalize, digitalize."

As we surfed he told me stories—about the inventor of hypertext, who had a severe attention deficit disorder and wanted information organized so that no one needed to remember anything, about a boy in a pornographic chat group who was mailed money to fly to Los Angeles and was found by police wandering around the airport and about how, thanks to computer lessons, Rachel could say hello in five languages.

Nancy came into the room and said, "We argue some about Rachel and the computer. I'd rather she read and practiced the piano."

Jonathan said, "We limit her to two hours a day."

"But she's only seven years old," said Nancy. She turned to me. "Last year for her birthday Rachel had kids over for pizza and to play Magic Cards on the computer. They loved it but I was less than thrilled. I don't like her looking at a screen so much. I think it hurts her attention span. I think she needs exercise and real conversation."

Nancy was computer competent but much less computer affectionate. She preferred to talk to people on the phone and used e-mail only for business. She worried that Jonathan might be addicted to his computers. She recommended that I read *Silicon Snake Oil*. Jonathan sniffed. "That guy is out of date."

I asked if the computer affected their relationship as a couple. Nancy looked at Jonathan. "After Rachel goes to bed, Jonathan chats with people all over the world. But I don't mind. I just want to watch my show." She laughed. "I confess I love *Mary Tyler Moore*."

Jonathan said, "Nancy complains that we don't have enough couple time and she's right in a way. We don't eat meals together or have mutual friends. Except for Rachel, we have pretty separate lives."

Nancy said, "We've talked about getting a regular sitter and having a Friday night date. But our weeks are pretty frantic. Rachel spends a lot of time in a seat belt or with paid caretakers. By the weekend, it feels good to nest."

We returned to the living room for coffee and cheesecake. I thanked Nancy and Jonathan for sharing their evening with me. These were good caring people, but they seemed utterly alone in a rapidly changing universe. Even though they didn't ask for advice, I offered some. I thought Rachel needed contact with the extended family, especially the cousins her age. I encouraged them to buy the plane tickets and invite kids to come spend summers with them. Jonathan and Nancy were older parents and someday Rachel would be alone. She would need some lifelong relationships that she could count on no matter what kind of person she turned out to be.

Jonathan said, "She loves my mother, who is coming to visit soon."

Nancy was thoughtful. "Maybe we should make more of an effort to get to Alaska. Maybe I should try harder to stay in touch with my relatives."

Jonathan laughed. "Can I pick the ones we stay in touch with?"

Part III

SOLUTIONS: WHAT WILL
SURVIVE OF US IS LOVE

RAISING HEALTHY CHILDREN is a labor-intensive operation. Contrary to the news from the broader culture, most of what children need, money cannot buy. Children need time and space, attention, affection, guidance and conversation. They need sheltered places where they can be safe as they learn what they need to know to survive. They need jokes, play and touching. They need to have stories told to them by adults who know and love them in all their particularity and who have a real interest in their moral development.

In the current family-hurting culture, families must do two things to survive: They must protect themselves from what is most hurtful to the health of the family and they must connect with what is good outside the family. These tasks require time and energy, both of which are scarce commodities in an era when many parents work long hours at jobs far from their homes.

This protection and connection to others will change the culture. Families can be really healthy only when children once again have communities of real people who care about them. Chapter Eleven is about protection, about making wise choices about what to consume and what to reject. It's about building walls to shelter families—walls that protect time and space, walls of rituals, ceremonies and traditions. Chapter Twelve is about connecting, about finding resources within extended families, friendships and communities that help families survive and grow. It's about the responsibility of all of us to heal the culture.

Chapter Eleven

PROTECTING FAMILIES—HOUSES WITH WALLS

In 1992 my mother was dying. I called her daily and once a week I made the long drive to her state to hold her hand and coax her to eat. I thought of my mother on the Fourth of July as, strong and healthy, I sat in a red-and-white tent by a blue lake. The fiddler, dressed in a cream-colored summer suit, played "music for the shady side of the house while drinking lemonade." He played "Red Wing," "Boil That Cabbage Down" and "Granny Will Your Dog Bite." A cool breeze blew off the lake and through the pines. I thought to myself, My mother would enjoy this, especially "Red Wing," which she used to sing.

That summer Mother and I had been having important talks. She told me about her regrets—she had never been to Europe or read the books she planned to read when she retired. We talked about her victories—she was proud of her medical career, her work in Korea and her seven children. I congratulated her on her courage during her long hospital stay. She was stoic like her mother, who also died slowly. I asked her what she believed would happen after death. She expected to be with my father and her beloved parents. Otherwise, she said, "I don't know what the architecture will be like up there."

She fretted that she was losing her medical knowledge. She couldn't remember the difference between alveoli and capillaries. During the long nights she gave herself math problems to keep mentally alert. She said she had always loved life, but not life as a patient in a hospital. She liked picnics, family gatherings and walks beside clear water.

At noon on that Fourth of July, when she was ill and too far away for me to see, my husband and I rode on a barge filled with bluegrass musicians. The sunlight danced on the water and turned our shoulders red. We stopped at the island to eat hot dogs and drink pop. I found myself watching a mother in a black bikini play with her little daughter in the water. She swirled her around, splashed her and encouraged her to dunk her head. They seemed so connected and happy. I wished they could remain that way forever. I wanted to shout at them, "Love each other while you can."

Later, at the citywide fireworks display, I lay on a blanket with my husband. The air smelled like gunpowder from all the fireworks. We were surrounded by storms—to the north and east were lightning and hail, to the south a wall cloud and to the west, ominous dark thunderheads—but that night we were spared rain. We admired the show—the golden palms that cascade slowly to the ground, the hearts and stars, the bursts of blues, greens, silvers and reds.

As we watched, I thought of my mother far away, sleeping with her oxygen tubes and IVs. I wanted to remember every image of this lovely day and carry them to her hospital room. My husband said that blues were the hardest color of fireworks to make and hold. He was right; blue fireworks were rare indeed and lasted only a moment.

WHAT FAMILIES ARE FOR

Families are about caring for people, about feeding and sheltering the young, the old and the needy. In addition to these roles, families have had two other major roles—to protect and to socialize. In today's families those two roles are often at odds with each other. To protect is not to socialize and vice versa. Parents must figure out how to protect their children from values that are harmful to their well-being, and they must help their children connect with a meaningful world outside the family. This connecting of children to a larger world of meaning is actually one definition of the word "socialize."

This is an unusual time. For most of the history of civilization, parents haven't been able to give their children enough information. Now parents have trouble because there is too much information. It arrives continuously in a chaotic way. The job of good parents becomes to siphon meaning from a flood of dross.

Parents have less control and more responsibility. In a family-hurting culture with limited community support, parents must work harder to raise healthy children. Unfortunately in the last few years many good parents have blamed themselves for their children's troubles instead of looking at the larger forces acting on families.

Families teach children their earliest lessons—how to bathe, eat with silverware, tie their shoes and speak their language. Families hold lives together, teach moral virtues and inspire their members to action in important ways. Ideally, the education of the heart is done in families. Ideally, children learn from their families what to love and value. Some parents have the impression that they shouldn't impose their values on their children. But if parents don't teach their children values, the culture will. Calvin Klein and RJ Reynolds teach values. Good parents are what Ellen Goodman called counterculture; they counter the culture with deeper, richer values.

Families give feedback to their members. They tell the truth as they see it about irritating habits, obnoxious behaviors and poor choices. Currently that kind of feedback is much scorned, but I suggest that this honest feedback is what keeps most of us sensible. People who are isolated from such feedback are in trouble. For example, celebrities are often outside ordinary feedback loops and consequently they are vulnerable to certain mental health problems, such as grandiosity and arrogance.

As discussed earlier, one of the greatest blessings of family is that members are in by virtue of birth. They don't have to do anything— be beautiful, witty or rich—to be included. Because of this, even when people are upset with them, families are often their safety nets. Shirley Abbott described family love in *The Bookmaker's Daughter:* "Love was what you felt for your father and mother—that mix of need, fear, anxiety, trust, anger and ease."

Families, whether biological or chosen, are what give most people's lives their shape. They produce enormous pain and joy and all the emotions in between for their members. Most of our happiest and most tragic experiences are somehow connected with family. Families are flawed, complex, intense organic units whose members often fail each other in important ways. But family affection is the glue that holds lives together. After losing his wife of fifty years, poet John Neihardt said, "She had built herself into the walls of my world." Families make me think of a Leonard Cohen line: "If your life is a leaf that the seasons tear off and condemn, then they'll bind you with love that's as graceful and green as a stem."

I would never argue that families are great, only that they are human. And I would argue that children do better in families, whether formed or biological, than they do anywhere else. Children grow best in a matrix of connected relationships. They exhibit failure to thrive in a world of strangers and talking machines. With some exceptions, families are more likely than anyone else to be nurturing with their children. As institutions, families are far superior to their alternatives—the state or the corporate world. At least until something better comes along, I am for families.

FAMILY VIRTUES

When I think of family virtues I think of the Johnson family. They are not without problems. Mrs. Johnson's father was an alcoholic and left a legacy of family shame. Mr. Johnson flunked out of college and struggles to earn a living as the owner of a lawn care and snow removal business. Piet is sixteen now and Stella is fourteen. While Piet loves to hunt and play softball, Stella is a vegetarian who volunteers at the Humane Society. The two kids argue over meals and ethics. They attend our largest, most gang- and drug-ridden junior high. Both parents work full-time and they are sometimes frazzled and tired. But this family comes to mind because they are "gifted at loving."

They have a hundred family friends. They have rituals and celebrations with dozens of other families—a certain weekend for inner-tubing down the Platte, another for a camping trip to a state park, a pumpkin festival in October and a Christmas potluck for all their friends. They organize hikes, bike rides, anniversary events and "ripe tomato" parties. When one of their friends had cancer, they comforted him by visiting daily with gifts—garden flowers, homemade soup or back rubs. Because Mrs. Johnson has such sad memories of her childhood Christmases, they adopt a family every year and take them presents and a turkey.

When the children became adolescents, the parents handled some tough problems well. For example, Stella was friends with some girls who used drugs. The parents told her that they wanted her to be friends with anyone she chose and that when the parents were around to supervise, these girls were welcome in their home. But as the parents put it, "Their judgment isn't good and we don't want you with them in dangerous situations." Stella invited the girls over and soon they were spending most of their time at the Johnson house. Things settled down for the girls and Stella kept her friends.

Piet is handsome and lovable. By the time he was in seventh grade, girls were calling him, asking him to go steady and offering him sex. Piet was more interested in biking and basketball and he was unsure how to handle these offers. His parents carefully avoided teasing him. Instead they said, "You are too young to date. You can invite girls to do things with our family."

Piet did this and when the girls came over, the parents worked hard to desexualize things. As a family, they played Trivial Pursuit and included the girls in picnics and family parties. If a girl persisted in defining the relationship as sexual, Mrs. Johnson gently said to her, "We think Piet is too young to date. We want you to be friends with our family." By now Piet has a steady girlfriend and he has many close young women friends from his junior-high days.

Mr. and Mrs. Johnson find time for people and for celebrations. They define their lives by simple pleasures. Each family member has a birth month, when they are given special treatment by the others. The parents have the knack for making ordinary events special—for fixing good sandwiches and enjoying them, for making caring phone calls to friends, for making a family project of building a deck or painting the garage. They give the people they know gifts of attention and energy. The son and daughter in this family are well behaved, calm and gentle like the adults. Both of them like people and expect to enjoy themselves whatever they are doing.

This family has roughly the same number of external problems as most other families. They struggle with money and time. Their kids are in an overwhelmed school system. The grandparents are aging and needy. But they have resources that they have created for themselves—friends, rituals, holidays, activities and beautiful places they enjoy.

The Johnsons have the qualities that Nick Stinett and John De Frain present in *The Secrets of Strong Families*. They find that strong families have several things in common—appreciation, open communication, time together, a commitment to promoting happiness and welfare, spiritual wellness and ways to cope effectively with stress. De Frain talks about the 20-to-1 ratio. Strong families have roughly twenty positive comments for every negative one.

To form my own list I thought about the Johnsons and other happy families I know. Good families understand themselves and have strong value systems. Somehow family members manage to strike a balance between freedom and commitment to the family. People are allowed to be individuals and yet they are expected to contribute to the common good. Helping each other is not considered pathological, rather it's acknowledged as important. There is a strong sense that family members should pull their own weight. People pitch in and do the work that needs to be done.

In a healthy family self-definition is encouraged, but not worshiped. Diversity is tolerated, even valued. Differences are openly discussed and disagreement isn't framed as disloyalty. For example, the Johnsons had heated discussions about meat-eating and hunting. On the other hand, family loyalty is a given. I think of my aunt Margaret and uncle Fred, who during the Depression and war always had family members living with them in Los Angeles. Or my aunt Grace and uncle Otis, who had relatives whom they fed and cared for in a house the size of a boxcar. Or I think of my prosperous cousin, who has paid the bills to help many family members through college. The family loyalty involved in these choices is out of fashion today, but I would argue that these adults felt better about themselves than adults who spend money on home entertainment centers while their relatives suffer.

Families need core values that give members meaning and purpose and guide their choices as they navigate through our complex universe. The Delany family, described in *Having Our Say*, had a strong belief in God. Their creed endorsed self-improvement through education, civic mindedness and ethical living. Hap Delany said, "I've had a good life, done everything I wanted to do and done right by people. We Delanys can usually say that when our time comes." The father taught the children, "Your job is to help somebody."

Good parents try to be available emotionally but not omnipresent in their children's lives. That means struggling to find the right blend of closeness and distance. Parents should help when necessary, but not help when it's not necessary. Parents must calibrate the choices they give their children with their developmental needs. Too much challenge overwhelms children. Too little keeps them immature. Children need to be loved and held accountable. The best message that parents can send children is "I love you but I expect you to behave properly."

Strong families have the knack for optimism, for taking long views and a "big picture" perspective. Hopefulness isn't the same as a denial of reality. A realistic family acknowledges problems and deals with them. A family in denial pretends problems do not exist. Secrets keep families from solving their problems and cement shame. All families must work through disagreements. It's best to do this quickly and kindly, then return to a calm, peaceful state. What unhappy families do is just the opposite. They savor and nurse their pain and blow up small disagreements into battles. They build skyscrapers of pain on the meringues of small miseries.

Families teach people to manage pain. Much of the terrible craziness in the world comes from running from pain. Many people drink, do drugs or engage in other self-destructive behaviors so they can avoid facing pain. Healthy people acknowledge pain, accept it and talk about it. Running keeps people from learning.

Good families know that no experience is worthless if it teaches lessons. Extracting meaning from suffering ennobles and heals. Rather, to survive any great tragedy, whether it be the Holocaust or a riding accident such as Christopher Reeve's, a person must learn things. Properly attended, pain makes a person more tolerant, empathic and emotionally complex. Pain helps family members grow and become more fully human. Along with transcendence comes forgiveness, a compassion for others and an awareness of how flawed humans all are. Healing requires forgiveness, not for the sake of the causer of suffering, but for the sufferer. The alternative to forgiveness is anger, which can destroy from within the person who feels it.

Strong families teach their members to be people on whom nothing is lost. What is bad and what is good is not a simple matter. A person who wins the lottery may lose his motivation to work and become an alcoholic. A person fired from a job may find a better one. A kidnapped man may lose his addictions to nicotine and alcohol. Because his wife worked for his release, he may realize that she truly loves him. My own experience is that all the things that have happened to me have been important in making me who I am. To wish that certain things didn't happen is to wish that I am not myself.

That which doesn't kill us makes us stronger. The difference between denial and resilience is that the resilient person processes experience realistically. Strong families produce members who neither ignore nor catastrophize. They fix that which is fixable and accept what they must. They know that to a certain extent stress is what a person decides is stressful. A friend said of her father's Alzheimer's, "We might as well laugh as cry about it." My aunt Henrietta said of her childhood poverty, "We might have been poor, but we had each other. We loved potato soup."

Good families are about joy. Strong families find ways to make time sacred, to make days special. People eat meals together, sing or play baseball or violins. They make jokes and hug, smile at the thought of a get-together. Strong families find something to appreciate in every day and teach their members to wrest beauty from a mottled reality.

STRATEGIES FOR PROTECTING FAMILIES

Today family members are often living in the same house, but often they are not interacting. Interruptions and pressures keep people from spending time together and even from knowing each other. The outside world pours into the living room, the kitchen and the bedroom. People define themselves by their possessions and lose all that matters.

To be strong the family must build walls that give the family definition, identity and power. These walls are built by making conscious choices about what will be accepted and rejected. They can be built in a variety of ways—by time, space, celebrations, stories, traditions and connecting rituals.

Walls can be built by discussing the effects on family members of the machines the family invites into the home. Most families ask—Can we afford it? But I think better questions might be—Will the benefits of this machine be worth the hours of work spent to buy it? Will a TV in a bedroom keep a child away from the family? Will a computer make a restless, impatient person more so? Will a car phone take away the relaxed, contemplative time Dad or Mom has on his/her way to work?

1. Time shelters families.

Good cooking takes time. Pollsters report that the average couple spends twenty minutes a day together. Parents spend 40 percent less time with their children than did parents in the 1950s. Fathers particularly are often unavailable—the average father spends less than thirty minutes a week talking to his children. Ironically, today children need more parental time because they have fewer other adults to rely upon and their world is more complex. Most kids need more adult time and less money.

One mother said of her family's schedule, "We're missing the seasons, the sunsets and the stars. We're slicing our time thinner and thinner until by now it's transparent. Our schedules don't protect us. They are stealing our lives."

There are a variety of ways to protect time—limiting the activities of family members, having one day of the week be family day when no one schedules anything or having a regular mealtime when family members don't answer the phone. I recommend that families design time experiments to discover what works best for them. It's good to try something for a month and then evaluate it. For example, some families really like game nights, others prefer going out for meals or hikes. Family meetings work beautifully in some, but not all, families.

Family rituals protect time. Every morning our neighbor's young children line up in the front window and wave to him as he drives off to work. I suspect they think this ritual is necessary to their father's well-being, and indeed it probably is. Bedtalk protects time for children. Bedtalk means that a parent sits by the bed of a child as he/she falls asleep. The parent can rub the child's head or hold hands. Mainly the parent can listen as the child shares the last thoughts of the day—children often speak most freely as they relax and fall asleep. Parents can say anything left over from the day that needs to be said. Parents can praise: "I liked how brave you were when you had your shots." Or they can calm: "Nobody's perfect. Everyone makes mistakes. Tomorrow will be a better day." Having bedtalk with children every night is a way to give each day a closing ceremony.

Meals, touches and conversations can be rituals. Children love conversations and stories. They love snuggling times, group hugs and good-bye kisses—at least they do until they are socialized to see these things as uncool. I know a grandfather who walks to the ice-cream store every night with his grandson. I know a family who spends Sunday afternoons in Central Park. I know a formed family of close friends who meet every evening and prepare a meal together.

Making school lunches, tying shoes, walking the dog, doing the dishes—any act that's done with love becomes a ritual. Watching the children dance in the back yard early evenings is a ritual. Drinking cocoa and listening to Gregorian chants on the night of the first snowfall of the year is a ritual. Watching a grasshopper lay eggs or looking for fossils is a ritual. Car dancing to Ry Cooder or starting every trip with a special song is a ritual. Saying grace is a ritual, as are Sunday dinners, toasts and good-bye kisses. Reading aloud as a family is a lovely custom, once very common and now quite unusual. Anything can be a ritual if the family puts energy into making it meaningful. Ritual sanctifies time.

One couple I saw in therapy talked about their perfect-rose competitions. They rode bikes with their children to the community rose garden. Then everyone would walk among the flowers, looking at and smelling roses to find their nomination for perfection. Everyone would gravely discuss with the others why his/her selection should win. Of course it didn't matter whose rose won, but what did matter was how carefully the family learned to look at roses together.

One poll found that the average family spends seven to eight hours a day, or 40 percent of their private time, watching TV. It's amazing how much time families have if they turn off their televisions, radios, VCRs and computers. I recommend that families I see turn off these appliances for a month and keep a record of how their time is spent. Then after a month they can decide what role they want TV and other machines to play in their lives.

One way to have more time is to work together. Rather than divide chores, everyone can help with the dishes, yard work, laundry and home repair. Children like communal work that's genuinely useful. They learn things with this work. And while they work, they can visit with adults. Many of my clients grew up on farms and they talk of working in the fields with their families. There is often pride and a sense of community in their descriptions of the plantings and the harvests. Their families' survival depended on their efforts.

Routines protect time. As a girl, I loved to visit my grandparents. I knew that we would eat at five at night and all do dishes by seven. Then Grandfather would pull out the card table and we'd play dominoes or hearts. Before bed, Grandmother would serve lemonade and ginger cookies. The repetitive nature of those evenings was deeply comforting to me. Children like to be able to predict events. It gives them a sense of control.

Important time isn't continuous; rather it is a series of conscious moments. Sometimes we're on automatic pilot, asleep to our own experience. There are only certain moments when we are tuned into what is happening. Those moments are what we live for. The trick is to make these moments happen and also to notice those moments that happen serendipitously. In our family when those moments happen, our joke is to say, "We're having a moment." Indeed, with our family, many of those moments have to do with jokes and fun. We remember moments from vacations, picnics, bike rides and fishing trips. Good jokes and even bad ones stick around for years.

Marsha created such a moment. She's a beleaguered single mother who worked long hours at a horrendous job. When she picked up her son at day care one evening, instead of going home to face the chores and bills, she drove the car to a small park. The two of them got out and sat on a picnic table. They breathed the fresh, cool air. Neither spoke for a while. Then the mother said, "It's so quiet here, not like the factory, where my ears hurt from the noise." Her son said, "Not like my day care, where babies cry all the time." As dusk fell, they watched robins and sparrows hop in the grass and the squirrels chase each other in the trees.

2. Places shelter families.
A friend returned from Bulgaria and described the housing situation. Three or four generations of family lived under one roof, each family with its own tiny apartment. The grandparents watched the grandchildren while parents worked. At night the cousins all played together. Adults cooked or played cards while kids scrambled underfoot. She said, "The children were happy, surrounded by adults who cared for them." My friend's story reminded me of something our ten-year-old son said when

we moved from our small house to a larger one. He said, "I liked our small house more. I could hear Dad and you talking when I was falling asleep. When you were in the kitchen I could ask you about my homework. In this new house, we are so far apart."

Children's needs are not necessarily what we assume. Children like coziness, adults nearby and safe places to hide out and watch activities. They like routines, predictability and familiar places. This gives them a sense of control. They like tree houses, alleys and places under stairways. Oftentimes with children smaller is better because smaller means closer and more navigable. The spaces we construct for children and the spaces that we leave alone for them affect their mental health.

Places can protect families as well. Families can have their spots—particular restaurants, parks, museums, front porches or street corners— where they like to be together. I know a family who spends every clear Friday night at the observatory looking through the giant telescopes and identifying constellations. Another family I know can't make it through a Saturday night without a walk to its favorite pizza parlor. When the owner sees them walk in the door, she knows what to prepare.

These sacred places can be anywhere—kitchens, ball fields, state parks or bowling alleys. My bias is that the best spots are in natural settings. One of the greatest gifts parents can give their children is to teach them to love the natural world. Sometimes families are lucky enough to own places out in the country, a possession more valuable than jewels. I have some friends who built a large cabin beside Rocky Mountain National Park. We can hike from their land onto its trails. They have befriended the trout in the stream running through their land and given them names. This couple's children come to visit on summer weekends and their friends drive across the continent for the pleasure of drinking coffee on their porch as the sun rises.

I know another family who owns a cabin on the Missouri River. The parents and four children all leave their city lives and head for the cabin on Fridays. In the winter they cross-country ski and ice-skate on the ponds. They build huge fires in the fireplace, pop popcorn and read. In the spring they hike and search for morel mushrooms. In the summer they swim, and in the fall they watch the geese fly south over golden trees. There's a pond for bass fishing, an enormous porch for sleeping and a deck for star gazing. It's impossible to be at their cabin and not feel safe, temporarily at ease in our difficult universe.

Other families have a long tradition of renting cabins in the White Mountains, by the sea or by a lake in the Upper Peninsula or west Texas. My father always took us camping in the Ozarks. My bothers and sisters and I can remember a hundred stories of snapping turtles, giant catfish, water moccasins, rainstorms and crawdads in clear, rocky streams. Those stories form the walls of our family shelter and hold together what we have of love in our lives.

I know a family that goes rock climbing every summer in the Garden of the Gods. I know a mother and daughter who have a tradition of a mother-daughter campout every summer at a Minnesota park. A client recently told me that her son in crisis called to ask her if she would go with him to the Wind River Range camp they'd frequented when he was a child. He said, "That's the place I need to be to think this through."

But shelters do not need to be in the natural world. I have a friend whose parents ran the city café in her small Iowa town. She spent her childhood pouring coffee, serving pancakes and pies and listening to townspeople tell jokes and stories. Now when she is troubled she goes to cafés and is comforted. I have a client whose family found refuge in the public library. They went there as a family every Wednesday night and they selected books together. Many families find shelter in their churches or synagogues. Many clients have memories of certain houses as refuges, places where they could go and feel at peace. Often when they tell me of these old places, their breathing changes and their facial muscles relax.

3. Interests shelter families.

As I write this I think of three men who have been friends and family to each other since their teenage years. As boys they drummed in their parents' garages. When they are together as adults, they talk drums, watch drummers and go to bars and listen to drummers far into the night. They attend each other's performances and record each other's drum solos. When they are apart, they send each other articles and information on drummers. They are saving to visit the Zildjian cymbal factory.

Hunting often connects boys to their fathers. In fact, I am convinced that the reason so many men love hunting is that it was the one time their father spent days with them. Many Midwestern men have memories of fathers waking them before dawn, sharing big breakfasts and driving to the duck blind or hiking through snowy fields looking for pheasants. All day fathers and sons hiked, sat and watched the sky, shared coffee or whiskey and talked. The lure of those days, often golden in the memories of men, wasn't so much the hunting as the happy time with their fathers.

Many families' lives revolve around ball fields. I know a family in which everyone in three generations plays softball. They keep master calendars so that they can attend each other's games. The highlight of their year is a trip to Kansas City for the opening game of the season and a meal at Gates Bar-B-Q. I know another family who lives and breathes soccer. The dad and mother both coach teams and all the children play. They have a special room for soccer trophies. All the jerseys are saved and everyone collects soccer memorabilia. Their favorite annual event is the World Cup. They can't afford to go, but they watch it on TV.

Gardening is an activity that connects people with their families. I think of a poet I know who traveled to North Carolina for her grandmother's daylily bulbs. Many people love to grow flowers and vegetables to share with their families and friends. In Nebraska it's dangerous to visit families with gardens in July. If you do, your kitchen will be filled with zucchini and tomatoes. I think of my aunts who laboriously pick and clean gooseberries and can them for pies. I think of my friend Twyla, teaching her granddaughter Kathleen the names of prairie grasses and what to look for in the trees.

Some families organize around their pets. When I was a child, we had a Chihuahua named Coco Rosarita. We took her everywhere with us— on trips, to the lake to water-ski and on our go-cart at the county fairground. When our family could agree on nothing else, we could agree that we loved Coco. I think of our friend's ill-natured, one-eyed beagle Ned, who is much loved and discussed, much photographed and held, by a family of dog-loving sentimentalists. Sometimes it seems as if a pet becomes a metaphor for the family's love for each other.

4. Celebrations protect families.

On a cool September evening I attended the fiftieth wedding anniversary of a farm couple. The picnic tables in the front yard were decorated with garden flowers and candles. Two hundred people chatted over roast pork sandwiches and cake. The couple hugged each other frequently and smiled with pride at all the children and grandchildren.

In the distance, the lights of the town sparkled like fireflies. The corn was high, the crickets whirred and the moon flowers slowly opened in the cool dusk. Children in their good clothes chased each other under a rising half-moon. A band played the Pennsylvania Polka and "Jeepers Creepers." The older couple and their children danced in the driveway. I was happy for this couple and for all the beauty they had created on the planet.

In our rapidly changing world, people who stay married for fifty years really have multiple marriages to the same mate. They have a romantic relationship, a child-rearing relationship, and later one strong in companionship and caretaking. One marriage ceremony at the beginning is not enough to hold such a marriage in place. Couples need new ceremonies and rites of passage, second honeymoons and even third and fourth ones. It's good to renew vows and write new vows every few years.

Sibling relationships need much more support and celebration than they receive in our culture. Often as adults, we find that our siblings are the people who have known us the longest, know the most about us and share the most life events with us. Particularly in our mobile society, sibling relationships offer us a shelter that few other relationships can provide. If we are lucky, our siblings are our built-in lifelong friends. And yet as a culture, we have virtually no ways to celebrate or validate these primary relationships. In fact, if anything we have a cultural tradition of jokes that suggest visits from extended family are punishing, at least for the in-laws.

Sibling relationships can be strengthened in a hundred ways—by regular phone calls, visits and letters, by reunions and shared celebrations. I know of some brothers who take their mutual children on trips on historic steam trains every summer. I know some sisters in their seventies who send each other round robin letters every week. Each sister adds a new section as she sends the letter along. These sisters are writing their life stories. When they finish, they will read them aloud to each other and make a book of family history for the grandchildren, nieces and nephews to read.

In spite of the lack of cultural support, siblings find ways to work together. I know sisters who get together to can peaches and beans. In late August they travel to Kansas City and shop for school clothes for their children. Many siblings become "godparents" for their nieces and nephews, a wonderful tradition for these difficult times.

Celebrations build walls for families. Those can be the usual national holidays or celebrations such as graduations, weddings or anniversaries. Kwanza, celebrated by 14 million African-Americans, begins the day after Christmas and lasts seven days. It celebrates unity, self-determination, collective work, responsibility, cooperative economics, purpose, creativity and faith.

It's important that national holidays be celebrated in the family's own way. Too often now holidays and celebrations mean buying a card and some candy. There's nothing wrong with that, but the more energy that the family puts into designing a meaningful celebration, the more powerful it becomes. One family I know has a tradition of making New Year's videotapes. Each family member talks about the year, its high and low points, goals obtained and deferred. Then family members say what they want to accomplish in the coming year. Every year the children play the same song on their band instruments; every year the song is more beautiful.

Family photos capture time and underscore the importance of a particular moment. Over the years family photo albums become many families' greatest treasures and the major links between generations. There is power in looking at the face of a Civil War soldier who resembles one's son or the face of a young pioneer woman with the eyes of one's daughter. These pictures give people a sense of family over time and relationships that last beyond the present. Many people whose homes have burned say that what they miss most is the family picture albums.

Judaism seems especially good at promoting family celebrations. Bar and Bas Mitzvahs bring together families and friends in joyous celebrations of children's passage into adulthood. I attended one recently where a big band played and the children danced with their grandparents, aunts and uncles. An old man with a long beard taught a new generation the chicken dance. As the band played "Limbo Rock," a balding guy in a tight suit led children in party clothes under the limbo pole. The Shabbat dinner with its prayers, candles, bread, wine and singing is a ritual of protection. A friend once told me the Jewish religion is about the sacredness of time. It's true that many Jewish rituals celebrate time and sanctify ordinary moments.

Families need celebrations that signify rites of passage. Without these celebrations, time runs together and the significance of events is not noted. Most families celebrate birthdays but they miss the opportunity to create meaning. Much more can be done with a birthday than simply having a cake and presents. Poems and thank-you letters can be delivered. Photos can be taken and flowers and trees planted in honor of the day. One family I know gives the children a new right and a new responsibility every year on their birthdays.

Weddings and anniversaries connect families too, especially if they aren't too elaborate. The more time people spend in formal clothes the less fun they have. Simple ceremonies are often the most fun and most meaningful. One of my favorite weddings was held in a city park with a cake and sandwich reception at the recreation center nearby. The bride and groom's friends and family supplied everything—garden flowers, music, handmade dresses, photographs and ham salad sandwiches.

Anniversary ceremonies can also be important. It's great when families have open houses, receptions and celebrations for the longtime married. I remember my aunt Agnes and uncle Clair's fiftieth anniversary. Friends and family came from all over the county to their small Colorado town. People stayed in the homes of friends or camped in the park. For several days we sat under the ash trees in their yard and visited with relatives we hadn't seen for years. Children played together under the sun and stars. Old people brought out photo albums and told stories. We ate meat loaf, fried chicken, huckleberry pie and homemade ice cream. On Sunday we attended a ceremony planned by their children at the church and a reception for all their friends from the town. Agnes and Clair dressed up and posed for a family picture.

Funerals also can bring families together. When I attended my grandfather's funeral, the church was full of people who knew Fred, his family and each other. The Masons, the country club families, neighbors and the children he'd taught in Sunday school filled the pews. After the service, we ate dinner served by the church ladies and told stories about Fred. When we returned to his house it was filled with Jell-O salads, muffins and country ham, all gifts from neighbors. The family stayed for a couple of days and played music and cards and talked. My grandfather would have loved it.

We have celebrations for birth, death and marriage, but not for many events in between, defining events that should be honored. We need a celebration for Aunt Betty's retirement, for Kevin's new job, for Stephanie's driver's license and for the day Melanie leaves for college. In a way, this absence of cultural traditions is sad. Many events are either not marked or marked the easy way, with a card or a box of candy, the omnipresent celebratory gift. But in another way there is a silver lining to this cloud. In the absence of tradition, each family can define its own celebrations around these events. There's room for plenty of creativity.

Finally families can invent their own holidays. I know a family who drives to Minnesota every fall for their own Applefest. They travel to orchards and sample, then buy, all kinds of beautiful fruit, enough to dry, freeze and can so that it will last them through the long Nebraska winter. One family I know never misses a chess tournament. Another family hits all the Midwestern bluegrass festivals. They play music in the contests and sing around the campfires far into the night with the friends they have met from year to year at each festival. Many Lakota families travel around the country attending powwows. They camp, dance and feast with other families, and their children learn their traditions.

A family I know in St. Louis has Cornfest every July. They have a meal that is nothing but four dozen ears of fresh-picked and steamed roasting ears. Another family has a wienie roast every fall as a back-to-school celebration. Each child receives a hand-carved personalized wienie stick the year he/she begins school, a stick that is carefully saved from year to year. Many young families build rituals around the first and last days of school. For any occasion, it's good to have speeches, plays, songs and writing. Awards, toasts and rituals make events special and memorable. I don't think a family can over-celebrate.

5. Connecting rituals protect families.

These rituals connect family to each other, to extended family, to family friends and to the community. They can also connect the old to the young, the rich to the poor, ethnic minorities to ethnic majorities and even the dead to the living. Toasts to departed loved ones or loved ones far away can be connecting rituals. Reading letters, poems, histories and diaries of old family members can be connecting rituals.

Interviewing family can be a connecting ritual. As a teenager, one man I know interviewed all his immigrant aunts and uncles about their European experiences before they came to this country. Through these interviews he developed a fierce closeness to his kin and an interest in family history that led him to a career as a historian. Another man I know found a picture of a relative in a Civil War uniform. He researched this relative's story and now has a love of Civil War history. He collects Civil War memorabilia, visits battlefields and participates in enactments. He knows a great deal about his great-uncle Zeke, who fought long ago.

Often I ask that family members write their autobiographies and share them with the other family members. I suggest that families visit places the parents lived as children. Parents can also visit the places their children spend time so that they understand that world. It's very good, for example, for parents to spend a day shadowing their junior-high student. I know a therapist who helped a mother-daughter pair publish their poetry together in a chapbook. Another therapist asks parents to bring in their high-school yearbooks and talk to their children about their experiences as teenagers. The parents also talk about their feelings toward their parents when they were adolescents.

A good connecting ritual is sending children for long visits with relatives. I have clients who send their children to be with grandparents in the summer. Children can learn from their older relatives in another part of the country. I know of one great-aunt who has visiting nephews and nieces help her build a trail on her wild North Carolina land. After they work with her all summer, she names that segment of the trail for them.

I urge people in mourning to pick something in the natural world that reminds them of their loved ones. When they see that object—the moon, a constellation or a kind of wildflower—they can pay their respects. This idea came to me on my way to my father's funeral. As we drove to his funeral, I saw geese flying north for the summer. Ever since then, that high V in the April sky reminds me of him. I have another connecting ritual for my father. We always fished together, and now when I catch a beautiful fish I lift it up into the sky for him to appreciate.

After my mother died, I went canoeing on the Niobrara. I couldn't have chosen a more healing activity—the water, the sandy cliffs, the hawks and trembling cottonwoods all washed away my pain. Now, whenever I go to the Niobrara I think of my mother. She has become part of the canyon walls and the clear waterfalls.

At the time of her death, my husband's grandmother was a source of much family history. Maude knew seven generations of family—her great-grandparents', her grandparents' and parents' generations plus her own generation and that of her children, her grandchildren and her great-grandchildren. She had been one of seven daughters. The night after her funeral I noticed how brightly the Seven Sisters glowed in our winter sky. For me, Maude is now connected to the Pleiades.

The love of grandparents and grandchildren is often incredibly pure and powerful. I've noticed that most children who have known their grandparents grow up loving older people. They are like kittens who have been gentled and have learned to love humans. Children who haven't had that privilege often regard older people as scary or, at best, irrelevant. They have no idea what they are missing. Unfortunately, many things—such as divorce, time and distance—work against what can be an important and beautiful intergenerational bond.

Reunions are wonderful connecting rituals. As I write this I think of a snapshot from a family reunion on Table Rock Lake in the Ozarks. This picture was taken on a sunny May afternoon when we rented a pontoon and motored it to a rocky point. We lazed around. Occasionally we saw cottonmouths on the surface of the lake, snaking around our fishing lines. We talked about how cold the water was and teased each other about being chicken. Finally we got wet. My cousin Paul dove in first, then my brother John, then his wife, Joy, then my daughter, Sara, then my cousin's daughter Melanie and finally me. At first we could barely breathe, but soon we were laughing and splashing each other, all of us grinning at our bravery and foolishness. From the boat, Karlene took a picture of us waving Mao Tse-tung–style from the dark green water. We were doing something together that we would never do alone.

It's odd in this culture that many people mock these celebrations of family. There are many jokes about family reunions, family holidays and family videos being a drag. But at reunions people often have memorable experiences. They say the things that need to be said. One brother spoke of his brother. He began, "The best luck a man could have is to have Randy for a brother." One granddaughter spoke at her one-hundred-year-old grandmother's birthday. "When I was drinking and strung out, her image gave me the strength to fight my addiction."

As a girl I was fascinated by the diverse and complicated relatives I met at reunions. As the women cooked, I would hang around the kitchen and listen to what they said about their husbands and children. I would drive with the men out to the fields and listen as they competed to tell the funniest stories. At dinner, my family would argue politics and family history, and after dinner the adults would play cards or horseshoes. I loved to fall asleep to the sounds of grown-ups talking to my parents in the next room.

I feel sorry for children today who, when the aunts and uncles come, are sent to the basement with a Disney video. Children learn from grown-ups. They hear their stories, their jokes, their trials and tribulations. They learn the rich and idiosyncratic use of language that occurs in families. They hear the cautionary tales and moral fables. They learn the wrong and the right ways to do things. For example, one time after a family celebration, my daughter observed, "Everyone loves to talk to Aunt Pam. She asks them what they are most interested in discussing. She knows how to listen."

Reunions let children know that there are people besides their parents who care about them. They give them a community of kin, a tiospaye for non-Lakota peoples. If children are not fortunate in their own parents, reunions are places where children may find other adults who will understand them. If children are different from their own families, perhaps at reunions they will find kindred spirits.

Reunions reconnect the family to extended family and to the natural world and disconnect them from the corporate, generic world. Compared to computer time, everything happens in slow motion. Families talk about who looks like whom, who walks like whom, who talks like whom and who thinks like whom. They compare cobbler recipes and discuss the best way to toilet-train toddlers. They tell embarrassing stories about the adults present. This talk is familial cement. It helps everyone stick together.

6. Stories and metaphors protect families.

All families have stories that they tell over and over—"Remember the time we went camping and the fire ants ate through the bottom of our tent. . . ." "Remember the night of the eclipse when we sailed all night long and watched the meteor showers. . . ." "Remember when the blizzard stranded us in Chicago for a week. . . ." "Remember Aunt Minnie's long visits and her stewed prunes every morning. . . ." "Remember when

Zeke woke up the alligator at Reptile Gardens. . . ." "Remember the night we fished all night and caught fifty-two white bass on Lake McConanghy. . . ."

At get-togethers family members tell certain stories as if on cue. Sometimes other members invite the stories, other times they roll their eyes in frustration. Occasionally someone will be so rude as to say they have heard the story a thousand times. They are utterly missing the point and the storyteller will ignore them. After many years everyone knows the words exactly; they'll jump in if the teller misspeaks, even a little. Why are certain stories so important? Why are they polished over the years, like pebbles in a stream, into smooth, round unbreakable metaphors?

Stories reveal what a family wants to believe about itself. They say something about the family, about its character, history and virtues. For example, one genre of family stories is vacation-disaster stories, which are told and retold with more zeal than the disaster-free stories. Families love the stories about the car breaking down in the desert, the flat tire on a mountain road, the hotel from *Psycho* with cockroaches between the sheets, the time lightning almost struck the tent or the time the pet rabbit got lost in a visitor-center parking lot. These stories are important because they say this family can not only survive adversity but they can laugh at it and keep on loving each other.

Some stories are about adventures, awards and good deeds. They announce they are an important family, a smart family or a beautiful family. Some are about the family heroes, and these teach the family what behavior is considered heroic. In some families, artists or writers are heroes. In others, it's the uncle who makes a million dollars or the great-aunt who cares tenderly for her senile husband. There are stories about the founders of the family—the grandfather who came over from Ireland, the great-grandmother who was a slave, the quirky inventor who made the family fortune or the beloved grandfather who was orphaned by cholera as a boy.

Many stories are cautionary tales. They tell of the cousin who gambled heavily and lost his home, the uncle who quit a good job and couldn't find another, the daughter who married too young and was never happy in her marriage. Families have hardship stories that underscore how hard the family has worked to survive. Often these are immigration stories, escape stories, Depression and dust bowl stories. Older family members want the young to hear these stories so they know that families don't survive without hard work. They teach that family doesn't come easily, but is hard won and therefore should be valued.

Families also have metaphors that stand for what the family loves and values. Sometimes that metaphor is a person who is deeply loved by all the family members. This person's virtues the family admires. Often the family saint is a grandparent. While the grandparent is alive, the family organizes around him/her, and after death, they mention the name in hushed tones. Family members unite around their memories and the love they share for the departed. On holidays they drink toasts to them and tell the jokes that they loved.

Sometimes a family's metaphor is an activity. With the Kennedys it was football. With the Bushes it was sailing. One family I love cooks together. Holidays mean that the members bake cakes and pies, smoke turkeys and hams, bake corn and potato casseroles and compare with great intensity recipes for cranberry relish or watermelon pickles. The daughter in this family is now pregnant in a faraway state and her mother is preparing a book of family and friend recipes of healthy foods for pregnant women. Love may be encoded as camping, baking, making music, sewing or barbecuing. They are all family prayers.

The metaphor can be a place, such as the kitchen or Uncle Lloyd's back porch. It can be an object—such as the round dining table, the old Chevrolet, the ash tree in the front yard, the blue quilt or Mother's diamond ring. These objects symbolize and concretize the family's love and power. Parenthetically, they are often hotly disputed at funerals. And anyone who argues about them on the basis of their monetary value is totally off base.

Food is often tied up with family metaphors. In our family it is pie. Everyone knows everyone else's favorite kinds, and the merits of these choices are hotly disputed. We compare pies with great intensity and all have our favorite pie chefs. Pie means that an event is special, that we are together and celebrating. In other families, Grandmother's noodles come to stand for Grandmother. The fresh-caught trout eaten in a mountain campground stands for a time when the family was young and happy. People speak with such longing of their mother's biscuits or their father's farm-raised chickens. It isn't just the food they are missing but the emotions that are connected to those meals and the people who served the food.

A friend of mine wrote about the healing powers of good food. He wrote: "We've done our share of things wrong as a family, but one of the things we did right was to insist that the evening meal be a family event. I cook these meals myself and I go to a great deal of trouble over them. We eat good food and we eat it together. My children, who can sometimes seem thankless, have often said how much they appreciate these efforts, and my daughter, who is now away at college, tells me all the time how much she misses dinners. This evening meal is a ritual so firmly established that it alters our way of vacationing. When we travel, we rent an apartment rather than stay in a hotel so that I can cook the evening meal. We have discovered that trips to local markets for food are a great part of our fun and there have come to be rituals within rituals. On our annual trip to Mexico, for example, one day is set aside for a trip to the sea to catch a fresh tuna for dinner. The rituals surrounding food are an essential part of our family's life."

In some ways metaphors are the most important protectors of families. When all else fails, there are always memories, stories and totemic objects. They can transcend time and distance, poverty and ill health. These metaphors of food, places, trips, beloved objects and beloved people become the connecting tissue of the family. They give family members' lives a context and meaning, a history and philosophy. The protective walls of a family are not made of stone, but of love.

Chapter Twelve

CONNECTING FAMILIES—CREATING A TIOSPAYE

THE MANOR

As I walked into the Manor at sunset, I felt tired from a long workday and gloomy about a broken water heater at home. The residents, most of them in wheelchairs, were gathered in a central area around the musicians. Lois, younger than I, waved from her wheelchair. Doris, a large woman in a pink blouse and yellow stretch pants, greeted her friends. Conrad, a thin, dignified man dressed in black, waved me over. He'd had a stroke and was hard to understand, but I could tell he was ready for music.

Crystal wheeled in the last of the residents. Crystal hugged InaJean and said, "She just broke her leg. This is her first time in a wheelchair. Music is just what the doctor ordered." Looking dapper with his snowy beard and red suspenders, Ray talked to the musicians as they tuned up.

The musicians, a fiddler, a guitar player and a man on bass, played on the first Tuesday of each month. They began with the Manor theme song, "Whiskey Before Breakfast," and Fiddling Dave told the monthly joke, "Somewhere in the world it's always time for breakfast."

The music changed everything. All the residents looked younger and more alert. Tired bodies sat up straight, heads bobbed, hands clapped, sober faces broke into smiles and toes in soft slippers tapped the floor. The residents sang along on "Wabash Cannonball." Many fine voices grew stronger as they sang. Memory for lyrics was amazingly good. Time dropped away.

The band played "Turkey in the Straw," "San Antonio Rose" and the "Tennessee Waltz." "I remember the night and the Tennessee Waltz, Only you know how much I have lost." There was lots of arm patting, hand holding and wiping of eyes. Lois requested "Dixie" and Doris wanted "Wild Irish Rose." I worried that InaJean would fall out of her wheelchair as she chair-danced to "Clarinet Polka," "Don't Fence Me In" and "Blue Ridge Cabin Home."

As everyone sang along to a jazzed-up version of "What a Friend We Have in Jesus," I helped pass out punch and cookies. InaJean shouted, "Are you weak and heavy laden, cumbered with a load of care? Precious savior still our refuge. Take it to the Lord in prayer."

While the residents struggled with their plastic cups and cookies, there was a lull in requests. The bass player said, "When in doubt, play a Hank Williams tune." The musicians ended the night with "Your Cheatin' Heart." Afterward, we visited with the residents. We touched their hands, made silly jokes and asked about relatives.

By the time we said good night, I was lighthearted. Whatever self-pity I brought into the Manor I left in the meeting room. I respected the courage of Ray with his red suspenders, of Lois, whose story was sadder than I wanted to hear, of Conrad and InaJean. I felt grateful to be healthy and forty-eight. Suddenly, being able to walk seemed like a miracle. When I left, it was cool outside. The cicadas hummed and a blue moon sailed behind black-and-white clouds.

THE YA SHOOR BIKE TOUR

Saturday was the third Ya Shoor bike tour. This event gives Lincolnites a chance to ride north from Lincoln to the "motherland" of Oakland, Nebraska, and the Swedish festival. Many of the riders have been friends since kindergarten. We met at six-thirty in the HyVee parking lot. Fifty bicyclists circled the sag wagon for drinks and last-minute instructions. This year the wagon was driven by two Viking Maidens, one who wore black motorcycle boots, jeans and a homemade breastplate, "Ya Shoor Noire," as one biker put it. The other wore blue-and-gold yarn braids, a silver tunic that matched her war bonnet horns and an amazing satin cloak of purple and gold. She belted out Swedish arias. Both women brandished spears and bows and arrows to get us started.

We rode north past meadows and old farmsteads. After weeks of gray sogginess, the hero of the day was the sun. In the sunrise, the oats sparkled with dew. Mist hovered over farm ponds. We saw and heard red-winged blackbirds, meadowlarks and mourning doves. We almost ran over bull snakes sunning by the road.

Our spirits were high as we pulled into Wahoo, Nebraska, for breakfast at the Wigwam Café. It's a historic café with wooden carvings on the walls and a dream catcher over the kitchen door. We had pancakes or the $2.50 breakfast special of sausage, eggs, toast and home fries. We drank lots of coffee and ordered raisin pie for dessert. The locals looked a little baffled by all the middle-aged people in biking shorts eating pie at nine in the morning.

We rode on past goats and sheep near Cedar Bluff, past the Pawnee sacred site on Highway 109 and past our sag wagon with the Viking women handing out cookies, bananas and water. As we rode we waved to each other. Thumbs up meant "Ya, you betcha." Thumbs down meant "Stop, I need a drink." The sun grew hotter. By noon there was more traffic, the hills seemed higher and we were riding into a head wind. Knees burned and behinds ached. The caravan spread out, with the serious bikers far ahead of stragglers. A few of us "hit the wall."

At the corner bar in Uehling we were all together again. Our bikes and bodies filled the main street. Fifty more Oakies and their children joined us there, including ten-year-old Jules, who showed us his homemade tattoo that said "Biking Vikings." Three beautiful babies were new to our community since the last tour. Chloe, Mara and Amazing Grace were passed around and admired. We put on our official green Ya Shoor T-shirts and took a group photo.

In the late afternoon we rode into Oakland. We paraded past the sign that said VELCOMMEN TO OAKLAND, SWEDISH CAPITAL OF NEBRASKA and past the water tower with a *dahla* painted on it. *Dahla* is Swedish for little painted wooden horse. Spears in hand, our Viking Maidens danced and sang. One hundred fifty sweaty bicyclists turned onto Main Street. After eighty-five miles of hard riding we were ready for anything—cold drinks, music by Champaign Jerry and the Vegetarians and the smorgasbord with its ostakaka and herring. We were old friends, hot, sore, happy and hungry. What's Swedish for carpe diem?

MAKING CONNECTIONS

"Love the earth and the animals, despise riches, give alms to everyone that asks, stand up for the stupid and crazy, devote your income and labor to others, hate tyrants and argue not concerning God."—Walt Whitman

The two stories above are about community, about people benefiting from the shelter of each other. They are stories of hope, a commodity in short supply in our confusing times. Despair, on the other hand, is easy to find. As a people we share a collective sense of victimization, helplessness and resignation. Our institutions are failing us and our collective culture is having a nervous breakdown. We mistrust each other. As things fall apart, people look for someone to blame. It's easier to be a cynical outsider than to go inside and try to make things work. We all wonder, as Greg Brown asked, "if bad change comes on so fast, why does good change take so long?"

In *A Distant Mirror*, Barbara Tuchman compared our time to the Middle Ages. The fourteenth century was characterized by economic chaos, frenetic gaiety, debauchery, social and religious hysteria, greed and the decay of manners. In the Middle Ages, people were better than their institutions. The times were violent, tormented and disintegrating. But after the Middle Ages came the Renaissance.

As Yeats wrote in "The Second Coming," "The blood-dimmed tide is loosed, and everywhere/The ceremony of innocence is drowned;/The best lack all conviction, while the worst/Are full of passionate intensity." In the 1980s many people retreated into private life. They tried to go first class on the *Titanic*, but that didn't work. By now it is clear that our public world must be saved. As Hillman wrote, the self is the internalization of the community. We cannot be healthy in a community full of pathology. We are all joined at the hip.

Many smart people live at the level of detail. They enjoy the tiny events, the small moments and the jokes. These friends deliberately do not integrate these details and extrapolate meaning from their lives. They do not connect the dots because to do so is too overwhelming. Instead they talk passionately of their children's swim meets, their hiking boots, their cappuccino makers or their home improvements. It's important to connect one's life with the larger whole. Without integration there is no meaning; with no meaning there is despair.

Sometimes people who are concerned with the big picture are discouraged from acting. For example, a client recently said, "I am upset about Bosnia. I'm dreaming about pollution and murder. Is it just me or is the world going crazy? Are things getting worse?" Even two years ago I would have connected her despair about the world to her depression. I would have viewed her remarks as a metaphor about her own life and I would have encouraged her to personalize her sadness about the world. This time I took her remarks about her dreams and Bosnia at face value. We talked about the things she could do to make a difference.

Some friends feel that there is nothing they can do. Some people even proclaim that fact proudly. But this profound hopelessness creates its own reality and becomes a self-fulfilling prophecy. We can act if we believe we can act. We can build new good things. The cure for cynicism, depression and narcissism is social action. Action solves two problems. It makes communities better and it gives people a sense of meaning and purpose.

When my daughter was thirteen we went to San Francisco. Sara had never seen homeless people before and she could not get used to it. Every time we passed a beggar she insisted I give money. At first I agreed, but finally I said no, that we needed the rest of our money. She was upset and I promised that when we returned home, we'd work together at a soup kitchen.

We worked at one for a year. We showed up early in the morning, made coffee and passed around donuts and fruit. It was the best thing that happened to Sara during her difficult seventh-grade year. The experience had four main effects: One, it removed her from a shallow and mean-spirited peer culture and allowed her to spend time with people of all ages. Two, it gave her an education about drugs and alcohol. The people at the shelter who used chemicals didn't look cool or sophisticated, they looked sick and messed up.

- Three, the work gave her time with adults who were not in a hurry. Homeless people were the first people she'd ever met who had plenty of time for children. No one looked at his/her watch constantly. A woman helped her learn to draw horses. Old men taught her card tricks or told her stories of ranch life in the 1920s. People had time for dominoes, double solitaire, hearts and pitch. And four, Sara learned that she could make a difference. She could give hungry people food and sad people some companionship. This saved her from cynicism.

Volunteers are happy people. The person who turns off daytime TV and teaches an immigrant to read feels better about his/her life. Sometimes volunteers unite against a common enemy, such as tornadoes, floods or fires. Sometimes they unite around a desire to do good work— to build a trail, paint a house or do health screenings for children. Working with others can rekindle idealism and rebuild a sense of community. Work cures despair.

Joy Harjo wrote, "There is no separation. We are all from the same place." In her Native American community, people who worked for the community were highly valued. Visionaries and artists were respected because they represented the community's situation. Joy Harjo wrote, "As long as there is respect and acknowledgment of connections, things continue working. When that stops we all die."

This century has suffered from what Foucault called "dividing practices." We have been separated from each other and the natural world. Nietzsche wrote that "sin is that which separates." But we can reintegrate our world and reweave a coat of meaning that we can all wear for protection from the elements.

For this purpose, Carol Bly and Meridel Le Sueur are more useful to us than Jack Kerouac and Charles Bukowski. O'Keeffe is more helpful than Picasso. The challenge now is to connect, to repair, to bring people back together—rich and poor, young and old, black and white, liberal and conservative. We have much more in common than is generally suggested. As Willa Cather wrote, "The prayers of all good people are good prayers."

When you are backpacking in the wilderness, the first rule in any crisis is "Don't panic." The greatest danger is losing one's head. Panic disorganizes thinking and leads to self-defeating behavior. When I backpack I never travel alone. It's always good to have someone along to help. These guidelines apply to our present desperate situation as a society. When we panic, we act hastily, make mistakes and get ourselves in even worse trouble. We can work our way out of the woods if we think carefully, talk calmly and work together.

America has long been about much more than money. The values of early America—self-restraint, self-control, work and frugality—were different from current profit-driven values. When the Pilgrims served the first Thanksgiving dinner, they didn't charge admission. The Constitution says nothing about the bottom line. It talks about ideas like equality, justice and the common good.

Our society is capable of great decency. We are the country of the Marshall Plan, the GI Bill and Social Security. We have made positive changes before. We've outlawed child labor and given women and minorities the right to vote. Racism and anti-Semitism are no longer socially acceptable in most places. We no longer allow cigarette ads on television. We don't dump DDT on our wheat fields or apple orchards.

Ideas have tremendous power in our culture. The ideas of Rachel Carson and Harriet Beecher Stowe, to name two of my favorites, have changed the landscape of our lives. Americans have long believed that the way to make our nation stronger is to make it better. But when we stopped working together in groups, things fell apart. We need to once again work community by community to make our country whole. It will be hard work, but America has done hard things before.

CREATING A COMMUNITY

"As long as there is one upright man, as long as there is one compassionate woman, the contagion may spread and the scene is not desolate. Hope is the thing that is left to us in a bad time."—E. B. White

A family I know spent a year in a rain forest in Brazil. They lived in a Stone Age village of eighty people on the banks of a muddy river. The mother told me how quickly her children adapted. In the United States, they were like other American kids—easily bored, acquisitive and reluctant to work. At first they were this way in Brazil. But it wasn't long before they realized they were in a new place—a place where adults slowly carved a papaya into a dozen pieces and shared it with everyone in the room, a place where families sat around fires far into the night telling stories about monkey kings and rabbits who jumped to the moon and a place where a person could grow up and marry before he or she ever rode in a motorized vehicle.

The children soon knew everyone in the village. They worked with the villagers building huts, seining for small fish and gathering firewood and fruit. The working parties included people of all ages who sang and joked together as they worked. Protecting and teaching adults were nearby. No one was in a hurry.

By American standards, everyone was poor. But the people didn't know this and they enjoyed themselves in spite of their lack of posses-' sions. For example, every night the couple next door ground just enough coffee beans for two strong cups of coffee. They prepared the coffee over a small fire and then climbed a hill to watch the sun go down. The children in the village played with rocks, sticks, leaves and water. People shared what little they had.

Soon the American children were offering whatever they had to the visitors who dropped by their hut. They stopped fighting with each other and whining for parental attention. Because there were no catalogs, commercials or ads to pique their attention, the children lost interest in consumer goods. They preferred people and activities. They were always outdoors with their friends and they were never bored. Life was more interesting in the village than in their Kansas City suburb. After a year the family returned to the United States. The mother ruefully said, "Within a week, they'd turned back into their American selves, arguing over the computer, who should take out the trash and who should get the last granola bar."

———

A friend of mine who is a single parent planned a coming-of-age ceremony for her daughter's thirteenth birthday. In the spring, she sent all her women friends who had known the daughter quilt pieces and asked them to stitch or draw a picture on the piece. The picture was to depict an experience the woman had had with the daughter. In the summer, all of these women met the mother and daughter for a weekend of camping, hiking and feasting.

Saturday night around the fire there was a ceremony. Each woman showed and explained her picture. Then she gave the girl a gift—a promise of one way she would help the daughter grow up. One woman said she would teach the daughter to garden; another offered to help her write papers and college applications; another could teach her French and another could help her learn to sail. The girl sat in the middle of the circle beside the fire. She listened to the stories and the offers. The women gave her hugs and congratulations. The next morning in the sunlight, they sewed the quilt together.

———

Communities are real places with particular landscapes, sounds and smells. Particular people live there and everyone knows their names. You may not always like each other, but you understand each other. Communities are about accountability, about what I owe you and what you owe me and about what we can and should do for each other.

Today many people leave their old neighborhoods and move to retirement areas in more beautiful places. When they get there, they are alone. As Greg Brown said, "You can't drink a cup of coffee with the landscape." Many young people leave their hometowns and move to cities or suburbia. There are more jobs in those places, but young people find themselves cut off from all that sustains them. If true wealth were defined as the quality of one's personal relationships, many young adults would choose to stay closer to home.

To have a real life, people must participate in real community. People who live in virtual communities have virtual lives. Black Elk talked to Neihardt about the time of tiospaye "when the people were still good." Children grew up surrounded by adults who cared for them. Proper behavior was made clear to children by aunts and uncles. When the tiospaye disappeared, children no longer were taught how to be good. How do we create a tiospaye for our children?

I visited a beautiful neighborhood in Connecticut. There were large houses with spacious yards on winding, tree-lined streets. But my hosts knew none of their neighbors. They wouldn't even recognize them on the street. Their children didn't know the neighborhood children. No one played out of doors. This was a "bedroom community" in which people spent the day away and then came home to their TVs, computers and stereo systems. Everyone was busy; they had their own little worlds but every family was alone.

And of course many parents were tired. The parents worked long hours and came home spent. The little time they did have they wanted for their children. Rather than go to a meeting, they supervised homework or prepared a meal. There is a season for civic involvement and parents with young children cannot do much. Later they can perhaps participate more in the life of their town. But even the busiest person could do a little. These parents could learn the names of the families on their block and wave to the children and retired people. They could help kids find lumber to build a fort or help an elderly neighbor into her apartment with her groceries.

These acts create a community. Adults can talk for a few minutes to the children who deliver newspapers or fliers. Parents of teenagers can meet once a month and talk about how the children are doing. Families can put their lawn chairs in the front yards rather than on their fenced-in back patios. Families can organize block parties—potlucks, parades or star-gazing evenings. Families can do all the things that people do for each other in connected communities. They can carry zucchini bread or garden flowers to each other's houses. They can offer to watch each other's children, and when the children are over, actually play games with them or teach them something. Families can offer to help their neighbors with home improvement projects or write them notes of news, sympathy or congratulations. Children can set up lemonade stands and all the adults can stop for drinks.

Simple tools would help people know each other. For example, when we moved into our neighborhood, the man next door drew us a map of our street. On every house, Ron wrote the names of the parents and what they did, the names and ages of the children and the phone numbers. He knew which parents were home during the day and which families had pets. Later Ron gave us a list of unusual or expensive items that neighbors were willing to loan. Over the years we shared ladders, microphones, video cameras, snow blowers, pickups, Halloween costumes and wheelbarrows. These small matters helped a great deal. Once we knew our neighbors' names we had something to build upon. Sharing goods saved us all money and gave us a sense of connection.

Ursula K. Le Guin said, "Love doesn't just sit there like a stone: it has to be made like bread, remade all the time, made new." Many of the things that would change the quality of our neighborhoods are simple but not easy. Architects could design homes that reach out into the community, homes with front porches or homes built around courtyards so that children can play together in protected places. Developers can save wild areas for children and set aside common space for families to enjoy.

The essential step is really the change in attitude, the wish to connect, and from that architecture will follow.

Martin Buber wrote of I-it relationships in which people were merely objects used for certain purposes. These he opposed to I-thou relationships, in which the other was a real person with a life like one's own. He argued that life is rich in proportion to the number of I-thou relationships a person has. What Buber said about relationships can be extended to cultures. A culture in which most people spend their time in I-it relationships is a deeply impoverished culture. Whether it's rural Colorado or the pygmy culture described in *The Forest People*, a culture of I-thou relationships is a rich culture. In fact, a new cultural definition of wealth could be not the GNP, but how many people truly know and care about each other.

This definition of cultural wealth is related to Margaret Mead's definition of an ideal human culture as one in which there is a place for every human gift. It is hard to realize the gifts of people whom we do not know. In an ideal culture people know each other enough to acknowledge and support each other in the development of their individual gifts. This way of looking at wealth also connects to Hillman's idea about the self as community internalized. There is more richness, variety and complexity to internalize when we know our neighbors.

Now this leads to some suggestions that don't even cost money about how to make America a better place. Turn off your machines, walk outside and visit with whoever is there. Talk to the children in your neighborhood. Ask the waiter at the place you buy your morning coffee about his family. Ask the waitress's name at the café you frequent. Ask of the people you meet, What is your experience? Go to a school board meeting, befriend the older people on your block, coach a ball team and offer help to whoever needs it.

I have heard many stories of adults who are making a difference in their communities. To do this, a person need not be rich or powerful, only eager. Bill's an example. His neighbor told me a moving story. Three years ago, just after she moved next door to Bill and his wife, her husband left her and her two toddlers. She said, "I was broke, pregnant and depressed. I knew no one in town."

Her doorbell rang and it was Bill with a bag of groceries. He introduced himself and said simply, "I understand that you are in trouble. What do you need?" She stood at the door speechless while he offered to shovel her snow, help with the children or give her money. She said, "He seemed great, but I was suspicious. Nobody is this nice. I wondered if he was dangerous, crazy or on the make." She smiled and said, "Now I am friends with Bill and his wife."

The saying "It takes a village to raise a child" has almost become trite with overuse. Our electronic village hasn't done a very good job raising children. To me the word "village" implies that children have many adults involved in helping them grow up. Everywhere villages are forming. Book clubs meet to read and discuss how to change our culture. Schools open their doors to children at all hours and churches mobilize to work for children. All over our country parents are meeting to discuss what our children need.

Let me share a few of the stories of projects that connect people to each other. These aren't necessarily the best projects or even a representative sample of the activities that are happening. In fact, most of the projects that I hear about are local projects. I live in a small middle-class city surrounded by farm land. Our town is relatively prosperous, and as of this writing we have had one murder in the last eighteen months. So we are safer, richer and more rural than many other places. Different areas have different needs, but I tell these stories as examples of what people can do. Certain solutions, such as more time in the mountains, are harder to implement in certain areas. Others are hard to implement without time or money. But I share these stories in the hope they give readers ideas and optimism about their ability to make a difference.

Six years ago Joe Ballard, a local school bus driver, organized sports teams for kids who were too poor to sign up for other teams. He now has more than six hundred kids playing on the forty-eight teams of his Youth Softball League. He also formed a Youth against Racism and Prejudice organization that has one thousand young members. Just recently a wealthy couple announced that they will pay Joe a salary and benefits so that he can work full-time with youth and sports. He was quoted as saying he is "still in shock and amazed. I am so grateful."

At Topeka High School, I spoke to a group of young women in Fearless, a club for the empowerment of teenage girls. Their school and community had many problems that hurt young women and they banded together to fight back. They have learned self-defense and assertiveness skills. They study the media and they fight ads they don't like with letters and protests. They work to raise the consciousness of other students about issues that affect young women—violence, addictions, eating disorders and sexual behavior. I loved my time with this energetic and idealistic group of young women who were helping each other to be strong.

One of my favorite stories is of a hundred teens in a small rural community. These teens were tired of a town that offered nothing positive for teens to do. They met at the local café and organized a group to build a recreation center. They want a place to play ball and read poetry. They have a board and an architect and they are in the midst of money-raising activities.

Many communities are finding communal spaces—for people of all ages to play ball, walk and talk, for horseshoes and boccie, for chess games and conversations. Often when older people sit on the benches around these spaces and talk, read their papers or knit, the dangerousness of the area decreases dramatically. I have heard stories of grandmothers moving into parks filled with drug dealers and changing the character of those parks by their benign presence.

In Cambridge, Massachusetts, parents organized a parents' forum that meets for support, education and activities. They offer parents exchanges of toys, books, videos and information. They also have listening partnerships in which adults and teenagers meet regularly to talk. (This is much less expensive than therapy.) They publish a newsletter and sponsor drug-free activities for teens. They also sponsor activist workshops, community letter writing campaigns and boycotts of products that hurt children.

"Every boy in his heart would rather steal second base than an automobile," said Tom Clark Teenagers need positive ways to be respected. Many communities are designing coming-of-age rituals for their youth. Unitarian churches now have a special coming-of-age ceremony for teens. The old-fashioned idea of pledges, something that was popular with youth fellowship groups when I was a girl, is coming back. Youths pledge not to do drugs or alcohol and to wait for sex until they are older. Many towns now have mentoring programs in which adults meet with young people and help them through their teen years. Some schools have programs in which business people come into the schools over their lunch hours and read aloud to children.

The Japanese celebrate the coming of age of their twenty-year-olds. In every community, young adults have a special day that includes a lecture on the rights and responsibilities of adults in Japanese society. Both the joys and duties of adulthood are clarified. The special day also includes athletic competitions, parties, prizes and trophies and acknowledgment of the honors of adulthood.

Some communities are honoring teenagers for their good behavior. Teens who volunteer, do well academically or create something important are featured in local news. The teens who are doing well, not the teens in trouble, are getting their names in the paper. For example, our public radio station asked teens to submit tapes of their own music. The ten best musicians were given an hour's show to perform their works over the air.

Many communities are realizing the value of projects that connect the young and the old. Older people are often wiser and less stressed than the rest of us and they have time and patience. Midwestern communities are developing intergenerational storytelling projects in which children are paired with older people in the community. The older people tell the children about the Depression, farm life, World War II, whatever they have experienced. The children are fascinated by these stories and began to seek out the company of the old.

My personal favorite intergenerational program comes from Ohio and is called the Environmental Mentor Program. Older people in town are paired with young people. They walk them around the town and talk about how the town used to be, where the rivers ran and what they were like, where wild spaces existed, where children played, what buildings are still in use and what ones are gone. The children learn the history of their town and the older people realize the changes for children in the town. Both generations are sensitized to the experiences of the other.

In a small Kansas town, every week the newspaper recognizes a citizen for random acts of kindness. Everyone wants in on this project and it's almost impossible to carry your own groceries to the car. Eager helpers are everywhere. It's dangerous to say that you want something. Someone is liable to give it to you.

There are good projects everywhere. Habitat for Humanity builds homes for the poor. The Children's Defense Fund coordinates national efforts to aid children. In Walnut Creek, California, citizens started a "gun swap for psychotherapy" program. My cabdriver in Takoma told me about his borrowers co-op, in which neighbors share cars, garden space and computers. Our Lincoln Action Program has set aside land for our Asian families to plant vegetables in a communal garden. In fact many communities are setting aside spots for collective gardening.

We have Jazz in June, free outdoor concerts every Tuesday night in June. Hundreds of people come with their lawn chairs and coolers. I love to go—to see all the babies being passed around, to watch young kids dancing or playing cards on blankets with their parents. I watch the old people talk to college kids, the punk drummers visit with the drummers in the bands. Our citizens love this chance to visit with each other and hear music.

Some communities in Minnesota are sponsoring "Turn Off Your TV Days." On these days, they encourage everyone to go out on their front porches and talk to their neighbors. These days give people a sense of community and control. They can do something about a world that has been overwhelming one family at a time.

One person can make a difference. Eleanor Roosevelt said, "Most of the good work in the world is done by people who weren't feeling all that well the day they did it." What's often important is not what we do when we feel great, but what we do when we feel lousy, when we've been up all night with a sick child or when we go to work with a migraine and hear that one of our co-workers is in trouble. People needn't be paragons of mental health to work for the common good. For one thing, self-actualizers are in short supply. People also needn't feel that they must change the world single-handedly. There are many people working on this project. Just because a person can't do everything doesn't mean he/she should do nothing.

Small events matter. Recycling helps. Feeding the poor helps. Protecting animals, plants and water helps. Making vows to be kinder helps. I know some junior-high girls who got together and pledged they wouldn't tease other girls for what they wore or how they looked. They didn't want to punish poor girls who didn't have designer clothes. I know a woman who, before she orders something from a catalog, thinks of sending a check to a charitable organization. She asks, "Do I want this blue sweater more than I want to send $40 to international relief? Do I want new hiking boots more than I want to contribute to Thanksgiving dinner for the poor? Which is more important to me?"

LaJean created a sanctuary at the high school where she works. She told me about it. "A few years ago there was this group of kids we called the Corner Crew. They were the kids who weren't into sports, music or studying. These kids hung out on the corner across the street and smoked. As I walked past them one day, this impulse grabbed me. Before I even thought, I invited them to the media center for a Christmas party. I said we'd have it just for them. They asked if they could bring their music and I said sure, that they could dance on the tables."

She chuckled. "Well, they all came. We bought punch and cookies and let them have the place for about three hours. They played their boom boxes and danced. We frosted a gingerbread house with them. It was funny to see these hard-core kids so excited about a gingerbread house. They ate all the cookies and played with the computers. After that they started coming by more often. We had a few more get-togethers. Soon all those kids were hanging out here." She said proudly, "Every one of them graduated from high school."

Chuck of Missoula, Montana, created something good in his town. While on a trip, he saw a beautiful carousel and realized that something important had been lost. He'd never carved wood before but he came home determined to learn and build something for the kids in his town. His wife bought him tools and he began to carve his first basswood horse. Soon other people heard about his project and offered to help. Letters and checks arrived. Chuck found seventy-seven-year-old machinery and the men got it cranked up and running. Men signed up for shifts sanding and painting the horses. Schoolchildren gathered one million pennies.

Now there is a community-built carousel in the city park for all the kids. The radio story that I heard focused on the beautiful carousel and the happy, awed children. But I think the real story was the process, the coming together of a community around a common purpose. As Chuck said, "The most important thing a person can do with his life is to leave something beautiful behind for children." He taught this to many other people.

NATURE

Thoreau said, "This curious world which we inhabit is more wonderful than it is convenient, more beautiful than it is useful; it is more to be admired and enjoyed than used."

On a lovely December Sunday I went cross-country skiing in Pioneer's Park. The sky was blue, the pines green and the snow, when the angle of the sun was right, sparkled with diamonds. I skied by the sledding hill. Hundreds of children and parents dotted the slope, their bright jackets like confetti on the snow. Near me, brothers on a toboggan took a tumble and roared with laughter. Parents warned kids to hold on. Kids squealed as they were pushed off the launching ramp. A boy in a red snowsuit, bundled up so tightly he waddled, pulled his sled to his dad and said, "This is the most fun we ever had." I smiled at all these people getting along so well. These families were the lucky ones, the families who knew to come outdoors. They were enjoying something families have loved for a thousand years.

As Mark Slouka sadly said, "Every place I've ever lived in this world has been paved over, malled over or disappeared." Many modern children find it safer and easier to stay indoors and watch television. I worry that children do not even know what they are missing. In the wilderness there is connection and complexity, challenge and serenity. In most of us there is a deep hunger for contact with the natural world. Everywhere people love to garden, to work with soil, to touch plants and make things grow. Gardening is healing. It's being involved with an old, old tradition, one that has always gone far beyond the practical need for food.

Children cannot love what they do not know. They cannot miss what they have never experienced. Families need wild places to visit and programs that connect children to the natural world. I know a program that helps infants and young children bond with the natural world. Older people take parents and young children out to the prairie to experience its immediacy—its waves of warmth and coolness, its smells of soil and plants, the sounds of wind through wild grasses, the birds, the field mice and the deer.

Disturbed children often find help in the wilderness. They learn new skills and they put some of their problems in a new perspective. In fact, programs such as Outward Bound are often more helpful to teenagers than hospitals. Many communities now offer camps for families or parent-child pairs. Families are taught to camp, hike, sail, canoe and rock climb. Members learn to love the outdoors together.

Environmentalist Wes Jackson of the Land Institute in Kansas advised young people to get an education, but to return to their hometowns and make things better. Bill and Jan Whitney have followed his advice. When they graduated from college with degrees in biology, they moved back to their hometown and founded Prairie Plains Resource Institute. They do research on preserving and restoring prairies and they publish a newsletter. One of their programs is SOAR, Summer Orientation About Rivers, in which they teach children to love our state's many streams and rivers.

There are many other local projects. Our town has beautiful walking trails that are filled with bikers, joggers and walkers of all ages. Local people are participating in the rails-to-trails program and developing places to ride bikes. We have a program called Wildlife Rescue in which families work to save injured birds, rabbits, squirrels and raccoons. We also have a nature center where families learn about the natural world. At night the center has star- and moon-gazing and animal-sounds tours. In the day, families learn to identify birds and wildflowers and study the ecology of a meadow and pond. These programs teach families to love the natural world, and ultimately those who love the natural world will be the ones who save it.

THE CULTURE

"Collective action is not all taking our Prozac at the same time."—Dick Simon

As I travel many people ask me, "What can I do?" People are eager to make a difference and will devote their time and money to help. But they are unsure of what would be truly useful. Often they do not know what others are doing. It's as if many of us have been working on our own piece of quilt. With that piece, we are doing the best we can, but between pieces there is despair and frustration. Somehow we need to combine our work and reweave the fabric of society and community. These quilt pieces need to be stitched together to make a connected country.

We yearn for the same things. Regardless of political ideology, most people believe that children should have certain rights—to physical and psychological safety, good schools, drug-free environments and moral teachings. Most of us respect the history and literary traditions of Western civilization and want to live in a free, tolerant democracy. We want government to be kind and just. Whether we are liberal or conservative,

Christian, Jew or atheist, we share basic moral values such as the belief in honesty, respect and compassion. Most of us want a link between effort and reward. We want to follow the Golden Rule and have others follow it as well. Most of us want a society that balances the sense of neighborhood of my grandparents' community and the tolerance and choices of the 1990s. The 1920s, with its emphasis on duties, led to some hypocrisy and stuffiness, but the 1920s also held most families' lives in place. The 1990s, with its emphasis on freedom, allows for more openness and options, but it also has more crime and social chaos.

WORK

"We Americans are easily pleased, a loaf of bread, a jug of wine and $50,000."—Greg Brown

"A great man is one who knows that he was not put on earth to be part of a process by which a child could be hurt."—Murray Kempton

There are three basic components to a good life—love, work and service to community. Currently in America, it's very difficult to do all three. Work and family demands often conflict. Many parents must work long hours far from home in order to be able to feed their families. Many people, overwhelmed by the demands of work and family, feel too shelled for community service. It's hard to balance duties as an employee, a citizen and a parent. The time problems are further complicated by the fact that so many Americans are discouraged in the work that they do. Workers are burned out and cynical about their workplaces. Often they are isolated and scared of losing jobs they don't even like. They are sick of the ethos of selfishness and eager to find work that serves the common good. As a young client said, "I want to help people. Telemarketing gives me stomachaches."

We have been encouraged to view work as a necessary evil and leisure time as what is really valuable. In some cases this fits. There are people who work at jobs they hate because they are terrified of losing their livelihoods. Their leisure time is the only good time they have. But the luckiest people are those who have work they love. We often label these people workaholics, but true pleasure involves doing work that means something.

Freud said that a healthy person can love and work. Finding work that one loves is one of the most important developmental tasks for adults. In *An Enemy of the People*, Ibsen defined work as "the creation of good on earth." Barry Lopez said, "We have to stop making things that sell and make things that help."

I would like young people to consider the following pledge when they graduate from high school or college: "I won't do work that hurts children." Of course some people wouldn't make that pledge and many others who made it would violate it. But at least it would suggest to young people that the morality of work is something they should consider, that it is a dimension they should evaluate, just as they evaluate pay, benefits and advancement potential.

Václav Havel wrote that modern society is held together by fear. He felt that people do many things to convince each other that they aren't afraid. From my vantage point, it seems like the world is organized around money. Money determines where people live and work, what they make, how they spend their time, whether they get health care and educations. I find myself asking—How did the world get organized this way in the first place? Who likes these stupid rules?

When greed is king, society falls apart. Children suffer the most because they are the most vulnerable. They must take what we adults dish out. They have no money, no lobbyists or power. And they aren't as organized as adults at being greedy. As a culture we must aid parents in their efforts to raise their children. It means that we protect children from adults who would harm them to make money. It means good day care, good schools and good neighborhoods. This means gun control and adequate social and medical services for all. This means that parents can leave work when babies are born and return later with no ill effects. This means we help poor kids and single-parent families with the burdens of poverty. We need a more even distribution of income so that no children go to bed hungry.

Arthur Miller's play *All My Sons* tells a story about a man who makes airplane equipment during World War II. As the war intensifies he falls behind schedule and he cuts corners to meet deadlines and increase profits. Young pilots die because of the faulty airplane parts he ships to the Pacific front. His son, who is a pilot in the Pacific, realizes what his father has done and kills himself by crashing his plane.

The play is about the family's attempt to come to terms with the loss of this son. Toward the end the father is trying to explain himself to his other son. He says that he did what he did for his sons, that he wanted them to have a house and security. Then he pauses and says, "I guess I didn't realize they were all my sons." All the world's children are all our sons and daughters. We must give children back childhood with safe space, protected time, good, nourishing information and lessons on how to behave.

MEDIA

"We are such beings as interact elaborately with what surrounds us."— William Stafford

Emerson said, "Life consists of what a person is thinking about all day."

I listen to a little girl and her father host a public access radio show. She selects "When You Wish Upon a Star" for him to play. I think how cute she is, how nice it is that a child is on the air. After the song she says, "Kids, tomorrow is Friday the thirteenth. Freddy Kreuger movies will be on and I'm gonna watch them. Sneak away from your parents and watch too." In the background her dad chuckles uncomfortably. I think about how the media's power to influence families has become stronger and how the family's power to influence the media has become weaker. When children are raised in front of machines and away from human contacts they become less than fully human. Their imaginations are co-opted by corporations, their dreams transformed into shopping goals.

I don't want to demonize the media. Most of the people working in the media are decent, good-hearted, intelligent people. Also, the media is a very broad category that includes the *Terminator* movies and *The Little Princess*, PBS and Shock Video. Media is *The Wall Street Journal* and the *National Enquirer*. Almost all of us have some media that enriches our lives. My favorites are National Public Radio and the Public Broadcasting System. Many adults enjoy sports, news, history and culture, and children benefit from shows such as *Reading Rainbow* and *Mr. Rogers*. But I believe that, just as teachers tend to be better than their schools and doctors better than their medical systems, so people in the media are often better than the messages they promulgate. Given the rules of the game they are playing, most media people do their best. When they are given a chance to work for the common good, they leap toward it en masse. But most work in the media is organized around money, not truth. Good people are hampered in efforts to do good.

Television will always be a baby-sitter for children and it's in our best interest to offer those children nourishing shows. As adults, we can demand enforcement of the Children's Television Act. We need to support PBS and anyone else who is making shows with children's needs in mind. Children's discernment is not yet fully developed and we adults must take care of them. We can censure, not censor, Hollywood movies that teach kids the wrong lessons. We can stop going to theaters that show movies that hurt our children.

The Europeans are much more protective with their children. The British have good after-school programs for kids, including news programs such as *Newsround*. Most European countries have commercial-free high-quality TV for kids between the time they get out of school and the time parents return home from work. There's more control of ads. Children are not marketed tobacco or alcohol. Children are taught consumer skills in schools. Norway, Sweden and Denmark took the Power Rangers off the air after a five-year-old girl froze to death on a playground. She'd been "power kicked" by several five-year-old boys.

The media could be transformed into a force that fosters community instead of crime and alienation. National media could foster a new ideology based on connectedness. We need heroes who value other people and who stick around to work for the common good. We need new definitions of success, such as helping others, and new definitions of wealth, such as having meaningful work.

We need a national reclamation project for our uniting values. Whether a society will survive is determined by how well it passes on time-honored values from generation to generation. We're now experiencing an "educational meltdown."

Children learn via media an alternate set of values that pits them against their parents and their own common sense. They learn values that will not sustain a democracy. But we can change. The human spirit has bounced back from worse things than TV.

STORIES

Yeats's epigram: "In dreams began responsibilities."

The Sunday morning I was finishing this chapter, the following story was on the front page of my newspaper. The headline read: RANGERS RESCUE LINCOLN COUPLE. The article began: "While their three children watched from the bank, the parents were rescued from the lip of a 75-foot waterfall in the Roaring River in Rocky Mountain National Park. They suffered hypothermia from spending 40 minutes in the cold rushing waters of the river, but were in stable condition at a Denver hospital."

The family had been hiking beside the waterfall when the mother slipped into the river above the falls, and to keep herself from going over she wedged herself between boulders. The father and other visitors tried to form a human chain to reach her, but the swift waters made that impossible. Others attempted to reach her with a rope made of belts and clothing, but that chain also broke. Then the father went into the water with a thin nylon cord tied around his waist, but that broke as well, leaving the couple stranded midstream at the top of the falls.

The reporter wrote: "The husband cradled his wife in his arms and bore the brunt of the pounding water." After the couple had been in the water for forty minutes, the husband could barely hold on to the boulders, but the wife talked calmly to him and helped him stay conscious. At last, a ranger in a wet suit, roped to rangers on the shore, moved into the water toward the couple. Another ranger got in the water below the waterfall, ready to catch them if they went over.

The exhausted couple made a plunge toward the ranger, who was able to hang on to them long enough for other rangers to pull them onto shore. They were given warm fluids by the rangers to counter the effects of hypothermia. Two helicopters then flew the couple to a hospital in Denver.

During the time their parents were in the water, the children watched from the shore. After the rescue, rangers took them to their camp and packed up the family's gear. The rangers told the children, "Your dad was a hero. He saved your mom."

The husband did what family members will do for each other. With only a thin nylon line for safety, he waded into ice water above a waterfall to save his wife's life. The wife also did what family members do—she talked her husband into holding on when hope was fading and he was ready to give in. Those acts of love and courage are the best things about families. Whether it is sensible or not, families will try to save each other.

This story is a good metaphor for the situation families are in. Often right now the waters surrounding families are cold and perilous. To survive, members must stick together, take risks and make sacrifices for each other. Partners must cradle each other and protect each other from our modern elements. But the family alone cannot save itself. Families routinely get into spots where they need resources outside themselves. Other people helped this couple to the shore, into the helicopter and to the hospital. The family was saved by their love for each other, by the kindness of strangers and even by the government.

Humans are story-telling animals. Since the beginning of time adults have told children stories. Around campfires, in dark caves and on grassy savannas, grown-ups have spun stories to instruct and entertain. The stories have been told to particular children by particular adults who knew and loved them. As they told the stories, they could see the children's faces. They could calibrate and adjust the stories to fit the children's ages, experiences, fears and hopes. If necessary, they could cuddle a frightened child in their arms or allow him to sleep beside them on the ground.

The stories that were passed from one generation to another survived because they were useful to individuals and to the culture. For example, "The Ugly Duckling" is a story about hope. It tells a child, You may not be valued now and you may feel like an outsider, but you will grow into someone who is beautiful and who finds your own kind. "Chicken Little," who shouts that the sky is falling in, teaches children not to be out of control emotionally and to evaluate the quality of information they receive before making judgments. "The Tortoise and the Hare" teaches children about steadiness and endurance.

Now the adults who are telling stories do not know the kids who are listening, do not love them and will not be there to comfort them if they are confused or upset by their stories. Another problem is that the stories that are told are designed to raise profits, not children. Most of the stories children hear are mass-produced to induce them to want good things instead of good lives.

Because I talk about the harmful stories that we are telling our children, I am often asked if I believe in censorship. In some ways I do. I don't think we should advertise to children. I think shows that brutalize children should be off the air and that, instead, we should have decent programming for children as they do in Europe. But mainly I am an advocate for more stories, not fewer. I like to hear that extended family, neighbors, old people, people from different backgrounds, poets, teachers and children are telling stories to each other. Everyone has stories to tell. Stories are about imagination and hope. They are, to quote poet William Stafford, "about discovering what the world is trying to be."

I believe that multinational entertainment corporations shouldn't be the only ones telling our children stories. Now too few stories are being told by too few people with motives that are too narrow. I would prefer that children hear stories told by adults who care for them. I would like more adults who care about children to have opportunities to tell their stories to children via films, TV shows and books. I like the adults around children to tell them their stories. These offer great diversity and hope. Right now our stories are too uniform and they are making us all sick. We need new stories.

Good stories have the power to save us. Reality is full of cautionary tales, heroes and difficult obstacles overcome through persistence. The best resource against the world's stupidity, meanness and despair is simply telling the truth with all its ambiguity and complexity. We all can make a difference by simply sharing our own stories with real people in real times and places.

There are many stories yet unborn. The best stories are stories that help us see the complexities faced by others. We need stories to connect us with each other, stories to heal the polarization that can overwhelm us all and stories to calm those who are frightened and who hate. These stories would offer us the possibility of reconciliation. We need stories that teach children empathy and accountability, how to act and how to be. Children are hungry for stories that help them feel hopeful and energetic. Let's turn off our appliances and invent these stories. Quilted together, these stories will shelter us all.

Further Books

Rebuilding the Nest, edited by David Blankenhorn, Steven Bayme and Jean Bethke Elshtain (Milwaukee: Family Service of America, 1990).

Secrets of Strong Families, by John De Frain and Nick Stinett (Boston: *Little Brown,* 1985).

Soul Searching, by William Doherty (New York: Basic Books ,1995).

The State of Families, vol 3: Losing Direction, by Ray Marshall (Milwaukee: Family Services of America ,1991).

The State of Families, vol 2: Work and Families, by Ray Marshall (Milwaukee: Family Services of America, 1987).

Grass Roots: The Universe of Home, by Paul Gruchow (Minneapolis: Milkweed Press, 1995).

Delinquency in Adolescence, by Scott Henggeler (New York: Sage, 1989).

We've Had a Hundred Years of Psychotherapy—and the World's Getting Worse, by James Hillman (HarperCollins, 1992).

Families, by Jane Howard (New York: Simon and Schuster, 1978).

Culture Ways, by James Davison Hunter (New York: Basic Books ,1991).

Culture of Complaint, by Robert Hughes (New York: Warner Books,1993).

Generation at the Crossroads, by Paul Rogat Loeb (New Brunswick, N.J.: Rutgers University Press,1994).

The Age of Missing Information, by Bill McKibben (New York: Random House, 1992).

No Sense of Place, by Joshua Meyrowitz (New York: Oxford University Press, 1985).

The Geography of Childhood: Why Children Need Wild Places, by Gary Nabham and Stephen Trimble (Boston: Beacon Press, 1994).

Amusing Ourselves to Death, by Neil Postman (New York: Penguin, 1986).

Disappearance of Childhood, by Neil Postman (New York. Vintage, 1982).

Intimate Strangers: The Culture of Celebrity, by Richard Schickel (Garden City, N.Y.: International Publishing Corporation, 1986).

Selling Out America's Children, by David Walsh (Minneapolis: Fairview Press, 1995).

Home Is Where We Start From, by D. W. Winnicott (New York: W.W. Norton, 1986).

INDEX

Randy Barger

About the Author

MARY PIPHER, PH.D., is a psychologist in private practice in Lincoln, Nebraska. She has taught at the University of Nebraska and Nebraska Wesleyan University, and has been a commentator for Nebraska Public
Radio. She is the author of *Hunger Pains* and *Reviving Ophelia*.